About the author

Lisa Welch is a paediatric Speech, Language and Communication Therapist, with over 15 years' experience working with children and their families. She has spent time working both privately and for the NHS, supporting communication skills in homes, nurseries, schools and clinic settings. At the centre of her therapy is a play-based, connection centred approach to support children; using their play passions to support their communication needs. Her experience has found that this not only nurtures progress but ensures children feel safe and regulated, allowing them to find joy in communication and thrive. Lisa was diagnosed as ADHD in her mid-30s and has two neurodivergent children. This further fuels her passion for finding affirming and supportive strategies for children and their families, celebrating and unmasking differences, and finding inclusive ways to encourage progress within settings. She runs the Instagram account @Peachy_Speech, where she shares her neurodiversity-affirming therapy ideas, her own ADHD journey of discovery and how she supports her own neurodiverse household. Her work focuses on connection – not perfection – when setting up play opportunities or daily strategies that nurture new skills.

Supporting Children's Communication

the Play Way

Neurodiversity-affirming, Connection-focused Speech and Language Strategies

Lisa Welch

Pavilion
PUBLISHING

Supporting Children's Communication

The Play Way

Published by:
Pavilion Publishing and Media Ltd
Blue Sky Offices, 25 Cecil Pashley Way, Shoreham by Sea,
West Sussex, BN43 5FF

Tel: +44 (0)1273 434943
Email: info@pavpub.com
Web: www.pavpub.com

Published 2025

A catalogue record for this book is available from the British Library.

ISBN: 978-1-803883-83-0

Pavilion Publishing and Media is a leading publisher of books, training materials and digital content in mental health, social care and allied fields. Pavilion and its imprints offer must-have knowledge and innovative learning solutions underpinned by sound research and professional values.

Author: Lisa Welch
Illustrator: Emma Rosendale, Ginger Rose Designs
Editors: Louisa Robertson and Mike Benge
Cover design: Emma Rosendale, Ginger Rose Designs
Page layout and typesetting: Tony Pitt, Pavilion Publishing and Media Ltd
Printing: Independent Publishers Group (IPG)

Contents

Prologue

Welcome to my book.

I'm Lisa, a speech, language and communication therapist. Speech and language therapy has been a part of my life since I was very young. I spent my early childhood absolutely fascinated by people, how they work and how I could help or care for them. I struggled with unclear speech at about age five and went to 'S – club sessions' at which I learnt how to make an *sssssss* sound in a tiny clinic above a library. I hated these sessions. I was so scared of the teacher and the work we did, and I remember one game in particular where they used paper scissors and pretended to snip your tongue off if it poked out while you were making the sound! Horrifying! However, even then, I loved teaching and helping, and I spent time after each session with my best friend teaching her how to make a clear S sound. She did the same thing as me but didn't have therapy – so I would demonstrate the techniques and explain how to change where your tongue was in your mouth and praise her for getting 'a really crisp *sssssss* sound!'. So really, she was my first ever 'work child'.

My first clear memory of knowing that I wanted to work with communication was at a presentation/concert in a big stadium at about age 13. There was a woman standing at the side of the stage signing for the speakers and singers as an interpreter and I remember being absolutely mesmerised by her. Watching intently and being blown away, that somewhere in this huge stadium was another person using those signs to understand, to receive the same message the words were giving me – and I fell in love with the amazing way we all communicate so differently.

During my work experience at secondary school, when everyone else at 15 was going on the preset placements to supermarkets and with their parents of local businesses, I asked if I could arrange my own placement. I got two trains and a bus to a primary school for children who are deaf. I met a speech and language therapist, watched her sessions, observed the lessons being delivered in British Sign Language, helped the children at lunchtime and fell even more in love with this idea that communication and play and interaction are entirely unique. I struggled through GCSEs and A-levels, trying hard to get the subjects and the grades I needed to do the vocational degrees of 'speech and language therapy' – a degree where all you are qualified to do after the four-year course is to be a therapist – it leaves very little wiggle room for changing your mind! But I knew. I knew this was my passion, and once I was working, the struggle of the academic work would be worth the joy of the practical experience.

I know now that that struggle exists because I am dyslexic and ADHD, so study is hard, exams are hard, but placements and doing the real job were wonderful, and the motivation I held on to, to keep going. The more I know and read about and experience Autism, the more I identify the behaviours, passions, struggles and joys within myself. I've read a great many posts and seen many Autistic women on social media talk about their journeys, and how perhaps highly masked Autism leads to a special interest in people. They describe how that special interest in communication, how people work and how to communicate in a way that allows you to 'fit in' becomes a strong passion that you absorb into your very existence. No one notices your needs because you become so skilled at morphing into exactly what is expected, by adapting, altering and deeply understanding social rules. But not instinctively. Not in the way that everyone else seems to just exist together, you understand them because you have spent almost every hour of your life collecting and

evaluating data. Every social situation is like a tiny experiment after which you evaluate and create rules to take forward into your next encounter. But that's exhausting, it's masking, it's not a sustainable way of life, and it often leads to co-occurring struggles with mental and physical health (which we now call 'burn out'). So I find myself relating deeply to my Autistic family members, my Autistic work children, and I find myself deeply passionate about speech, language and communication therapy and how people work. Maybe my special interest in people and how they communicate has Autistic roots that haven't been officially identified for me yet. That's a different personal chapter of a different book, but worth sharing with you as you read on and hear how I've developed my play-based neurodiversity-affirming way of creating connection through communication therapy. It's been created through a deep passion, not just from things I observe, but because I feel it too. It's more than just my work, or a research project. It's my everyday, my family, my life.

I've worked within the NHS and privately. I've worked as part of schools, nurseries, in families' homes and in clinics. I have two of my own children and support our neurodiverse home with our daily life. When my children were young and I was on maternity leave I started capturing moments on video – examples of key language strategies in action – for my NHS team to use in training sessions with other parents. Social media was growing and changing, and I created a page called "Peachy Speech". I knew that services were stretched and that there were plenty of simple play ideas I was enjoying with my boys that others might like to copy, to support speech, language and communication at home. Over the years this evolved and is now a place I can share my professional thoughts and ideas with parents/carers and professionals. My hope is that I can put together a book for you that combines my experiences as a therapist, a parent to neurodivergent children and a neurodivergent adult myself, to give you support and insight into helping your children with their communication. My therapy and strategy support has evolved over the years and is now entirely play based. It is entirely about building a connection to allow communication to grow. It is focused on creating therapy that regulates the nervous system to create calm and joy, allowing learning to occur within a happy brain.

A lot of my knowledge comes from on-the-job experience. Seeing real children in real therapy and real life, rather than being based on specific research papers or set of statistics. I do use theory – of course, the base knowledge needs to come from research and theory, and I will name their origin and describe these theories in my own way to pass this on. But, as you read this book, you may notice I don't cite research papers, statistics and figures. As much as these hold value and are important for progress, what I want to share here are everyday experiences with practical solutions that will transfer from these pages into your day-to-day life without too much adapting or interpreting.

Terminology and language – affirming, Autism-first language and why

In recent years, the language we use to talk about diagnostics has changed hugely. In this book, I will be using neurodiversity-affirming language, and 'Autism-first' language. Let me explain why...

Historically, we have always been taught that we should use person-first language – this means we name the person first and then refer to any condition they are diagnosed as having – for example 'a little girl with Autism' or 'a man with depression'. The person is first, the diagnosis follows. The idea around this is that it avoids the somewhat detached and often offensive way of talking about their diagnosis that had existed before, in times when these conditions were often talked about in a very derogatory way that could be really quite upsetting for the people they referred to. Putting the person first felt like a symbol of respect, that we were acknowledging that they were more than their diagnosis or struggles, that they had an identity outside of their diagnosis. This is how I learnt to write notes, reports and records while I was at university, where there was a push for this shift in language, and a message that this was a more holistic way of writing.

Fast forward to the present day and we are now listening to the Autistic community of adults who have grown up among all of this. It is widely agreed among Autistic adults that they prefer not to be separated from their diagnosis. That using person-first language can leave them feeling like they have a problem that needs fixing, that they have an extra thing that they carry around with them: 'I'm a person, and I carry Autism around *with* me – a person *with* Autism'. There is an implication that we should search for a cure – a child *with* a cold needs medicine to get rid of the cold, does that mean a child *with* Autism needs therapy to get rid of their Autism!? Absolutely not! And so that is how the start of 'Autism-first' language began. Where we refer to a person *being* Autistic. It is part of their being, an important part of who they are that cannot and should not be removed or solved. But understood, accepted, acknowledged and supported. The person and the Autism aren't separate. The person isn't carrying a bag of Autistic behaviours around with them for us to try and unload and unpack. The Autism exists as they do, at one with them and who they are. An Autistic child. An Autistic adult. A child who *is* Autistic. An adult who *is* Autistic.

In this book, I will use Autism-first language as well as referring to children *being* Autistic, or that a child *is* Autistic, rather than *having* Autism or *with* Autism. This aims to respect the wider voice of the Autistic community being expressed right now. I do understand that there are always personal preferences, and often there is change in the future, as we 'know better and do better' all the time. Some will always prefer to hear person-first language (the other way around) and use the reasons I described first as to why it feels more holistic to be person first. I believe that when you work with children and families, it's important to explain the two concepts above and allow individuals to make their own choices because, ultimately, it is language used to describe a person and being truly holistic and affirming is about what makes that individual feel the most valued and understood. I hope that having this explanation at the start of this book will support professionals and families to have these discussions and open up the conversation to allow individuals to take ownership of their diagnosis and what language makes them feel the most comfortable.

Along with this shift of language, new terminology has been developed to help us talk respectfully about the different ways that individuals learn and experience the world:

Neurodiversity – This is the understanding that a brain has a natural range of differences in the way it accesses information, processes and functions. This diversity leads to differences, strengths and areas of need.

Neurotypical – This is the term used for an individual who is not diagnosed as having a neurological difference. They access information, process and function in a broadly similar way to their peers.

Neurodivergent – An individual who experiences differences in the way their brain accesses information and processes the information in their environment. A neurodivergent individual will often have a diagnosis that reflects more specifically what neurotype they are. Such as a diagnosis of being Autistic: they have a brain that accesses the world in an Autistic way. A diagnosis of ADHD: they have a brain that accesses the world in an ADHD way. There is a huge range and variation across these terms. The term 'neurodivergent' gives us a broad understanding of the possible or potential differences but does not tell us the unique ways an individual needs support.

Neurodiversity affirming – This is an approach and a mindset to supporting children and adults that acknowledges that their strengths and needs are linked to their brain type. It is not something that can be changed. It is not something to try and change about them, but to nurture, understand and support. Being affirming means that support is holistic and person centred. Being affirming means we look to place an individual's wellbeing at the centre of inclusion. Being affirming means we look to adapt environments and systems to accommodate an individual's needs, rather than place expectations on them.

Chapter 1: Seeing the whole child...

It's really important when we start supporting a child, and throughout their communication journey, that we consider more than simply 'how they talk'. Although talking is a huge part of communication – and for many of us it will feel like our main way of engaging and interacting – it is actually only a very small part of how we share messages with each other.

Alongside our talking we have a range of skills and abilities that surround us, they help create who we are and how we perceive and interact with the world.

Imagine each of these skills forms a snowflake, and let's imagine our children surrounded by these snowflakes. Each snowflake is a unique part of their communication and personality profile. It tells us about who they are, what their needs are, what their strengths are and where their struggles lie. It's our job as the adults in their lives, to decipher this. When we understand them, their needs, their patterns, their systems, these snowflakes exist suspended peacefully surrounding the child, available for those around them to access, learn from and celebrate.

Each unique snowflake tells us something about the unique individual it accompanies.

Without a holistic mindset being used to notice and decode these snowflakes, often they become a whirling snowstorm of needs, whipped up into a tornado of misunderstood messages. We either end up with a child who is frantically fighting within a fog of chaos or one who curls up into a ball and hides away from us all. But all the while, the information is there. For every child, their code, their snowflakes, their unique set of needs is there, ready for us to explore and decipher so we can support them better. We, as the adults, need to invest the time and the skills to work through it. To calm the storm of needs and create that peaceful glitter of sparkling information that helps a child to thrive.

So where do we start? The storm is raging and we are desperate to help and find a way.

As part of this book, we will explore speech, language and communication with a holistic child-focused mindset. We will consider all the areas that influence a child's development, such as their emotional wellbeing, sensory needs and individual capacity. We will explore how we can use this information, as the adults in their lives, to create the best possible set up for their skills to thrive.

It's more than just setting language targets and getting children to do things. That's not real progress. Statistically, children 'gain' but often at a cost to other areas – their emotional wellbeing, their focus, their regulation. We need to create an opportunity for children to be so entirely safe in themselves and their settings that their skills have nothing else to do other than grow and swell and reach their full potential.

When I'm first meeting a child, I consider a vast number of needs, this helps me to see them. To see all of them – not just as a child who needs to learn to talk. But as a tiny human trying to work out how an entire world is working and how their brain type can access it within its own limitations.

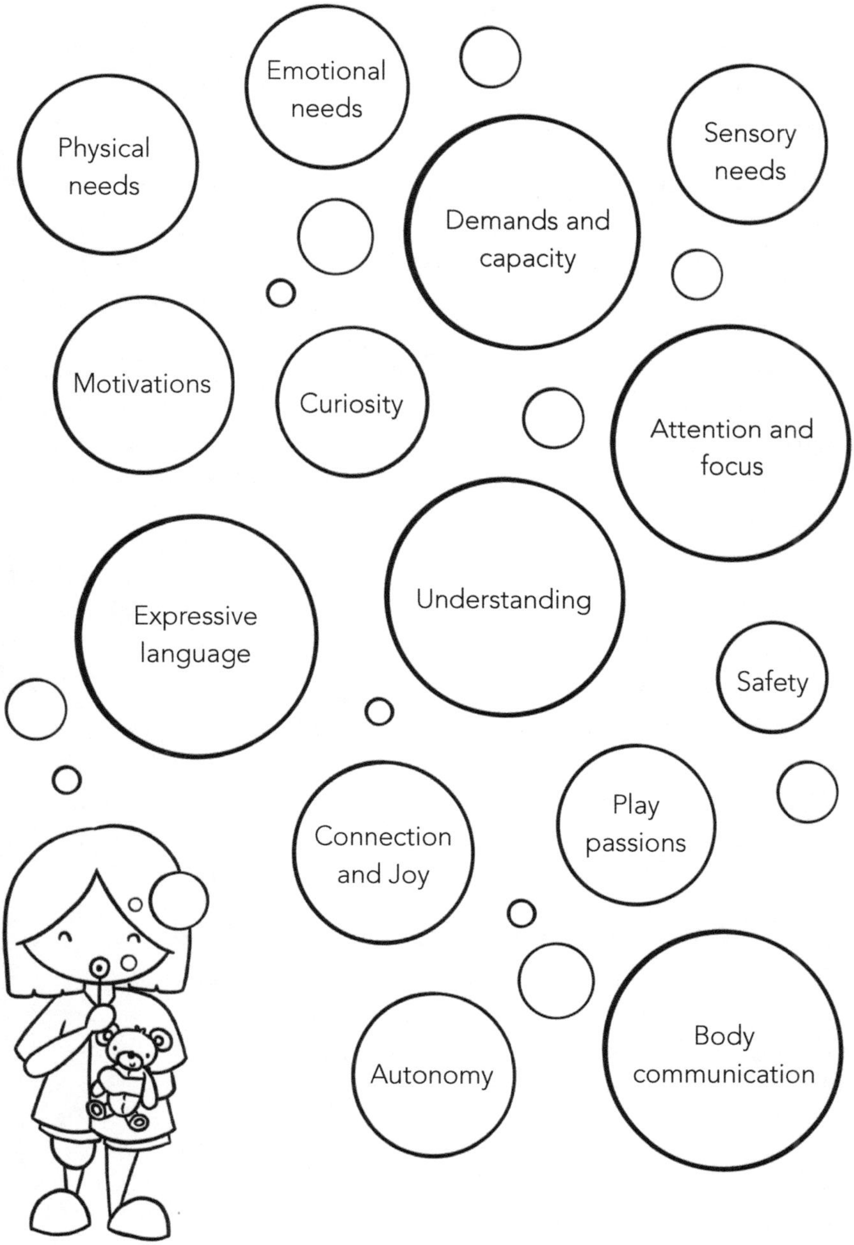

Fight, flight, freeze, fawn

How our brain and body reacts and responds

Let's start by exploring our fight, flight, freeze or fawn response system. This is a theory researched and written up by multiple psychologists and medical professionals over many years. Theory and knowledge about the brain is continuously evolving as new research and advances in technology offer a clearer insight. This will not be a detailed look into neuroscience, but a very simple glance to support our understanding of children's behaviour.

Different parts of the brain support us with different skills, responses and reactions. The way that messages are sent within the brain and body is extremely complicated and as neuroscience advances, we learn more and more about the complexity of these messaging systems and the parts of the brain that are involved. For our children, it is important to understand that their brains are still developing these systems. Their brain and body is constantly learning and developing a way of efficiently sending messages to predict, learn, process, react and respond to the information *around* them (exteroception), as well as the information and signals from *inside* them (interoception).

As we process this information we will then respond to it. Sometimes this response will be carefully considered and planned, and other times it will be an instinctive, reactive response. Each time we experience something, the messaging systems within our brain grow and learn. When we experience something that triggers a reactive response, our brain, body and nervous system activity will often fall into one of four categories: fight, flight, freeze or fawn. These are the reactive states that are programmed into us as responses in order to survive. This 'survival mode' is not sustainable for a long period of time and is not a state that we can learn in.

This theory was first described by Walter Cannon, but has been explored further and added to by many psychologists including Pete Walker who added 'fawning' in later research. Current research also details a "flop" response, where individuals my faint or pass out.

I have researched and read and watched psychologists and medical professionals talk about this theory and I want to share it with you because it truly changes the way you view a child's behaviour, reaction and interaction with the world around them. This is not my own theory, but I have learnt it and experienced over and over again with the children I support, and I have developed my own imagery for explaining it to you.

Fight	Our body responds by fighting – physically or verbally.
Flight	Our body responds by escaping any way it can – running or leaving.
Freeze	Our body responds with an inability to engage in other responses – staying very still or very quiet, maybe perceived as being unresponsive.
Fawn	Our body responds by trying to appease, soothe, calm the threat at any cost, even at the cost of their own wellbeing. The drive to stop the threat outweighs self-preservation/safety.

Visualise the concept

Let's imagine our brains are like jacks-in-the-box. When we are thinking clearly and steadily, the lid on the box is closed, the outside of our box is strong, steady, logical and peaceful. When we experience something that sets off a big emotion, the inside of the box is activated, and the lid opens. The inside of the box contains a busy clown on a spring, waiting to burst out and bounce around chaotically; it's not in control, it lurches forward and backwards, unpredictable. The unleashing of this jack-in-the-box is our fight, flight, freeze, fawn response. This is an automatic response, which effects the body's nervous system and changes the physiological state that our body sits in. Once we are in this state, the physical reactions we have will be different, our heart rate is faster, our impulse control is reduced and we are in a highly reactive state.

This is very similar to how the different parts of our brain work. When we are settled, safe, calm, happy, peaceful, our box is shut. We can access logical thought. We can learn new things. We can make balanced choices. We can consider next steps, maybe even predict consequences. When we are dysregulated, the lid on our box flies open, we no longer have access to logic or reasoning. Technically, it's there, the box hasn't broken and the lid hasn't disappeared, but our chaotic jack-in-the-box clown is lurching about on a spring, in a purely reactive state.

Imagine trying to reason with that jack-in-the-box! Imagine trying to explain something calmly as it bounces about and the spring propels it forward and backwards crashing and bashing into things – it feels impossible. We need to gather it up, calm it, gently soothe it so we are left with that logical box. This is how your child's brain works in terms of emotional responses, and it is why emotional regulation is so important when we are trying to teach, help or nurture skills. If that jack-in-the-box is open and the chaotic clown is bouncing around, we are already at a disadvantage in terms of being heard and understood by the child. They are at a disadvantage too, because their brain is not in a logical learning state, it is in a chaotic reactive state, so any learning will get flung about and will not be stored carefully in our box for another time.

Here's how this might look in a real example:

An adult and child are at a park. The adult, using their logical, closed up jack-in-the-box brain, makes some solid observations – it's almost lunch time, we've been here over a long time now, there is something else scheduled for this afternoon that we need energy for, it's starting to cloud over – all these logical observations lead to a reasonable choice that the time in the park should end. The idea is presented to the child – 'one more turn on the slide and then we need to leave...' The child's jack-in-the-box lid whizzes open and out springs a chaotic, disorganised and emotional response. The lid that seals in all the logic, all the concrete understanding and reason is no longer available, all that's left is that toy clown lurching backwards and forwards and all over the place, out of control. On the outside this looks like the child screaming 'No!' running away, crying, big, big feelings, lunging backwards and forwards with that spring clown, out the box, uncontained.

If, as the adult, we offer logical solutions like 'but it's lunch time and I've got your favourite crisps ready', even though that makes complete sense, because the lid of their jack-in-the-box is sprung open, the logic we offer, any reasons, any new information, will immediately be flung from the box by that coiled spring. We can keep offering it – 'and this afternoon we've got painting planned which is the best!' – but the lid is off, so whoosh, that logic isn't received and gets flung from the box as the clown toy bobs frantically about.

What we need to do, with our logic, and our calm, and our strength, is to help soothe their jack-in-box, back to a clam state. We can do this by stepping back from fighting the emotion with logic and instead meet it with understanding. This might sound like – 'Wow, that's a big feeling; you're in a panic because you want to stay at the park, I can see that, I can help'. That big emotional feeling will start to shrink as the child feels heard and understood, the spring on their jack-in-the-box slows down and isn't moving quite so frantically. The adult keeps meeting the emotion with understanding. We might then add in some connection and some empathy and the lid on their jack-in-the-box starts to close, like this: 'You've had the best time at the park and it's really hard when a nice time has to end, I've felt like that before'. They don't feel the intensity of the emotion and their whole body starts to calm. The message that their lid is closing starts to filter around their body and the busyness of the jack-in-the-box clown starts to fade, in place of a calm, safe state. The adult helps further with the final parts of calm in the body by offering connection and safety, which might sound like, 'Shall we have a cuddle? I'll help you do some breaths so we can feel steady.' And together they take some deep breathes and jack-in-the-box rests. The brain is now ready for logic and we try again: 'I've got your favourite crisps at home, I bet your tummy is hungry after all that playing, shall we go and get them?'

In an ideal world, that would be the end of the story and the adult and child skip off to do the next part of their day. But the reality is that the lid will often flip again when we present the transition idea a second time. This is OK; their brains are still young and they are still learning this very new skill of regulation. We will need to do these steps a second (and maybe even a third) time. But each time we do this, the 'calming pathway' in their brain becomes stronger. The burst and the energy from the spring becomes slightly less, and over time we help our child grow healthy regulating pathways, with skills to soothe and steady themselves. This means they can access their logic quicker, even after their jack-in-the-box has sprung out.

This is not suggesting that we want our children to keep a lid on their feelings, absolutely not. We are aiming for them to feel the feelings, but we are also showing them how to calm and feel safe again afterwards. This then means they can access their logic to process and understand what has happened. This is a life-long skill that applies to so many aspects of our lives.

Children who are Autistic often find this much harder to do and to learn. This is partly because of how they understand the world, but also because there are so many other factors involved. There are sensory aspects, there may be speech, language and communications needs, the way feelings and emotions are often experienced more intensely, and the way the feeling is perceived tends to be more instant. As such, knowing this theory is incredibly helpful because we can reassure ourselves, as the adults in their lives, that every time we help them to regulate we are helping them to learn a life-long skill.

When the jack-in-the-box lid flip open, our steps for calm and regulating are often:

1. Notice and name the emotion the child is having – 'Wow that's a big feeling, you are sad you dropped your ice cream…' 'Wow, you feel so angry right now, I can see it in your face and body.'
2. Tell the story and offer understanding of where the feeling came from – 'You were so excited to have an ice cream that it slipped out of your hands! What a shock! That's happened to me before.'
3. Create connection and calm – 'Let's have a cuddle/hold hands/sit together, and we can do some breathes/cuddle our toy/use the play dough.'
4. Offer peace and time – sit together and connect.
5. Notice the calming shift together – 'Your body seems more steady now.'
6. Monitor to see if the child is ready for logic and reasoning.

therapeutic thought

A child who doesn't conform is not a problem, they are a tiny human with a whole world to work out...

Within schools, nurseries, social situations, activity clubs etc, there is an incredibly high expectation placed on small children to 'follow the rules' – listen, wait, don't touch, don't climb, don't get too loud... Sometimes we need these rules for safety, to make things fair, to make systems work. But when a child struggles with these expectations, their motivation is not because they want to 'cause a fuss'... They are just a tiny human, with an immature brain, limited impulse control and an under-developed nervous system. They are working hard and working out how the world works and finding it tricky.

Immediately in my head I can hear the adults and teachers and parents saying, 'Yes, but the other kids, the lesson, the learning, the rules, the aim of the activity, the routine...' and those 'yes buts' are true to some extent.... But still, at the heart of the chaos is that tiny human, finding it hard. At the heart of the paperwork and the tick boxes and the systems and the behaviour plan and the ideas, is a tiny human, feeling a big feeling that they don't understand.

As adults we have our own big feelings and we all find things hard and we all juggle a lot, but tiny humans need the bigger humans to ground them. To be safe. To be a steady voice that isn't afraid of the chaos created, and that shows up even when the world seems to be falling apart.

It's not easy being that bigger human to a struggling tiny human. And if you have children or work with children, you are absolutely an incredible soul facing all manner of pressure... but that tiny human needs you to remember that they aren't a problem to fix. They are learning and struggling – and compassion and care will always be pivotal to that.

I'm not saying any of this to evoke guilt, but to evoke thought. Next time a big thing happens, hold this thought:

This isn't a problem, this is an invitation to help.

This doesn't need fixing or fighting, this tiny heart needs soothing.

You'll be so amazed how this mindset shift feels in those moments.

Chapter 2: Regulation

When we are trying to support a child, it's important that we begin by thinking about their regulation. Regulation refers to how a person feels within their own body. It links to how they manage and alter their internal systems in relation to what is happening in their external environment, responding and reacting to their body's signals and needs. When we are regulated, we feel at one with our body, bodily systems and the environment it exists in. When we are dysregulated, we are conflicted. Our body systems and its environment aren't aligned, leading to discomfort, disconnect, upset and a drive to resolve these problems.

We can't possibly encourage a child to learn and to thrive if their body and their mind are in turmoil. It would be like trying to ice a cake before it's even been baked. Working on language skills, working on math skills, working on academic work, working on friendships... All this is like icing and sprinkles, but if our cake mixture hasn't even been baked yet, how can we possibly start to layer on the decorations?

Our first job is really to think about what parts of a child needs supporting first. What parts of this child are dysregulated, are in a jumble, are not feeling OK? And we need to work on these as a foundation first. We need to identify and support those first, above and beyond any other sort of therapeutic play work or academic work. I use theory from 'Maslow's Hierarchy of needs' to help me organise my observations and support. Maslow described our needs as a hierarchical system that builds through different levels of need, and any gaps in lower-level needs make it harder for us to achieve a feeling of 'self-actualisation', which is where we can grow and learn.

1. **Physiological needs:** Needs that are vital for survival, such as food, water, breathing, warmth and shelter.
2. **Safety and security needs:** Needs concerned with safety and protection, such as personal security, health, stability and wellbeing.
3. **Love and belonging:** Social needs, such as friendships, family, a sense of connection, inclusion, acceptance and love.
4. **Esteem needs:** Needs concerned with recognition, such as self-esteem, confidence, achievement, respect for others, respect from others.
5. **Self-actualisation needs:** The desire to become the most one can be – growth, creativity and fulfilment.

With that in mind, I would often start by thinking about the child's **physical needs** and how their body must feel for them right now. Really simple things like the temperature – are they hot? Are they cold? Is there a draught in the room? What is the lighting like? Too bright or too dark? Could they be hungry or thirsty? What time in the day is it, and could they be fatigued from the day, had a late night and be tired? Are they recovering from a cold? These basic bodily feelings will have a huge impact on how ready a child is to receive new information. Not only will any level of discomfort be overwhelming in terms of regulation, it will also act as a huge distraction. For lots of us, having cold hands may be a small inconvenience. We carry on working and, as we focus on other things, our mind settles and quiets and we almost forget. For a lot of neurodivergent individuals, how their body feels in the world overrides all other stimulus. The feeling is amplified for them. So those cold hands may feel like they are holding an ice block while playing/doing maths. It will be like trying to play or answer a maths question with someone stood shouting 'COLD HANDS COLD HANDS COLD HANDS' in your ear over and over. An almost impossible distraction, holding your focus above all other tasks. These things are usually quite easy for us to support – grabbing their drinks bottles, having a snack, putting on or taking off their jumper. Noticing them and providing that support ahead of upset supports children to remain feeling steady and level, rather than having to peak in distress and then recover.

Once we have supported any physical needs, we are starting with a solid base ready for the next step, which is to consider how **safe and connected** they feel. As adults, we can sometimes assume that children know we are safe, but in my experience, children often need us to show and to prove this to them. This can be especially true for Autistic and neurodivergent children because so often in their lives they will have experiences being misunderstood and possibly being placed in uncomfortable situations or unrealistic demands. So we have to work for their trust, for their connection and for their joy. This is where my approach to therapy activities works for itself. It's all play focused, it's all connection focused and it's all centred around the child and their play passions.

Before we launch into connection play therapy, we need to think about the other signals we give to the child to ensure they feel safe and connected.

Things to consider:

- **How readily available you are to the child.** The simple gestures of connection by sitting on the floor instead of being stood at the door will show children that we are ready and wanting to connect with them.

- **Quickly and intentionally responding to them.** An easy way to build connection is to respond quickly and intentionally to *all* their communication or play attempts. By this, I mean giving your entire attention to any small gestures of communication or bids for your attention. For example, if they pass you a toy, act as though it is the most important thing you've ever received – stop your conversation with the other adult, turn to them, relish in the joy of whatever you've been gifted. Because in terms of connection and rapport building, it is not just about that toy. That toy represents an offering of connection. An invitation to show that you are interested and respond; to indicate that you understand them. These small acts can build an incredibly important part of relationships with the children we work with and support. Understandably, this is not possible at all times and we can never aim for this 100% of the time, but it is important to be mindful of this concept and it should be our most common response. It's a way to signal to children that we, as adults, are safe and trustworthy and that we value them for exactly who they are.
- **How we talk about children in front of children.** When working in school and nursery settings, it is often required to offer discussions and handovers. These are essential for support and care to be carried over across different staff and settings. The time for them can feel almost impossible to find and often quick discussions are had with the child present, or among play and interaction. However, the impact of feeding back sensitive or difficult information about a child in front of that child can be really damaging to the connection you are trying to build with them. It is really important to consider how that may impact how the child feels about you and how safe you feel to them. What we know from listening to Autistic adults is that often, even when they were non-speaking, they heard, they knew, and they absorbed that information. They felt which teachers found joy in them and which therapists spoke poorly about them. With this in mind, it is really important that we nurture our relationship with children, to keep them feeling safe, connected and understood by us.

The senses and their role in regulation

Our senses and how we process sensory information plays a crucial role in how we feel and how regulated we are.

Senses are usually viewed in eight key categories (further research is being done in this area all the time and more categories are being explored and discovered, so this is certainly an area to do further reading and research about on a regular basis.) Occupational therapists are specialists in this area and a really important part of a supportive therapeutic team!

Here is a brief summary of our senses to consider when we are supporting children's systems and regulation. This is a huge area that fills many books all by itself. My summary here will be short but will hopefully inspire some further research. (Books, blogs and social media accounts written by occupational therapists who support Autistic families, or who are Autistic themselves are a brilliant place to start.)

The eight senses:

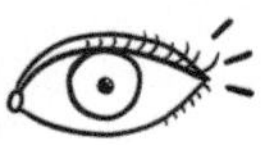

Visual: This allows us to see and understand the difference between things. The sense of sight that allows us to see colours, shapes and motion.

Olfactory (smell): This allows us to sense and interpret smell.

Gustatory (taste): The sense of taste that allows us to identify flavours, textures and temperatures.

Auditory (hearing): The sense of hearing that allows us to interpret sounds, their frequency and volume.

Tactile (touch): The sense of touch that allows us to respond to physical stimuli through the receptors of our skin. It allows us to understand sensations like pressure, temperature, pain and texture.

Proprioceptive (body awareness and coordination feedback): Allows us to understand our body in relation to itself. The proprioception system is located in our muscles and joints. It's the sense of movement that allows us to understand where our body is in space without using our sight to guide us. This gives us a sense of body awareness and allows us to notice and react to force and pressure.

Vestibular (balance and movement feedback): Allows us to understand forces acting upon us, in order to understand our movement in space. The vestibular system is located in the middle ear and is our sense of balance and motion. It gives us the ability to recognise our spatial awareness. It's the sense of balance and movement that allows us to understand where our body is and how fast it's moving.

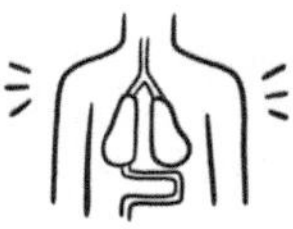

Interoceptive (body signals feedback): Allows us to understand the messages from our body, such as hunger, thirst, toileting and breathing. It's the sense of internal body signals that allows us to understand our physical needs and emotions

Why our knowledge of the senses is important

Not every child will have the ability to notice or identify what feeling they are having and how it links to their other sense. As described above, this is called **interoception**. This is where our body sends us a message about an internal physical or emotional feeling – hunger, thirst, heat, cold, pain, need the toilet etc... and we make a plan for how to resolve that feeling. It is understood that neurodiverse brains don't send and receive these messages in the same way, and often they are less effective at organising these feelings into actions. It means that often the signals will build up before they are acted upon, and the action may then appear very extreme or urgent. A good example of this is going to the toilet. A child will often miss the small signal that they are starting to need the toilet and these will go undetected, meaning that a request for the bathroom and a plan to resolve these small signals isn't made. Then they will receive a huge, urgent signal that they must go immediately or an accident will occur, and they act on that, and to surrounding adults it will feel very sudden and unexpected.

This means as the adults in their lives, we must dedicate time to being a detective and working out how to optimise the environment for our little ones and their sensory system needs.

There are therefore many areas of need that are linked to our key senses:

Basic physical needs: Thirsty, hungry, tired, unwell, needing the toilet, clothing (labels, itchy material, seasonal changes like recently moving from short to trousers and how that feels different for the individual).

The environment: Lighting, heating, noise/busyness, seating comfort, smell of location (are you sat in the dinner hall before or after lunch, near the medical room, near the painting/art room?).

Movement needs: Big movement needs that involve their whole body, such as spinning, rolling, climbing, running. Small movement needs that concentrate movement into a smaller zone of the body, such as foot tapping, hand-held fidgets, tactile play like sand or play dough.

(This is not an exhaustive list, but a starting point.)

All of these factors and more will impact how regulated, settled and steady a child presents at any given time. These variables are also changeable within environments and on a daily basis, so, as supporting adults, it is important for us to increase our skill at noticing and observing which sensory areas seem to impact our children's regulation. You can either do this 'on the go' and keep a check in your own mind. Or, if you are part of a team, it is really useful to note down your observations to share with the rest of the supporting team. I recommend writing down the eight senses as headings and noting down any sensitivities or joys that you observe your child experiencing within those areas. This will give you a 'sensory map' of how this child is experiencing the world. (Be mindful that as their skills evolve, so too will this map, and it will be an ever-evolving set of observations, rather than a one-time job.)

How needs are communicated to us by our children

It's important to notice that the way these needs are communicated to us may not exactly as we expect. They may come to us in a code that we need to decipher. Our children will often not really realise that the feeling they have is linked to a need that isn't being fulfilled. In the example above when we talked about a child having cold hands, they might not have the words or concept knowledge for 'cold hands', so inside their head they just have an 'owwwww' noise raging. They may communicate their discomfort by scratching at you with their hands because that's the part of their body that doesn't feel right. They may refuse to pick up a pencil because their fingers are uncomfortable. They may curl up into a ball to be able to put their hands under their armpits.

They will show you somehow that they are not OK – it just might not be in the way you are expecting.

If we see this behaviour as 'being naughty' or 'being defiant' or 'not following instructions', we are likely going to make things more difficult for them. Things will escalate fast. Insisting or distracting or guiding a child to continue with an adult-led task/routine/structure at this point is unlikely to be successful. Considering all the theory we have covered in this section so far, we can see that needs linked to comfort, safety, self-esteem, validation and sensory regulation are all missing from the child's system in this moment. Aiming for 'self-actualisation', which is that optimum moment for progress and learning, is not possible. Their behaviour is telling us, but perhaps in a unique way to them.

So when you notice a behaviour, *get curious*! I will write this phrase a lot in this book – *all behaviour is communication*. It's a message, being sent to us by the child. This message is often not superficially clear, but if we invest time and energy decoding it, working it out, pealing away the layers, we will understand and be able to offer support to nurture progress and new skills, rather than resorting to behaviour-linked consequences, which rarely offer meaningful or transferable learning to our neurodivergent children.

All behaviour is communication.

Children thrive on connection and being understood – behaviour is the message they gift us to help us understand them. It's communication from them to us that they need help and to be understood. As the supporting adults we can use this as a signal that we need to get curious and get exploring:

Ask yourself:

- What's going on for this little human right now?
- Within their systems, which part, and what, isn't feeling quite right?
- How can I connect and collaborate with them to help the world feel better, safer, more comfortable?

Sensory capacity

When considering sensory regulation and how the senses and our sensory experiences affect us, we will need to notice differences between individual's systems. How stimulated, over-stimulated or under-stimulated a child is within the different sensory areas (i.e. areas linked to each of the eight senses). Due to sensory processing differences, our Autistic, ADHD and neurodivergent individuals frequently experience sensory input with more sensitivity.

When we're considering this, it's therefore useful to think about **sensory capacity**. Simply put, this is each individual's unique ability to tolerate different levels of input, exposure or demand on each of those eight senses.

Psychologist Dr Segal described there to be a 'window of tolerance' for individuals. There is a zone for us where we receive a feeling of everything being 'just right'. We can apply this to our sensory capacity. More input than that leads us to feeling **over-stimulated** (often termed hyper-arousal). Less input than that can lead us to feeling **under-stimulated** (often termed hypo-arousal).

We will have all experienced being over-stimulated and under-stimulated by sensory input at times in our lives. The difference for our neurodiverse children is that they will experience this feeling more intensely and more frequently because of the way their brain and body experience and process the world.

Experiencing our own window of tolerance

Imagine you have a piece of gravel in your shoe. The laces are done up, and as you step, you get a sharp pain in your foot, it's a woosh of discomfort and you react to it. However, even when you aren't moving or putting any weight on it you can still feel that it's there, it pushes and creates a pressure that doesn't hurt but is very present and on your mind. You notice how it rolls and moves as you do, and although it's a felt sensation, it may even disrupt your thought process.

Think back to a time when you've been somewhere with sudden bright lights or sound effects, maybe as part of a show. It will have made jump, put your hands up to your ears or partly close your eyes.

Think of a time you've had a cramp in your leg or foot or hand – maybe you were in a place where you couldn't move straight away, an important meeting or mid-conversation. The urge to move, wiggle and stretch to relieve the discomfort will feel like an intense drive within your body.

Those are all times where your sensory stimulation has not been 'just right' – because if that gravel had been a foot massage ball, that level of spiky-ness or pressure would have been OK. If that light had been a sunny day and you'd had sunglasses on, you'd be managing the input in a controlled way for yourself. When we exercise or stretch as part of a class, the extension in our muscles feels OK. You can see that we all exist in this careful balance of trying to find a sensory load, a sensory experience that is 'just right' for us. Neurodivergent individuals process information differently and therefore their systems are often more receptive to changes and shifts in input, so they often have to work harder to maintain that balance.

Visualise the concept

We are often asked to imagine each person having a 'sensory cup' that gets filled up over time by all the sensory experiences going on around us, and that if we keep filling it up, eventually it will spill over. However, I think that this imagery oversimplifies the concept and would like to explore visualising it in a different way...

Let's visualise instead that every person – adult or child – holds their own sensory balloon. Every person's balloon is a different shape, size and strength. Every person's balloon has a different capacity for air, depending on its dimensions. Every person's balloon holds onto the air differently depending on how the knot is tied or how tightly it is held on to. Every balloon takes a different amount of effort to blow up and fully inflate it with air. How easily it blows up differs depending on what kind of material it is made of.

Neurodivergent people's balloons come in a huge range of shapes, sizes and capacities, varying enormously between different individuals. For some children, too much air and the balloon explodes, for other children, too little air and the balloon doesn't inflate at all. Different types of sensory input will equate to different puffs of air in each child's balloon, because they receive the information in a unique way.

For example: Turning the big florescent lights on in a classroom will be a tiny bit of air for some children, and for others it will equate to a huge burst of air that fills their balloon entirely. Not only that, but children's balloons will be different sizes. So that tiny bit of air as the light flicks on, for a child with a large balloon, won't have an impact. But for a child with a small balloon that is already full, it could be the final puff that makes it pop!

For example: Some children will have balloons that only fill up with very big movement-based sensory play, but this play would burst their peer's balloon. Other children may need play with much smaller sensations to fill their balloon slowly and comfortably, but this play would not be enough to even begin to inflate their peer's balloon.

Sensory regulation is often a key difficulty for our beautiful neurodivergent children. What I have experienced is that their sensory balloons can vary hugely! Part of our job as supporting adults is to work out what 'just right' feels like for that child and what input gets us there.

What *amount* of input and what *type* of input mean that they are feeling regulated? We want to set our children up with a balloon that floats gently next to them. Ideally, we can learn all about our children's sensory needs and communicative behaviours, allowing us to add to their balloon when we see it start to flop, as well as anticipate and gently release some air if we see the pressure building, before it pops!

Here are some important considerations when exploring your child's unique sensory balloon (not real balloons):

- What sensory area are they seeking? (We can use these to fill their balloon up.)
- What sensory area are they avoiding? (These might burst their balloon.)
- What is the child's capacity for stimulation, how much of the thing the seek do they need? (How big or small is their balloon.)
- What is the child's capacity for remaining regulated? (Once their balloon is full and floating gently, how long does it stay that way? How well is the balloon tied up?)

Important: When a child is dysregulated, they very often will not have the skills, capacity or energy to find regulation for themselves. They will need help. It is an unreasonable expectation that they find their own 'just right' when they are in an extreme state of 'not right at all'. In these moment of dysregulation, external support, strategies, ideas and care will be a necessity, not a luxury.

How does this impact our play and therapy?

Knowing about our child's sensory balloon and how sensory input links to their regulation, means we can use sensory experience to enhance their learning environment and support them in play therapy. We are able to make adaptations that allow them to remain feeling 'just right' for as much of their day as possible. It also allows us to make adaptations and create strategies that support recovery from dysregulation as and when it happens.

Sensory play is not a quick fix, or a one-programme-for-all solution, and here is a child-based example to show why:

Child A: Has a large sensory balloon so they need a lot of input to get their 'just right' feeling. It is made of stretchy material so needs a lot of big movements and stimulation. They seek body movements and rotations. They avoid sticky textures at all costs, as this immediately bursts their balloon.

Child B: Has a small sensory balloon and only needs a small amount of input to feel 'just right'. In fact, it is so small that often just being in a group with other children makes their balloon close to popping. They seek small sensory experiences linked to touch like sand, slime or play dough. They seek loud music to dance to by themselves – the sound input of the music slowly fills their small balloon. But music at parties or carpet time with others is distressing – the visual/touch input of the people fills their balloon too quickly.

Both these children present with sensory differences at school/home and would benefit from sensory support. However, offering these two children the same sensory tray of making slime potions, with scoops and little bottles, cut flowers and glitter is going to result in very different outcomes. Child A is likely to feel over-stimulated, emotional and overwhelmed after this play. But Child B will be soothed, engaged and ready for learning through the play. The same activity does not suit them both, because their sensory capacity is different. The way they process sensory information is individual. The way they experience the different senses is unique to them. Their balloons are different.

Table 2.1: Ideas that support children linked to the senses

Sight / Lighting	
If there is too much	Use lamps rather than overhead lighting. Use florescent lighting covers to dim the glare. Allow child to wear a peaked cap or to put their hood up. Create a cosy space with less light, like a tent or den.
If there is not enough	Use flashing toys. Sensory room lights. Activities where you hide in and out of blankets so there is quick lighting shifts. Explore colours. Use glitter and sensory bottles. Use torches with colour slides.

Hearing / Sound	
If there is too much	Offer ear defenders. Model using their own hands, or offer yours if they prefer. Allow the child to wear a hood up to soften surrounding sounds. Create quiet spaces for respite. Make sure paper towels are available rather than hand dryers in the bathroom. Give notice before creating a loud noise – e.g. using the hoover or emptying a toy box.
If there is not enough	Use music on the TV, radio etc. Use musical and noisy toys. Activities with sudden noises or songs. Activities with clapping, drumming and musical instruments. Allow children to layer noises – they may enjoy having the TV on, noisy toys playing and a song on their tablet.

Smell	
If there is too much	Be mindful of where you complete activities – consider if you are close to the kitchen, toilets, art room. Be mindful that environmental smells may take a lot of your child's capacity and lower their tolerance for other input – if you are on a school trip to a farm, the smells may impact their ability to follow in-structions. Find preferred smells and incorpo-rate these into play activities.
If there is not enough	Use scented play dough. Use soaps and fragranced products in water trays. Use herbs in sensory trays Play games that involve smelling – putting different foods into covered cups and trying to identify them by smell.

Taste	
If there is too much	Be mindful that trying new foods may take a lot of capacity and lower their tolerance for other input. You may notice extreme food sensitivities and need to support specialist advice from a feeding therapist and dietician. You may notice sensitivities to toothpaste and need to seek a milder flavour.
If there is not enough	Play dough that is taste-safe because it is likely to be explored orally. Your child may seek a large range of flavours and textures in their food – they may show a preference to more extremes, like spicy food or salty food. Your child may benefit from safe chewing – crunchy foods or chew jewellery.

Touch	
If there is too much	Consider clothing and its impact – removing labels, allowing joggers not school trousers, allowing trainers not shoes. Allowing adaptations for sensory activities – offering a spoon to mix with rather than hands. Offering towels to wipe paint on. Using 'clean sensory play' by putting items in zip bags to be explored without the intensity and after mess. Being mindful of your positioning and the amount of contact you have with the child as part of your interactions.
If there is not enough	A wide range of sensory play trays to explore textures. A wide range of sensory play trays to explore temperatures – ice play vs. warm water play. A wide range exploration in different environments to experience contrast in touch – tree bark, soil, leaves vs. plastic toys, paper books.

Proprioception	
Over-responsive: child is avoiding	Offer warning and support when completing movement-based activities. More reassurance, support and explanation may be needed for PE/playground or group activities. Support them to advocate for their body boundaries by teaching them phrases with actions like 'I don't like it' or 'I need more space' or 'no touch'.
Under-responsive: child is seeking	Jumping activities. Using crash mats/pads. Pushing toys in a box along the floor. Carrying heavy items in a backpack. Using a weighted blanket. Big cuddles and squeezes.

Interoception	
Over-responsive: child is avoiding	Children may need adults to prompt them for body needs such as drinking, eating and using the toilet. Use visuals and reminders to support independence as well as adult prompts. Children may be under-responsive to pain/injuries and need extra support to pause and rest/have medical care. Relying only on their perception of the severity/outward reaction to the event may not be appropriate. Request that school systems and policies are adapted to allow children to respond to their needs in the moment – systems such as 'use the toilet only at break time' or 'drinks bottles are kept for scheduled times'. Adults can prompt children to check in with their needs, to support awareness – 'how do you feel, what does your body need?' Adults can label and narrate what they think a need may be to support their understanding – 'You did a lot of running, I wonder if your body feels thirsty… you need a drink!'
Under-responsive: child is seeking	Children may need support with anxieties around how their body feels – extra care, compassion and validation can be given at times of emotional and physical distress. Children may appear to have extreme responses to pain, cold or emotional discomfort. These will need validating and soothing. Adults can prompt children to check in with their needs, to support awareness – 'How do you feel, what does your body need?' Adults can label and narrate what they think a feeling may be to support their understanding, validating the extremity of the feeling and offering a soothing narrative – 'You fell over and it was a shock and a hurt. That felt like such a lot for your body. I'm going to help, it feels really big now but it will slowly get smaller.' (Alongside other appropriate support for the situation.)

Vestibular 	
Over-responsive: child is avoiding	Offer care and compassion during busy movement activities in PE. Allow children to 'opt out' of activities that intentionally induce dizziness. Allowing more time for activities like going down the stairs. Allowing more time for climbing on or using play equipment.
Under-responsive: child is seeking	Providing activities that allow safe rocking and swinging movements – such as rocking chairs, swings, balance boards. Play balancing games on the beam, or standing on stepping stones or tip toes. Play jumping and bouncing games – hopscotch, the floor is lava, trampolines. Yoga and gymnastic poses that gently move our head down to the floor and back up again – touching toes, making a bridge, 'downward dog' yoga pose.

Because there is such variation between children, I cannot create a list of play activities that will support every child. The table above can be used as a starting point, but children will often need a combination of these things, which may even feel a little conflicting. For example, one child may like loud music, but not like the loud singing of their peers at carpet time. Each child will need a unique combination of sensory factors to be considered. My hope is that the information and the categories I have outlined in this chapter will help you *detect and discover* what your child's sensory needs are to then create play-based activities inspired by other things I share with you as you read on.

Supporting children to notice and advocate for their own sensory needs

I have observed that children often know exactly what they need to help their body feel steady and regulated. However, they may not always seek it in a way that is deemed socially expected or socially safe, and so over time we accidentally guide them away from what they actually need. Consider a young child who often feels overwhelmed and who lays on the floor and has a big cry when they do. This instinctive reaction is a very grounding way to respond to distress. Their body gets feedback from the floor, the contact and pressure soothes their vestibular and proprioception systems, the cry releases the emotion and triggers the release of hormones to soothe them. Older children may ask you to sit with them while the complete self-care tasks or daily tasks, not in order for you to help them, but just as company – this is now a well-known system within the ADHD community called 'body doubling'. But so often we will encourage children to be more independent or explain that at X age they should be able to complete a task without an adult there. It is interesting to me that so often we teach our children out of these systems because of social expectation and then, later, we need to reintroduce them, or find ourselves searching for alternatives because the skills aren't progressing. But actually, often, the child's instincts were right all along! We come back to *'all behaviour is communication'*. Their behaviour is communicating a need to us, and rather than stopping it, we can look to *redirect* it to become a more functional or appropriate strategy that works alongside the child and their environment.

Remember it is also important to question whether action is needed at all. We can ask ourselves, is the behaviour, action, noise or movement putting anyone at risk? If it isn't, is there a genuine need to redirect it, or can we work towards accepting it as part of how the child exists, regulates and expresses themselves.

Stimming

Closely linked to this behaviour concept is stimming. Stimming is a repeated movement/action/noise made by an individual to support regulation and bring joy or comfort. You can stim in all sorts of ways to bring feedback to your body and stimulate different senses.

Examples of stimming for different senses:

- **Touch:** Fidgeting, hair twirling, tapping, stroking or holding material/toys.
- **Audio:** Listening to the same song or sound over and over, repeating words/sound, clicking, play involving sound like kicking leaves to hear them crunch.
- **Visual:** Watching sparkles, playing with lights or shadows, watching water/sand move.
- **Body movement and balance:** Hand flapping, rocking, spinning, climbing, seeking pressure and weight.
- **Oral:** Tongue, lip or mouth movements/chewing, biting nails, sucking thumb or fingers, singing, humming, whistling, screaming, seeking strong tastes/textures.
- **Smell:** Smelling toys, food, clothes, hair, and other items in their environment.

Different people stim for different reasons. Some will stim to support their concentration and focus. Some may stim when they are distressed because the repetition brings calm and regulation to their body. Some may stim to show and experience the height of emotions like joy and excitement. Some people may stim when they are board and not fulfilled by their environment.

When we see a child or any individual stimming, it is so important to value this as this person's unique way of expressing and regulating themselves. It is also an indication that they are working really hard to make sure their body feels right as they process everything in their environment. Interrupting or stopping a person stimming can be extremely distressing and damaging. It is important that as supporting adults we advocate for our children to stim as a valid form of communication and regulation. Only if a stim is putting the child or others at risk should we interrupt their process, and this should be done with compassion and the option to try an alternative, safer stim. Stimming will be happening for a reason: our role is not to stop it, but to get curious about why and either celebrate it or show we understand its importance by offering a safer alternative.

In the examples that follow, I would recommend using simple, clear spoken language supported with visuals such as a communication board, regardless of the child's own expressive language skills. This is because it provides a story of compassion and understanding. We can never know what a child's internal language system is and how much they understand but don't yet use. It is important to *assume their competence*, in which case, offering this kind of narrative will make it clear that the expectation is not to continue with something distressing; it is a communicative signal from the adults that we are in tune with their needs.

Strategy: Adult narration

When you notice a child's sensory or regulatory behaviour, name it and add an action for them. I often use the phrase: 'Your body seems X, let's try X to help'. For example, a child comes in from break time and is super busy, running around, spinning, jumping and throwing. This is a signal that they are over-stimulated and can't calm that feeling in their body – they will feel almost stuck in this busy feeling, a tornado of energy. Think of the sensory balloons – for this child, it's been filled up with so much air at play time that they have let go of the knot and the balloon is now flying about the room uncontrollably. His behaviour is like he is leaping around trying to catch it. Telling that child and his balloon that he must calm down and stop moving or running is not going to help him catch that balloon. He is very unlikely to have the skill set to catch such a chaotic balloon all by himself. He needs help. His behaviour is asking for it, but in a very chaotic way. We can try supporting his knowledge and understanding of regulation by explaining his feelings to him. 'Your body seems super busy! Play time must have felt big and you can't make it small and steady. Let's try five star jumps and then a big stretch to help it.'

This action offers structure and grounding. The number of star jumps offers a clear boundary, the collaboration offers reassurance, the stretch offers a chance to breathe and be still but still receive a level of feedback. This sequence helps the child to catch their balloon and hold onto it again, at a time that they couldn't independently. It helps them notice their body and how the feeling they have changes. We can prompt them afterwards to consider 'How do you feel now?' to complete the story of regulation.

Different children will need different levels of support and input depending on what their sensory profile is and what type of input they are seeking or avoiding in order to settle and feel balanced again. Always keep in mind that sensory balloon they are holding – we are aiming to help them maintain it, floating gently by their side.

Strategy: What do I need poster

Create a visual prompt for recognising that dysregulation has occurred and how to help.

Use key phrases like: 'I don't feel right!' or 'My body feels busy/slow/sad/achy'.

Then offer solution phrases: 'I need a… drink, hug, some quiet time, some time in the dark, to go to the toilet, help to find what to play, space, to move my body'.

Strategy: Advocating phrases

In play-based therapy and throughout your day with your child, it is important to model and support phrases and communication systems that encourage children share their sensory and regulation needs with us. In play, this might look like the adult noticing that a child does not like the noise and fright of a pop-up toy. When you see their reaction, we can model key advocating phrases such as: 'I don't like it', 'I need to go', 'no touch', 'too big', 'stop', 'I need more space', 'no more', 'help me', 'I'm scared', 'I need a break'.

We can model these verbally, but also with actions/signs, as well as making sure these phrases are available and accessible on communication boards and AAC devices. (There's more on this on pp.85-86.) It is also important that we offer choice and that we respect the sensory boundary being shared with us. In play therapy, this may look like saying 'This toy is so noisy! Shall we do more or stop?' The child then has the opportunity to decide for themselves if they have capacity to experience it again, or if they want to move away from it. Be sure to use all their communication to help you gauge this, and interpret their body language and facial expressions as well as what words or symbols they choose. You can respond accordingly: 'You want to stop? I understand. You're telling me "I need a break!"... let's play something different.'

The science of fun

When we think of a child becoming dysregulated, we often think of this presenting in terms of upset and distress when they don't enjoy an activity. But this is not always how dysregulation manifests. I have observed and experienced that neurodivergent children can easily become dysregulated with excitement or anticipation in equal measure. This might look like repeating a play sequence over and over again and not seeming like they can stop. They might be spinning or running themselves to crash into the sofa/crash pad. Although the activity is initially joyful for them, the happiness and joy can grow and grow until it's almost overwhelming. The crash gets bigger and the spin gets faster until it's actually an unpleasant experience. Maybe they watch a funny video or ask you to make a funny sound over and over and laugh so intensely that suddenly the laugh evolves into tears and crying and sadness. The feeling has grown too big to manage, even though it was a joyful one to start with, it almost outgrew the child's capacity to hold it. (In terms of their sensory balloons, the joyful feeling got so big the balloon burst.) It feels a contradictory concept to have too much joy, but I have experienced this often when playing, supporting or observing children.

Visualise the concept

I often visualise this by imagining a double-sided step ladder. As we play and engage in something joyful, it's like we are climbing the steps on one side together. There comes a point where we are nearing the top and things are at the very best they can be. Each child's capacity to remain at the top safely will be different. I look for warning signs of dysregulation starting to set in – are their actions getting bigger, louder and more intense? Are they able to pause and catch a breath before the next turn? Are they adapting the game to make it bigger, more forceful or more explosive each turn? These are the warning signs that the joy is becoming dysregulating and overwhelming. If we carry on or they are left to carry on by themselves, they are very likely to tip toe on the very top of the step ladder and topple off with a crash – this often looks like the activity becoming dangerous, they may injure themselves by accident or maybe even on purpose (self-biting or banging their head) because the feelings are overwhelming even though they started positive. As the supporting adults, we want to look for these signals and help them slowly, turn and start stepping down the steps on the other side of the step ladder. We've built ourselves up, up, up, and now we need to carefully steady ourselves down, down, down the other side. When supporting them to climb down, be mindful that stopping the game abruptly because 'It's getting too much!' will feel like pushing them off the step ladder and it will likely end in a big dysregulation of sadness and confusion. The change from fun to nothing is too sudden. It's really important that we walk through it with them, slow and steady, add some calm and structure to the fun the ease ourselves away from it.

There are a few ways we support this process:

- We can do this by slowing our own rate of speech as we play, lowering our tone and our volume, and making our happy reactions a little bit smaller. Still connective and positive, but smaller.
- We can add in some sensory soothing input for that child, like rubbing their back, or a slow and gentle hug to help them regulate again. (This will need to be child-specific depending on sensory preferences.)
- Offer a different idea that will give a smaller, more controlled version of the play. For example, if they are running, suggest they do six jumps or start to march around. Movement is still involved, but it is more controlled than freely running and full speed.
- We can narrate as we start to do this, using ourselves as a model, to support awareness and independent regulation in the future. Sounding something like this: 'Woah! This got so busy, my body feels so happy and wooshy [big breath]... It's getting a bit much for me! Time to get a bit steady... Let's do X more and then try X.'

Our aim in modelling this is that our children will observe the build up and gentle lowering down in their own systems and be able to use this in future more independently – I like to imagine that we are supporting them to turn their step ladder into a slide – one day, their skills will be such that they can get to the top, enjoy the peak of excitement and then, without help, gently slide down the slide to the ground by themselves.

Depending on your child's age and skill set, you can even use this theory with them directly. Draw out the ladder and talk about the build up and link it to their play. This gives you a subtle prompt to use when they need to regulate during an activity. You might say, 'I think we might be at the top of the ladder here, shall we get ourselves down safely before we topple over?' They too can use that visualisation to support self-regulation.

Grounding and getting steady

The movement from peak excitement to a steadier state is often referred to as 'grounding'. When describing this to children, I often refer to this as us feeling 'busy and whooshy', and then 'feeling steady', and then 'feeling calm and ready'. We can notice throughout the day and throughout our play therapy activities that a child may be at their peak level of stimulation and need support to slowly regain control over their body and emotions. This has been researched and written about by many specialists including occupational therapists based on theoretical knowledge linking sensory integration and sensory processing. Therapists have developed programmes of activities that move children from a state of alert, slowly ground them and then achieving calm, which gets them ready for learning and supports regulation. These steps are often referred to as 1) Alerting 2) Organising 3) Calming.

This three-step approach can be used and borrowed not only as its own individual programme of activities, but also throughout the day and for our play.

Table 2.2: Three-step approach to grounding

Alerting activities: Feeling busy and whooshy	
■ Bouncing on a trampoline ■ Spinning in a chair ■ Jumping jacks ■ Hopping on a space hopper ■ Skipping ■ Rolling forward and back over a gym ball	■ Using a slide, swing or play equipment ■ Going on a scooter or bike ■ Jumping on the spot ■ Running

Organising activities: Feeling steady	
▪ Walking on a balance beam ▪ Crawling through a tunnel ▪ Playing with a clay, dough or putty ▪ Throwing bean bags into a bin or hoop	▪ Listening to music ▪ Balancing – on one leg or on a balance board ▪ Wobble boards ▪ Heavy work – carrying heavy objects, or pushing heavy boxes
Calming/grounding activities: Feeling calm and ready	
▪ Rolling a gym ball on the back and limbs ▪ Using different fidget toys or toys with differing textures ▪ Doing press-ups or planks ▪ Pushing against the wall or table ▪ Sorting shapes ▪ Playing listening games – 'point to your nose, point to the ceiling, touch your toes'	▪ Reading a book together ▪ Listening to nature sounds ▪ Stretching and yoga poses ▪ Blowing bubbles and breath work ▪ Sensory play tray linked to sensory preferences ▪ Using a blanket or weighted blanket

We can use this knowledge to support our children successfully regulate in between activities and across their day.

How this might look in therapy

In therapy, you can arrange your activities to follow these three stages, such as:

1. Playing with chasing balloons (**alerting**).
2. Going on a balance board (**organising**).
3. Interactive storytelling with sensory props (**calming**).

You can also combine these three stages within one activity – such as using bubbles. To start with, you blow bubbles for the child so they run about catching them; you notice that they are becoming overwhelmed by the joy and excitement and are very **alert** within play. So you start to gently help them **organise** to feel more steady. Rather than blowing the bubbles freely, you offer guidance for stamping on the balloons to pop them. Following this, you guide them to stretch to the ceiling to catch them up high and then encourage them to blow the bubbles themselves, supporting a deep breath and **calming** puff of air out. Rather than allowing the activity to peak and become too much, you are able to use these steps and knowledge of sensory processing to support the child back to feeling regulated within the task itself.

How this might look at school

When a child has been on the playground for break or lunch, they will have naturally engaged in a lot of high-energy activities, which will have awoken their sensory systems. A typical routine involves them coming in from lunch and starting their afternoon lessons. However, for many children, this shift from high alert to the expectation of calm and focus will not be achievable without support. So using the three-stage approach we can get them ready for learning:

1. They are busy on the playground, involved in running, chasing and football activities, which activate their systems and makes them **alert and awake**.
2. At the door of the classroom, we support them to engage in a series of balance and stretches to help them **organise their systems** – hop four times, balance on one leg for six seconds, march on the spot, slow motion walk into the classroom.
3. Once in the classroom, we offer **calming movement activities** to get them ready for learning. This might involve yoga poses, stretches, breathing with visuals (sensory bottles and balls).

How this might look at home

When you return home from the park or meet up with friends, your child may have been very busy – physically and emotionally. You may notice that they are busy and 'whooshy', in a state of alert. Going straight to lunchtime or play activities may not work because it is too big a transition, the whoosh will come with us – maybe the plate of food gets thrown on the floor, or a tower of bricks gets knocked into a sibling. So we can use our knowledge of these three stages to help the child gently step down from their state of high alert. We need to offer some 'organising' activities before we can go to calm activities and then a state of readiness. This might look like rolling them up in a blanket for a playful cuddle-squeeze (organising), and then settling down for a story (calming). This might look like getting some play dough out for them to squash out flat on the table/floor with their hands, pressing down very hard (organising), and then adding small pieces to make a fairy garden (calming). This might look like having time on a balance board or stepping stones (organising), and then exploring fidget toys.

We use these three stages as stepping stones to help their body move into a more calm and regulated state so it is soothed and ready for its next activity.

Remember: Children won't understand this about themselves yet. They will need adult help and support to move through these stages. Without guidance, they may stay in the alert state even when it doesn't feel right and isn't safe for the surroundings – running around the classroom, throwing things indoors. They may not have the skill set to process instructions to stop, and action strategies to self-organise and self-calm by themselves. They will need an adult to guide them through the stages. To help them down from the top of that step ladder! (See p.40.)

Key strategy: Practice your calming and grounding activities *before* a child desperately needs them. When a child is very alert, busy and highly active, within that moment they are often unable to access the learning part of their brain to process instructions and information. Therefore, if you wait for a child to be in this state before you teach them to organise and calm, the teaching will feel clunky, difficult and may be unsuccessful. Make time to practice your regulating activities when your child is *already* regulated. This way they have prior knowledge of the movements, expectations and resources. This can make such a difference to the success of this process.

Connection and its role in regulation

Safety and connection are just as important as a child's physical and sensory needs. Considering for them whether they need the toilet or whether they need a snack helps regulate them physically. Considering, whether they feel safe with this grown-up, whether they feel safe within this environmental setting, whether they feel safe with these toys, or with their peers, helps regulate them emotionally and plays a crucial role in what state their brain is going to be in and whether it is going to have capacity then to take on new skills.

This links all the way back to our basic theory of a child's nervous system and whether they're in fight, flight, freeze or fawn mode. So, how do we create a feeling of safety? How do we create a feeling of connection for children?

The first thing that we want to do is consider what, for that individual, makes them feel safe? What makes them feel understood and accepted? This will be completely different for every single child so we will need to spend time observing them and gathering this information as we play and learn with them.

You will notice different themes that create connection for a child, some examples might be:

- A child who needs a gentle touch. You notice that when you place your hand on their back as you chat, they relax and settle quicker.
- A child who needs a certain topic of conversation, a passion that they have, which talking about or playing within makes them feel calm and settled.
- A child who needs their communication partner to be loud and laughing and enthusiastic.
- A child who needs their communication partner to be calm, peaceful and settled, who doesn't make lots of big and unpredictable noises when they play.
- A child who needs you to be really close to them while they play; they may sit on you or very close next to you so they can reach for your hand for help, or the feeling of you rather than the chair helps them settle.
- A child who needs distance and space between you and finds physical touch or contact a shock that disrupts their connection.

All of those characteristics and options are completely valid in forming a connection, but some are opposite to each other. It is important for us to match up with the child's needs as a way of offering safety. Being an excitable character for a child who needs a gap between them with steady voices from an adult in order to feel safe will make therapy less supportive. It is going to be harder to create a connection if you haven't worked out the coding for what that child needs for safety. This is why it's really important to individualise your therapy plan and to really invest time, in observing your child to discover what makes them feel happy, safe and connected.

This mindset shift should help redirect your approach to therapy because, rather than asking yourself 'How can I teach this child the skill X?' or 'to cope with X?', we start to think, 'What's going on for this child that makes X so tricky? What kind of support do they need that will mean they are more regulated within this situation/setting/ with these people?'

Chapter 3:
Communication pyramid

The communication pyramid is the foundational theory for much of the therapy that speech and language therapists do, helping us track the pathway of typical language and communication development. Neurodiverse children will often follow their own unique pathways. They are often more individual, and don't tend to follow the step-by-step systems of neurotypical development. However, it is still useful to know this theory as understanding how they are jumping and zigzagging across the pathways can give us a greater understanding of how we can help, as well as a greater empathy for how confusing language and communication may feel for them. So, although the little ones we are supporting may not follow this theory, that's OK, knowing it is still helpful when planning our therapy activities.

Our communication skills are more than the talking and the sounds we make. They are a set of skills that are all linked together to form the way that we communicate with each other.

It is more than just the words we have or the way that we say them. It is a combination of skills that we can visualise as a pyramid tower, carefully stacking

on top of each other, building a firm foundation at the bottom to create a steady place on top of which our more complex communications skills can balance.

There are skills involved at the bottom of the pyramid that form a foundation of knowledge and ability. They are harder for us to see and to measure, but they are crucial for the development of the more obvious skills that build onto them.

The layers of the pyramid

1. Attention and listening skills

At the bottom of the pyramid we have our **attention and listening skills**.

These include our ability to focus and attend to things in our environment, paying attention to something that we have chosen to do for ourselves, as well as our ability to attend to something someone else has asked of us or suggested to us. In terms of listening, this skill doesn't refer to being able to hear words or sounds – which is a separate physical skill linked to our physiology – no, in this context, listening refers to our ability to notice and identify sounds in our environment. Be aware of sounds and words and have an interest in them. It is absolutely crucial for this skill to be part of our communication, because we, as adults, can offer all the language and play opportunities in the world, but if the child we are supporting is not accessing them, is not attending to them, is not even really noticing them, it will be almost impossible for them to absorb and acquire them to then use for themselves.

2. Play and social skills

Above attention and listening skills, we've got **play and social skills** and how we interact with people around us.

Play is such a huge area of skills; it covers so much of a child's development, and, for me, in therapy it is the key to unlocking children's communication capacity and potential. There are different styles of play, different types of play and play patterns that I will explore this in lots of detail. Social skills here relate to how we interact and engage with other people and things in our environment. It often refers to how often or how much we want other people to be part of our play and interaction. It refers to how we incorporate others into our lives, take turns, invite people in, initiate interaction, how we greet people, how we say goodbye. In a really broad sense, it refers to any way that we connect with other people.

3. Understanding skills

The next layer of the pyramid is our **understanding skills.**

This refers to our understanding of language. When words and language are in our environment, can we respond to them? Can we link words to pictures and pictures to objects? Can we understand concepts and definitions? For example, do we notice and understand that a four-legged creature can be a cat or a dog? Can we understand and decipher what makes a cat different from a dog? This section of language learning refers to our ability to hear an instruction and pick out the key parts, interpret that information and then follow instructions. It refers to knowing what words mean, having a vocabulary that we can refer to. As well as understanding the world around us, for example learning that food goes into the freezer to get cold or that, when we let go of a ball, it rolls out of our hands. Children are using their understanding skills to answer questions as well as interpret and evaluate their surroundings.

4. Expressive language skills

Building further, we've then got our **expressive language skills.**

The most obvious part of this skill set is where our words feature. It's where we find talking skills, making sounds, linking sounds together to create meaningful words, linking words together to make meaningful sentences, telling stories, telling jokes, giving instructions, asking and answering questions.

If children are following a step-by-step process of language learning, they will move through a slow and steady process of acquiring their talking skills. This flow will often look like this:

1. Sounds and noises: Gurgling sounds, often vowel sounds like ooos and ahhs. This also includes crying and laughing, as these are noises that communicate.
2. Symbolic noises: Sounds and noises that link to real objects, a great example of this being animal noises, saying 'ba ba' for a sheep or calling a car a 'brum'.

3. Part words: This is when we hear incomplete words, but children use them consistently to represent the same thing over and over again. They might call a snack a 'na'. They have heard the word and are using the sounds they have to create a word as close to the one they've heard as possible.
4. Single words: Children start to name objects, people and simple actions around them with clearer, single words – 'car' 'mum' 'go' 'bye'.
5. Putting two words together: When children are more confident with their single words, they tend to start linking their words together to make two-word phrases. These often include a noun (naming words) and a verb (action word) – 'teddy gone' 'baby sleeping' 'more snack'.
6. Creating short sentences: As language skills build, children start to link more of their words together to create three- and four-word sentences, gradually increasing in complexity.
7. Longer sentences, including more complicated grammar structures: As sentences increase in length and complexity, children will often attempt to talk about a larger range of topics, too. So, rather than simply talking about what they see in front of them, they make attempts to recall past events they have experienced, such as something that happened at school or on holiday. They also start using language to predict future events as well as create imaginary stories or scenarios, using their language creatively.

When we are supporting neurodiverse children with their language skills, they will often jump around on this flow system, using a mixture of early and later skills. This is when it's important to know and understand the theory and flow of language learning but not force children to move through them sequentially, or at a certain speed. We need to meet children where they are and aim to add to what they are already able to do without the expectation that they will move in a straight line of the known stages.

Total communication

As part of expressive language skills, we also have 'non speaking ' ways of communicating. These are particularly important to notice and honour when we are supporting our children who are Autistic, as they will often use these to support their communication before they have a spoken word system. Non speaking ways to communicate may include:

- Using signs
- Using gestures
- Using drawing and writing
- Using looking – eye gazing or face gazing in the direction of the item that they want or are noticing
- Using body language and facial expressions
- Using noises
- Using stimming movements to share emotions
- Using photographs, pictures, picture boards or symbols
- Using objects to indicate needs – showing their shoes to indicate they want to go out to play
- Using technology – AAC devices, apps and buttons

It is important that we value and nurture all of these ways of communicating. These are the ways of communicating that often are used first or alongside spoken words and are often the first times that children experience being able to share their message with other people. It is often through these methods that we can support children to embrace communication as they experience the empowering feeling of connecting, requesting or showing another person something. If we only focus on spoken words, we can often miss or overlook a child's attempts at these none-talking ways of communicating messages with us, and missing these means we miss an opportunity to celebrate connection and communication. We miss an opportunity to encourage and nurture them to use that method of sharing a message again. It is important to encourage, demonstrate and celebrate *all methods* of communication, because that is where the real joy in connection and empowerment of communication can start from and grow for our children.

5. Clarity of speech

Right on the top of the pyramid of skills we've got our sounds, which is often referred to as the **clarity of our speech**.

Very simply, this refers to being able to identify, process, produce and blend all the sounds in all the right places at all the right times – for example, being able to produce a C sound, an A sound and a T sound and blend all of these sounds together to produce the word 'cat'. This is a huge area for speech and language therapists and there are many books specialising in just this type of therapy alone. This is often the very last skill that we would consider supporting independently in therapy because it relies on a child being able to efficiently use all the underlying skills of this pyramid independently. Speech sound production is a different skill set to reading, writing and literacy in school, and although there is much crossover, we consider these as different skills. Often, but not always, speech clarity and speech sound production skills are not necessarily a focus for a child who is Autistic as we would want and need to support the underlying skills for communication and their communication system first. In this book, I will not cover therapy ideas and support for speech clarity, specific speech sound production and speech sound discrimination. It is a huge area and would fill many books all by itself. However, a lot of my play, regulation and connection-based approach could be combined with a 'speech sound target' practice to support an Autistic child's speech clarity, should that be an appropriate focus for therapy for that individual.

Building the pyramid

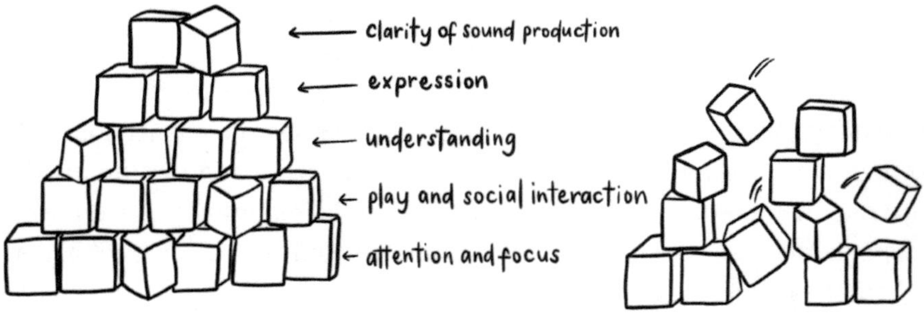

When neurotypical children are developing their communication skills, they tend to follow the pyramid structure, acquiring skills in this sequence and gradually building the skills on to each other. They won't learn each skill exclusively before they move onto the next skills; they don't have to develop completely perfect attention listening skills before they then move on to play skills. That would be too structured and strict. However, it is often the case that children develop a solid enough foundation in each skill before they can start to develop the next. To visualise this, let's imagine that the skills learnt for communication are like building blocks. Children are learning new skills to build a pyramid shaped tower with these blocks.

When skills in attention and listening have been acquired these form a base layer of our imaginary building blocks at the bottom of the child's communication pyramid structure. The next layer of skills is play and social interaction which forms a second layer of building blocks balanced on top. Because these blocks have been acquired first, they fit snugly together, creating a strong and solid base . This creates a foundation for the next set of skills to build up onto. These are the skills that we are often watching and waiting for – the understanding of language skills, as well as the talking and sound skills.

Now imagine we've not got this very solid structure at the bottom; imagine it's patchy, blocks are missing all across the bottom two layers of the pyramid tower. When we come to add additional skills to this base, it is very quickly going to crumble and topple. Our child may have some of these skills, they may be attending at times, playing at times and interacting and engaging at times, but there are a lot of skills that haven't formed and created the foundation skill set yet. With this image in mind, we can imagine how fragile that structure is, and if we then trying to teach new skills, like following instructions or learning new words, it is easy to see why those new skills don't seem to get stored and stay with the child. Because the foundation isn't there, they may be able to balance that skill for a moment but then their tower topples, the skills crumble when we load too much for them.

Relating this theory to a neurotypical child and how they are playing/ learning might look like this: a child has sat with an adult to do an inset puzzle. They are looking at the puzzle and then looking at the adult. The adult picks up a puzzle piece as says, 'Look, it's a bus'. The child looks at the bus picture and hears the adult's spoken words at the same time. What we are seeing here is a child who has developed enough of their attention and listening skills and enough of their social interaction skills to then have capacity to access the language being provided in their environment. They are focused and connected and motivated, and therefore, when the language is used by the adult and they see the picture of the bus, they are able to start to build an understanding of what that word means. If that adult then repeats the word a few times, the child's understanding will have built enough that they will feel confident enough to attempt to say the word for themselves.

Children learning in this pattern with a neurotypical brain will have a predisposition to follow this pyramid structure as they learn language. They will be driven to gain other people's attention in their environment; they will be driven to acquire the connection within play and maintain that focus with another adult or child for as long as possible. It means that, naturally, they are building those bottom layers of their pyramid and getting themselves ready for understanding the language that is in their environment.

How does this theory help us to support neurodiverse children?

Neurodiverse and Autistic children will not necessarily follow this pattern for their language and communication learning. They will zig-zag in a unique way across communication development. They will explore attention and listening skills in their own way. They will investigate and include people in their own unique way to develop their social skills. However, this pyramid theory is useful because we can use it while we design our play-based therapy to layer the skills throughout.

Historically, in therapy, when children are working through the pyramid structure in a step-by-step process, if we observed that there was a skill set in their pyramid that needed support, therapy would usually focus on that, building one skill at a time. We might design activities to work on attention and listening skills, for example, or we might work on turn-taking by rolling a ball between children, or passing toys between children to label 'your turn – my turn'. This doesn't tend to be successful for children who are Autistic because their skill set is uniquely patterned. Their pyramid is a wonderful patchwork of blocks rather than a solid wall. They will have real strengths in some areas and much greater needs in others. What I have found, then, is that activities that focus on one skill at a time tend to be either under-stimulating or over-stimulating. This leads to a child opting out and searching for a more preferred way to play so that they can get that 'just right' feeling.

Designing play therapy

With this all in mind, when I am designing therapy, I don't choose just one element from the pyramid, but consider **all the elements needing to be covered for EACH play idea**. Each play idea needs to capture their attention, have an element of social play and interaction, an opportunity for understanding, and opportunities for expressive language in a range of ways.

Layering in attention

When developing an activity for a child, we want to create a play therapy concept that will be appealing and engaging for the child.

I take time to consider:

- What the child enjoys.
- What they are motivated by.
- What captures their attention.
- What creates focus and engagement for them naturally.
- What do they choose to play.

In doing this, we are already setting ourselves up for successful play. Because *within* that activity we are building the foundation of the pyramid. This is different to therapy before, where you might complete activities designed to stretch and focus a child's attention and listening skills. I am not going to design activities that 'work on attention and listening' because that skill hasn't developed yet. I am going to design an activity that I know will *naturally capture their attention and focus*. They won't have to work hard to attend, because the play will be something they already want to do. They will *choose* to attend, rather than be *taught* to attend. This means that the foundation layer of the communication pyramid is built and achieved within that task. It also means that we start off connected rather than in a power struggle. Insisting a child attend to something teaches a very different skill. It is still an attention-based skill, but it adult-guided rather than child-chosen. For our neurodiversity-affirming therapy, we want children to *choose* to be part of the play with us, not complete the tasks because they have to, or as a means to receive a reward.

Mindset shift: If an activity is not sparking their attention, it is not that they need to learn to attend more, it is that we need to adjust our therapy activity to be more appealing. We need to create something that captures their attention by choice and sparks their play joy.

Layering in social interaction

Once their attention is focused because they choose to engage with the activity, I consider the next skill on our pyramid – play and social interaction. I now want to build this skill *within* the play activity in the same way.

I will do this by considering:

- What dose the child enjoy?
- What will they accept and enjoy from my presence?
- How can I try and add myself as being part of their play?

Some simple ways to add yourself to the play are:

1. Work out how you can help within the play. Are you able to help them open things, are you able to help them by passing objects to them, are you able to help them by moving irritating items out the way, can you help by getting them extra parts for their game. Consider yourself the 'play assistant' and they are the 'play director'!
2. Work out how to make the play funny or a little bit silly. Consider how you can create some joy and silliness within the activity. This will flood the child's brain with all sorts of happy hormones and inspire them to carry on with a drive to repeat the activity with you again.

Ask if it's OK to join and respect their space. Regardless of the child's skill set, I will always check in with them verbally and with my body language to gain their consent for my involvement in the game/play. As part of this, I will never take an item from a child's hand (even to help them). I wait with my hands out and ask 'help?' If they don't offer it to me, I wait. If they give up and put it down, I then have a chance to pick it up from neutral ground and show them, saying, 'I can help with this', and do a quick demo. Alternatively, I try and find something similar and do my own version of their play to show I have some knowledge to share. So if they are trying to use a spinning top, I use a different one next to them, or pick up a sensory bottle and spin that. Again, this signals I want to help, but also that I respect their space.

Why? Because so much of young children's lives involves adults organising them and being closely involved with them – wiping their face, putting on shoes, giving them things to hold, helping them open packets. We need to be very close and involved and it isn't always what the child wants or expects – so this is a gesture in play that offers a partnership and collaboration, rather than a takeover. It's a small gesture of respect through providing physical space and waiting.

A chance to initiate

Initiating communication and play means being the person to go first. Being the person to start a collaboration. Very often for children who are Autistic, this can be a skill that isn't always prioritised. They often have advanced skills in areas such as pattern sequencing; understanding how technology or toys work; as well as a resilience and drive to complete tasks or challenges independently. What this often results in is a different approach to their supporting adults in their environment. A neurotypical child may try to reach a toy on a high shelf, see an adult sitting on the sofa and request help by pointing, asking or looking. An Autistic child will often continue to pursue the item independently, reaching or climbing the shelf, or will decide to move on and seek their play elsewhere. The choice to initiate the interaction won't necessarily be prioritised.

This can often establish patterns that eliminate the chance to practice initiating. For example, the adult in this example might ask 'Do you need help?' or 'What's the matter?' Although this is supportive, the adult is the one who has started the conversation. If this happens, it can often become such a regular pattern that the child may learn or create a rule for themselves that they need to wait to be asked, which can be disempowering and frustrating. To create more balance in the interactions, it is important to *create playful opportunities* for the child to start the interactions, or take the lead in the communication. A great way to do this is *using your body language but not your words*. In the example above, rather than asking 'Do you need help?', I would move from the sofa to be right next to the shelf where the toy was, hold my hands out so they looked ready to help, and then just pause in this 'almost ready' position. This gives the signal to the child that we are available and a possible source of help, without directly asking them to ask us. Ideally, in this example, the child will notice my availability and push my hands or body towards the item they want, they may just make a noise, or they may stare at the item they are trying to get. All three of those behaviours are valid forms of communication and indicate that the child is starting an interaction with us, noticing that we are there and inviting us to be part of the solution. It's important that we respond straight away to any initiated communication to show that we value it and that it is worth prioritising in the future. In this instance, we would respond by getting the item they need and modelling additional communication such as, 'I want that,' or 'Help!' or 'Toy!' Our response is *never* conditional to an expectation placed on the child. We respond regardless of what mode of communication the child chooses to use.

In this example, if the child did not respond to us being nearby and available but continues to climb the shelf, we can use this as a chance to demonstrate that we want to collaborate with them – so without hesitation, we reach for the toy, pass it to them and model 'help'. Although in this instance we have not had a chance for the child to practice initiating, we have had a chance to show we want to be a play partner. Over time, this builds our connection and will increase the possibility that the child will initiate communication with us in the future. (This is very different to outdated therapy advice that is not neurodiversity affirming – see Chapter 13 where I discuss this further.)

Another way to allow for initiation in play is to create an interesting or curious play sequence and then pause, leaving an opportunity for the child to approach you to join in or request completion. For this to be their initiation, we must not call their name or call for their attention to look. They need to be the ones who see us, choose to join and be the instigator of the collaboration/interaction.

This might look like: The adult building a tower of bricks, singing a song but not knocking it over, pausing, waiting to see if the child approaches and knocks it for us. The moment they do, they have started a conversation with us. A play conversation has begun. I can build the tower again and leave it for them to crash – it's a back and forth through play that they initiated by choosing to join.

This might look like: The adult lines up alphabet tiles because they know this will bring the child joy. When the child sees the line, they reach for the next tiles and add it to the line. The moment they do, they have started that play conversation with us. But not because we asked them or told them. Because we presented an opportunity for them to initiate, and they took it!

Our mindset here:
To be available, but not insisting.
To be ready to respond, but not rush in and go first.

Ideas for layering people into play

Because one of our key foundation layers for learning language skills is the social aspect of sharing a message with another person, speaking and none-speaking skills are included in this. We also want to create an element of *'people – ness'* to the game. If a child is enjoying their play but they haven't really noticed that the help or part of the joy is including us as another person, they are less likely to respond or absorb the language that is coming from us. Here are a few simple ways to do this:

- Bring toys and items of interest from the floor up to near your face or body as you try to help with them in the play. The aim here is not to encourage the child to look at our eyes or our mouth. This needs to be very clear, because there is research and evidence that this can feel incredibly uncomfortable and upsetting for children who are Autistic. Our aim here is really just to show that the object and the person are separate and different things: 'My hands are part of my body and face, and that's where the communication and the help are coming from', rather than, 'My hands and the toy are one of the same thing'. I would only ever recommend you do this fleetingly and I would never recommend allowing this to disrupt the flow of your play or create distress for your child. This strategy should be used with care and attention should be given to how the child responds to this and we should act with respect and compassion accordingly.

- Use your body as part of the play. For example, placing a toy on top of your head and wiggling so it falls off. Placing a blanket over you to hide yourself and allow the child to find you.
- Use yourself as a sensory play support. For example, if your child likes weighted blankets and deep pressure, they may enjoy a game where you hug or squeeze them. Your arms can cuddle them and then release, allowing the child to then indicate that they would like more or to finish. For example, your child may love to jump on the exercise ball, but they need to hold your hands to do so safely, so people become an integral part of this play fun.
- Find equipment that needs two people for success. For example, blowing up balloons with a pump is often too tricky for a child to coordinate and do alone, so adding an adult to use the balloon pump with them creates a chance for collaboration. It is important that within this play we don't withhold the activity or insist a child act a certain way before we collaborate. *Our help and collaboration is unconditional of any communication.*

Make sure adding people to play enhances the child's play experience. If you see your role in the play becoming a frustration, it is time to gently step back.

Making those foundation layers combine

Say sorry when it goes wrong – It's OK to get the balance wrong by accident every now and then. Maybe the help didn't help in quite the right way. Maybe you added the toy to the line and it knocked a different one over by mistake. Maybe the song wasn't quite the right tune... Acknowledge the mistake openly with the child. Use words, signs and symbols to do this. It might sound like, 'Oh, I'm sorry! I tried to balance the toy and it fell. You wanted it in the line. I understand. I'm sorry.' Try and repair the play sequence if you can, or take a brief step back to allow the child to repair the sequence themselves. Then gradually add yourself back in to the play.

This simple act of apologising adds respect to your play. It shows that you value the importance of their play patterns and sequences. It shows that you are there to collaborate and support them.

Do this regardless of a child's expressive language skills – we often never truly know what their understanding is, so let's assume their competence and that these words will be meaningful to them.

To cement those two foundation layers together, we now want to create *connection and anticipation.* Countdowns and build-ups are great for this. Having the option to use 'ready steady go' or '3, 2, 1' gives a predictable way for your child to know the climax of the play sequence is on its way. Ideally, we are looking to create an element of anticipation, pause to allow expectation to grow, and then fulfil the expectation with the final action.

At this point in the play, in this moment, we have managed to build an entire pyramid – their attention is there, their focus is on us in play, they understand and expect the next thing, and we add language to indicate more/go/woosh. Therefore, within the moment, a child is at the optimum learning capacity for their communication skills.

More strategies for creating connection and anticipation

We can have the best therapy toys, the most wonderful sensory set up and a magnificent play environment, but if we are not connecting with our child, the communication progress we make will be slower and feel harder. During play-based speech therapy, there are some key strategies I use to try and build a connection with children.

- **Mirror, echo and copy, actions, play, sounds, gestures.** Mirroring and copying a child's play can be a really supportive gesture of connection to children and shows through actions that we value their ideas and that we want to be part of their play/world/communication.
- **Play alongside not always involved.** It is tempting to make ourselves fully involved all the time as part of our mission to stay connected. However, this can sometimes be overpowering, and taking a step back to watch and be alongside a child in play is just as affirming. Watch for signals from your child as to how involved they would like you to be and don't be afraid to step back and allow them time to process or play independently.
- **Balance involvement and space.** Imagine yourself as a yoyo when you play, sometimes you will be within the play, among it and hands on, but other times there will need to be some space to allow the child to regulate, reset or organise themselves for the next idea they are having.
- **Don't call their name and tell them to look.** Calling a child and asking them to look is a play-based demand. It puts us in control and can accidentally break the flow of attention within their play. Instead, use noises like 'ooooo' and 'wow!' to create excitement. You can use the sequence of 'point, gasp and wait' or use toys that make a noise as they tap the floor to encourage attention to shift naturally through curiosity, rather than through demand.
- **Monitor tone – reduce language but don't use a harsher tone.** Be mindful of your own tone. Often when we interact with children who are learning language or finding it tricky, we will be encouraged to shorten our sentences. For example: rather than saying, 'Let's go and get your coat on now', we will change it to 'Coat on'. It is important that we monitor our tone with

this language reduction. Very often, we will instinctively shift to using a harsher, more instructive tone because of the language reduction. Be careful that, even though your language load shifts, you keep a gentle, connective tone, intonation and facial expression. Less language doesn't mean a more serious tone. Keep it light and sing-song.

- **Let them initiate – be ready but don't dive in.** We cover this on p.78, but here is a reminder that allowing your child to go first, to initiate communication, will help build a balanced feeling of playfulness between you both.
- **Consider how often your hands and body move into their space.** Even if we are trying to help, it's important to notice how often you lean in, or across, to reach for a toy or item in their space. This may feel like an invasion of their play space which can change the balance and feeling of collaboration within your play. This change can make you appear more dominant within play, rather than being a partner for the play.
- **Keep trust and respect at the centre of your actions.** We do this through requesting involvement. Assume competence, and give them time to process ideas as you play and assume that they have a purposeful plan – our job is not to direct them but to work out what their plan is, so we can facilitate it with them.
- **Adding ideas, but not changing the game – extending play.** When joining a child in their play, look for ways to follow their lead but add to play ideas to try and expand their play. It's a careful balance between honouring what they have already created and adding a little bit extra to make it a collaboration. Make sure the focus and end result of the play stays the same so the child maintains a feeling of ownership and pride in their play creation.

Style of play partner

As you play, there will be different styles of play partner that you will need to move between, these styles of play partner all help our connection with children. All of these play styles are valid and supportive in different ways. It is OK to shift between them, and you will often need to do so to maintain your connection. Don't feel that you need to be in among a child's play continuously. Being parallel or observing can be an important role, too. Let's explore these roles more:

- **Collaborative.** This is when you are working together to create a joint outcome. This might be that you are putting blocks onto the same tower. It might be that you are collecting all the green pompoms for the green pot. You are on the same team, working towards a shared goal.
- **Parallel.** This is when you play alongside the child. You may play the same game as them but have your own set of toys. Or you may play an entirely different game but be in the same room or at the same table as them. Being parallel to them can be a great way to mirror or echo their play without being actively involved in moving or touching toy items that feel important or precious to the child.
- **Observer/distanced.** This is when we sit back and watch. We remain present and interested in the play idea but are not actively involved. We are ready to respond and react should we be needed, but we remain still and quiet, giving the child their own space and time to play in their own way. This is a great time to notice what and how children love to play.
- **Helper.** This is when we present ourselves as useful for the play's success. It can often be our stepping stone into being more collaborative in play and help us to create our first connection with children in their play. It might be that we are needed to wind up a toy, or open a box, or reach something from a shelf, or use the balloon pump. We are involved because we add a helpful role to the play's success.

Tips for collaborating in play

If you feel stuck as an observer and a child is cautious about you joining in their game, here are a few ideas to help create collaborative engagement:

- Set up a play sequence but leave the last bit for them to finish. For example, lay out the number blocks 1-7, and leave 8, 9, 10 in an open box ready to offer to the child. This offers a quick bit of task completion for the child and brings you in to be part of the play creation. You started it and they completed it.
- Say engaging things in an engaging way with engaging actions/ expressions. Make yourself seem interesting and like you will add to the joy of the play – be mindful of what 'engaging' means for that child – loud isn't always what creates connection.

- While observing, work out what the 'point of motivation' is for that child and use this and recreate it – is it the build up, is it the celebration, is it the finished? When you see this, offer it to the child. For example, you see that a child loves popping bubbles but is struggling to blow them. Find a second pot and blow some for them to pop. Because they love to pop them, you are created a chance to move from observer to helper and are now more involved in the play.

Layering in more language

You have already built your solid foundation by choosing an activity you know captures your child's attention; it includes toys and items of interest and already includes you as a helper and fun provider.

You are now ready to add an element of storytelling to the play, which will lend itself to predictable and repetitive language.

Remember our pyramid – within this play moment, attention is built, play and interaction is built, and we are ready for understanding and expressive language to be layered in for children to experience as part of the play.

When developing a play story, we want it to be appealing to the child, so that they want to copy and repeat it. Here are some ideas:

- **A three-element sequence to the story.** Simply put, this is three bits of play that link together. For example: 1) Fill up the cup with rice. 2) Lift it up to a height. 3) Pour it all out slowly, watching it fall. Alternatively, you might: 1) Build a foam-brick tower. 2) Sit a teddy on the top. 3) The tower falls down. Using three-element sequences works well because this lends itself to the classic story frame – beginning, middle, end.
- **Movement as the grand finale – falling, crashing, flowing, bursting.** Including movement as the end of the story gives a clear marker for completion. This is often appealing in play and also means the play naturally prompts us to stop and start again. When this clear end marker is not used, play can escalate, getting bigger and bigger until it becomes unsafe or unsustainable. This structure supports repetition and maintenance.

- **Reaction – shock, joy, humour.** Including a social reaction at the end of the sequence creates a chance to connect in a very real way over a shared experience. Choose a set way you are going to react each time the play happens so you can repeat it after each play sequence. This makes you a predictable and enjoyable part of the play, which is so often not the case when people join play sequences.
- **Short language sequence or song.** As you complete each action in your story sequence, add repeated phrases. For the examples above, this could be:
  - **1)** Fill up the cup with rice saying, 'Fill it up, fill it up, fill it up' (said with every scoop). **2)** Lift it up to a height saying, 'Up it goes! Up, up, up!' (pause for suspense). **3)** Pour it all out slowly watching it fall saying, 'Down, down, sprinkle, sprinkle'.
  - **1)** Build a foam-brick tower saying, 'Build it bigger, build it bigger' (said with every brick). **2)** Sit a teddy on the top saying, 'Teddy on top!' (pause and sing Humpty Dumpty). **3)** The tower falls down, saying, 'Fall down! Crash!'

Layering in total communication

All the while, we want to be adding as many different modes of communication as we can:

- Consider what visuals you can use – making sure you have a core word communication board out and available as you play. This can be electronic or a printout (or combination). You may also use photographs, symbols and line drawings depending on the child's learning style.
- Make sure you are using simple gestures and signs.
- Make sure you are modelling eye gaze by looking at the toys as well as looking at the child for their response.
- Use your face and your body to show your emotions, clap your hands with joy, gasp and put your hands to your face in shock.
- Using your voice for words, sounds and noise.

Throughout therapy and interaction, it is important that you use all these modes of communication, as well as that you observe and respond to the child's attempts to use all of these. It is important to value all ways that children communicate with us. It is important to respond to an eye gaze with the same communicative enthusiasm as a spoken word. All communication is valued and nurtured.

Symbols and systems: Something is better than nothing!

Not every therapist will agree with this, and big companies who design systems will tell you that having it all the same, matching and exactly as they designed it, is the only way… But I strongly feel that something is better than nothing. If you are waiting for perfect resources, or to learn all the signs, or to make all the posters, or laminate all the symbols, the child misses out. Because, while we are waiting for the perfect set of something, in the moment, we have nothing. And nothing is not supportive at all. Something, no matter how quickly sketched the picture card is or approximate the sign is, is still a small extra something to support, that isn't there when only words are used.

So, if in doubt, sketch it on a whiteboard, have a notebook in your bag or pocket at all times and create a gesture that matches the action of the time. Yes, research it later, make it properly later, print off and laminate it later so the official way is available for next time. But in the moment, something is better than nothing.

Be creative and make something. I actually think it's a wonderful way to model resourcefulness to our children and that, in a time of trouble, conveying a message in the future, they too may reach for the whiteboard or notebook, or wave their arms into a made up sign/gesture to support themselves to be understood. Giving them in that moment a way to communicate with an imperfect something, rather than leaving them with a perfect nothing.

People are curious but tiring

One of the things I often notice when supporting children through play therapy is that, even when we are having a nice time together, even when we are playing, connecting and engaging, the child is working hard. Experiencing another person as part of their world and their environment can feel like a lot of work, even when that person is doing everything they can to be a calm and connected presence. What this means is that, during play therapy, children will often wander off for moments of self-regulation and to take some time to themselves. This is actually a really positive thing. This shows that they are in tune with what their body needs and we should nurture and encourage this. This isn't an indication that they have lost interest in a play, or that they can't focus their attention any longer, but is more a signal that their body is telling them to take a break. If we can honour this, allow them time to stim, allow them time to wonder, allow them to take the toy to the corner and have it all to themselves for a moment. When we notice this, we need to pause our talking, we need to lower our voice and shuffle back slightly to give them space to regain their strength. If we can honour that when they are young and learning, we will do two key things:

1. Improve their ability to notice their body's signals and need for space from social communication. This will significantly reduce their frequency of burn out as they get older, and teach them to value the signals they receive rather than push through to adhere to social rules.
2. Show that you, as a supporting adult, understand them and are a safe communication partner who is available for play and rest in equal measure.

Here are some ideas for how we can step back but still keep children safe:

- When we notice a child is creating distance between us, turning their back to us or walking to a different table/space, stay where you are to allow the space to grow. Keep watching and remain available to the child, but allow them to generate the space they need. If you follow them or move to be face-to-face again straight away, we aren't listening to what they are asking for – a physical break.
- After a busy amount of talking from an adult, or perhaps a very loud interactive game, it is important to reduce the amount of noise we make as the adults in their play. We can feel a lot of pressure to be always modelling language and being the most interactive we can be, all the time. But if a child goes quiet, or creates physical space between us, it is likely that they also need an auditory break. You can give them this break by keeping quiet. If they offer you a toy or look to you for words, respond to them but in a lower tone or whisper.
- It is important to keep watching and keep ready during these 'communication breaks' that children request.

In a play-based communication session, this might look something like the following example.

> An adult and a child are both on the floor and are connected in play. The adult has a balloon pump and a balloon and the child is waiting for the balloon to be blown up. The child reaches for the balloon and pushes the adult's hand onto the pump to request it is blown up. The adult models language 'let's go!' and starts pumping the balloon up. The child's excitement builds as they see the balloon grow. The adult says, 'Get ready, get steady.... And pauses...'. The child looks at the balloon and looks at the adult and a connection is created, excited energy builds and the adult says, 'Let's go!' The balloon whooshes around the room and the child screams and jumps and flaps their hands excitedly at the visual stimulation of the balloon zooming around. They collect the balloon and place it back in the adult's hand. The adult models 'more' and the child responds by pushing the balloon closer to the adult. The balloon-blowing sequence happens all over again. After the third time, the child collects the balloon, passes it to the adult but then lays their head

on the sofa and slowly starts moving a car across the front of their face. They watch the wheels move and their face is calm and still. This is a request for a moment's peace, for a little break from how intensely exhausting the interaction is.

This is not a signal that balloons aren't fun, or that the adult did something wrong, it is simply that interacting and connecting can feel like hard work and being alone is calming and regulating. It's a request for a little break and a moment's peace. It's important that the adult in this situation respects and understands this. If the adult here starts strongly encouraging another round of balloons, thinks to themselves, 'I want to stretch this child's attention a few more moments, see if we can expand the learning a little longer', then the child is going to become overwhelmed and either upset, or remove themselves further by going to another room or place in the room. This then creates a tiny damage to the connection that was built and the balloon activity may not be remembered as positive but as overwhelming. If the adult notices the rest and gently rubs the child back and then sits back quietly, allowing time and space for them to process their interaction and the new skills they just practised, then the child quickly restores their social energy and will, over time, learn that this grown up understands them. Getting the balance right here is crucial and it's much easier to do when we have the mindset that play and communication can be hard work for children who are Autistic or neurodivergent, and a break is often needed periodically throughout the play sequence no matter how enjoyable or well-planned it is. It's not necessarily that the activity is wrong, it's not that the child isn't ready or didn't enjoy it, it's just that they need a rest to charge up and play again. (We explore this more in Chapter 11: Demand, capacity, gentle stretch.)

Chapter 4:

Language strategies to layer into your play and your day

The language strategies in this chapter are well-known within speech and language therapy across the world. They are well researched by many therapists and therapy centres, for example Hannen therapy, Michael Palin Centre for Stammering, Elklan and many others. This type of therapy is often referred to as 'adult-child interaction therapy' because the aim is to equip the adult with key strategies to support the child's communication, rather than teach the child. The adult uses the strategies to create a communication set up and environment that makes communication as easy as possible. Over the years, I have used and adapted this theory and these strategies to ensure they are both supportive of language skills and neurodiversity affirming.

Some of these strategies feel very natural and will really just conform to your natural communication instincts. But others are a way of us adapting how we interact. Parents, carers and teachers will often become concerned after learning new strategies that they have 'been getting it wrong' before this strategy was introduced. But that isn't the case. For many children, our natural way of interacting and communicating will be supportive enough for their natural drive and predisposition to learn language to mean that communication, words and interaction occur and develop naturally. When a child has a language delay, or has a neurodiversity, it means that the way their brain processes communication information is done differently. It means that a lot of the subtle natural ways that parents and teachers interact with children may not necessarily lead to a child accessing and acquiring the skills. That's where specialist support comes in, that's where specialist information comes in, that's where specialist strategies come in. It doesn't mean that you have been doing it wrong before this, it means that the subtlety of language development isn't working for this particular child, and there are ways that we can adapt as the adults in their life to make it even more accessible for them. These strategies enhance their language environment and create play and life experiences that mean language is as easy as possible to access and acquire. But, before we launch into strategies, here are some words of kindness for you…

Should it feel this difficult?

I have messages and conversations all the time with parents, teachers and teaching assistants, asking me this – should it feel so difficult? Really apologetically, full of worry and guilt… 'Should it be this hard? All these strategies and play ideas, they are great but they take such a lot of work and the progress feels slow…'

There was no need to apologise because, yes, it feels difficult because it is hard work trying to engage in communication with a small person who can't respond. That is exhausting! Thinking about strategies, noticing patterns in play, longing to hear their little voice, wondering how long this will go on for… The journey for communication can feel difficult, and it's OK if that's where you are right now.

One of the things I remind parents and professionals that I support is that, when children are slower to talk than their peers, if means we have a longer period of time having one-sided interactions. As well, as longer periods of time using strategies for specific skills.

It means we work really hard for a tiny flicker of connection, or spend weeks nurturing an animal noise during nursery rhymes, or put in hours of play for a gesture or sign. That is tiring. Because all of those practices before we reach the moment when they respond, are sometimes met with nothing. We put on a full show with all our enthusiasm and best strategies and maybe we don't get any response at all... That's why it feels difficult.

So it's OK if this feels hard. It's OK if some days you miss the opportunity. Because giving and giving and waiting to get a little back is really hard work, it's amazing, it's a joy, it's a privilege, and.... it can also feel difficult.

Keep going. Be kind to yourself. You're doing amazingly.

Let's get ready to play!

Before we can play and use language strategies in play, we need to be ready! As adults, we live spinning a lot of plates, with lots of ideas and jobs and thoughts. If we are going to be a connected communication partner, we need to be in a place that most of those things can be paused. So when you are getting ready to play, set yourself up to be committed to the interaction. At home, this might look like putting your phone on silent or turning your smart watch notifications off. This might look like making sure you and the child you're supporting both have a bottle of water with you, don't have to rush off to an assembly or meeting. It might look like getting the right chair or cushion so you can sit comfortably for play.

Within school, it might be that you need to develop a phrase or code with your colleagues so that they don't pop in to ask a question or start a handover conversation with you while you are doing your therapy play. Because without meaning to, that interruption could shift your carefully set up communication environment. You could make a 'Play in Progress' poster to stick to your chair/table or door. Or use a phrase like, 'We are just connecting in play therapy right now, I'll find you later'. Agree it beforehand so that there are no misunderstandings or upsets among staff.

Sometimes, these 'setting up' parts of our play therapy can make such a huge difference to how successful we are, as adults, in staying focused! It's worth taking time to consider what will make it as easy as possible for you to give your child as much of your attention and focus as possible without feeling pulled in different directions.

Being visibly ready to communicate

By this, I mean considering a few things about the way you position your body during interaction and play. It is important that we are sending a message to the child that we are ready and available for any ways they may want us to be part of their play world. An easy part of this is to get down to the child's level to try and make your bodies at the same height. The reason this is helpful is because it gives a clear message of availability. The part of our body that a lot of communication comes from is your hour head – your words/sounds come from your mouth, facial expressions your face, hearing system from your ears. If we are at a mismatched height with our conversational partners, it can lead to feeling disconnected. If your child is finding communication difficult, there is already a level of disconnect and so we want to remove any possible obstacles that we can. So, very simply, if they are stood, you will need to keel. If they are sat, you will need to sit, crouch or lay down. This means your heads will be at about the same level and this will give a very clear message and signal that you are available to them.

It is also worth considering your body positioning. Once you are at the same level, you also want to seem open and ready for play/communication. This can be achieved by having an open body posture, arms uncrossed and leaning in towards the toy you are playing with. This gives a message of interest and shows a willingness to play and support them. I will often sit with my hands open, palms up, arms stretched in front of me as if I am waiting to be given something. This again, means that if in a moment of frustration or a time of need, I am very literally ready to receive an object, toy, or their hand. This readiness to help quite quickly creates a feeling of connection between us because I give the message that I am there for them.

WARNING: Use this strategy within reason!

This is where we 'know better and do better' when we listen to Autistic voices. Historically, this strategy would have been described as 'be face-to-face with your child, get into their face and their space so that they can see you easily'. However, although we want to be available and show a willingness and desire to connect. We do not want to create pressure to conform to what neurotypically feels like connection. For a neurotypical adult, connection may feel like making eye contact and looking at a person's face. For a child who is Autistic, this can be a very overpowering and a physically painful process. These things in turn create the opposite feeling of an unsafe pressure-filled interaction. If when you spend time with a child, they constantly move away from you, or position themselves with their back to you, it is important to respect the message that that behaviour gives us – they are telling us 'I need space'. If we want to create a feeling of safe connection, we *must* respect the messages we receive from children. Yes, we can know these strategies and we can understand that they have the potential to create 'optimal conditions for communication'... but they are also *general* strategies that will not be suitable for every single child. You may work and support a child who is their most connected to you while sitting with their back to you, leaning into you because they like the pressure and the warmth, tapping your hand to indicate they want you to wind up a toy again. This is still connection. This is still communication. It doesn't look like two people face-to-face making eye contact, but it is a beautiful moment where two people are sharing one aspect of play and a feeling of togetherness.

Children are not robots and we cannot programme them for communication. We can learn strategies, but we *must* watch and learn what works for them individually. Look for the signals they give us that they are connecting with us, even when they aren't what we expect from connection.

Neurotypical connection may look like:	Autistic connection may look like:
Looking at your face.	Leaning on you.
Smiling at you.	Happy stimming during play.
Hugging you.	Placing your hand on a toy.
Asking you to play or do more of a game.	Staring at the toy waiting for it to happen again.
Laughing in play.	Moving away from you to jump and regulate before the next turn.

Follow their lead in play: watching for play patterns

When we play for therapy, our first job is not to dive in and get started... First, we need to wait. Watch and wait and learn. Because, in order for us to be a partner in play, we need to know what 'play' means for this child with this toy... For about three to five minutes we can sit back and observe a child in their play and watch for key parts of their play style.

Observe and look for:

- WHAT toy they choose, but also HOW they choose to play with it.
- WHAT actions get repeated as part of their play.
- WHAT part of the toy or actions seems to bring them joy.
- WHAT sounds, words and/or actions naturally occur as they play by themselves.

Looking at how a child plays with a toy may sound odd because, as adults, we tend to have a preconception about a toy's functions/purpose in play. For example, cars are to be driven, blocks to be stacked and teddies to be cuddled. However, that's our adult, logical brain thinking about the rules and telling us that there is a 'right way' to play. But there isn't...

Our children are often much more creative than this, especially when they explore a new toy. Each child will also have a play passion and a play pattern that they currently favour. We need to watch what they do and how they play and try and look at what patterns and systems they seem to enjoy. What this means is that, when we join in, we are ready to be a partner and a helper, rather than accidentally getting in the way of their already formed play idea.

For example, a child has toy cars – they have them in a big pile, their play is to add to the pile and watch as a car falls from the pile and rolls slowly under the sofa. The joy for them is in the pattern of building, falling and rolling. If I jump straight in and take a car off the pile and start driving it around on the floor, I've accidentally got in the way of the game they have created.

As adults, we do this a lot – we don't mean to, but we do because we think we know the right way to play and we want to teach. But play is about being a partner, not a teacher.

In play therapy, take time to WATCH and WAIT. Look for what the play pattern is, and then join in as a HELPER.

For the example above, We may become a helper by rolling the cars back from under the sofa, or pass them to the child to put on the top of the pile, or simply watch and react with excitement as each car falls. This means we are *facilitating* their game, their idea, their play. They remain the creator of the play and we are seamlessly adding ourselves into the world that they have created.

Summary of getting ready for play

- We adjust our body position to mirror what the child is doing.
- We spend time watching to learn about the child's play.
- We notice what in the play brings them joy.
- We look for ways that we can be a helper/ facilitate their play.
- We are not aiming to change or teach them a new play idea here. We simply want to become part of what they are creating.

Now that we understand the play, we are being a helper and are connected through that play; we can look to feed our children language as they play.

Give language rather than *take* it: Asking questions

As adults in conversations, we rely on questions to keep our conversations going. We engage in a back-and-forth of asking and answering, and it is a valuable part of how we maintain conversations and relationships.

As adults talking to children, we use questions to check in on their knowledge. We ask questions to encourage further thinking and as a method of teaching.

What this leads to is that, as adults in play and interaction, we tend to ask *a lot* of questions. Although these have a useful role in other parts of our lives, when interacting with children, these questions act as demands. Each question we ask comes with a small amount of pressure for a response, an answer or an interaction. For lots of children, this may work and they will adapt and learn. However, for children who are finding language and communication skills more difficult, these small demands add up, and often the more questions we ask, the less they respond.

We can end up in a very unplayful cycle of adults asking questions, children not responding, and adults asking more questions in an attempt to gain a response, which leads to children withdrawing further – and on and on…

Instead of asking questions, here is what to do...

Adding language to what they do

Pretend you are a sports or nature commentator and very simply describe what you can see your child is doing. You can describe what they are doing, what you think they might say, what they might feel, what they might hear and what they are experiencing.

For example, if they are playing with a sand tray, I would avoid asking 'What's happening here? Is it falling? Is it cold?' because, although these questions hold some important vocabulary, the nature of the question will act as a demand and may limit how the child responds to you.

Instead, I may say, 'Wow, look at this sand! I can see it falling out the cups! Woooosh! Catch it! It's in your hand! Oh, it's cold!'

This on-the-go description of what the child is experiencing means that words/vocabulary are happening at the same time as the actions and experiences. This makes it as easy as possible for the child to link the words and the actions together, making it as easy as possible for them to store the two together in their communication system and giving as much chance as possible that they will retrieve it and use it themselves on another occasion.

Talk about play using a range of word types

When we are narrating and describing a child's play, it's important for us to try and use a range of words and concepts to allow them to experience as much relevant vocabulary as possible.

Try to include different types of words as you talk in play.

Type	Meaning	Example
Nouns	Naming objects and things	Sand, cup, hand,
Verbs	Actions and movements	Pour, falling,
Adjectives	Describing features	Soft, big
Concept words	Describing abstract features	Cold, empty
Symbolic	Noises and sounds	Wooosh, Oh! Pitter-patter
Social phrases	Useful play language	Help me! My turn, more, finished
Prepositions	Talking about location	In, on, under, behind

Using a range of volumes and intonation in play

Consider your own communication style and look at ways of making it varied and interesting for the child. If you naturally have a loud, clear voice, add times when it is softer or use a whisper. If your voice tends to contain a lot of 'sing song' to it (early years practitioners tend to build this into their talking style – like a children's TV presenter), consider contrasting it with a lower tone. The shifts and range will help make your communication interesting and curious.

Copying/intensive interaction

This strategy is about being a mirror to any of your child's play and communication sounds, actions or movements. Whatever your child does, we can echo it back to them as a connective response. We do this gently and with care, making sure that it is enjoyable. This type of interaction strategy creates a great connection between the adult and children because it shows that we are listening. Very often for children, this can be the first experience of a sound- or action-based conversation – where they make a sound and we make one back. They make another and we make that back too. They lift their head and we mirror the action; they smile and laugh and they see us do it too. The back-and-forth becomes an interactive game and conversation that the child remains completely in control of. It creates a great opportunity to explore and play with sound and actions. This type of interaction is validating of all communication because we copy and engage with sounds, actions, gestures, noises, words, songs and body movements. It is also a lovely way to demonstrate that we can copy each other, so often we model and demonstrate language in the hope that children will learn and copy from us. This strategy reverses those roles, to explore with the child leading.

Repeat and add to extent language/actions

This strategy is as simple as it sounds! Whatever your child says or does, copy it back to them and add an extra bit. This works no matter what level of language or play they are working at, and is a positive support for two key reasons:

1. Echoing back what they have said shows that you were listening to them and understand what they have said. It builds connection.
2. By adding an extra part to their word/action, you are collaborating while also teaching them a new skill.

They say/do	You respond – repeat and add
'Bus'	'Bus! Red bus!'
'Fall down'	'Tower fall down'
Point	Point and say 'look'
Clap hands and say, 'Yay'	Clap hands and say, 'Yay, we did it!'
'Today is a cold day'	'Today is a cold day, it's winter'

A choice of two things

Offering choices as we play and talk is a great alternative to asking a lot of questions. We still get information but in a more collaborative way. When we offer a choice of two things we also provide a language/action model which reduces the pressure attached to respond. It also gifts language to children rather than taking it from them.

For example, a question would be 'What do you want for a snack?' The skills needed here are:

- To interpret the question word – 'what' means it's an object.
- Interpret the key word 'snack' – is a food item.
- Access all food words in storage system.
- Retrieve accurate word.
- Produce word/action as a response.

Compare this to a choice of two: 'Time to choose a snack – biscuit or banana?'

The language has been presented, children are able to identify key items and use the language model from the adult to support vocabulary in their storage system, while still empowering them express a need/opinion.

Depending on your child's language level and language learning style, you can adapt this strategy to include more or less language. Your choices don't have to be single words, as this may restrict the language model and practice to single words. You could also give a choice of phrases. For example, if a child was struggling to open a toy box, I may respond saying, 'Oh no, it's not opening – I need help… OR… I can do it…' Modelling two key PHRASES rather than single words so the child to use or copy.

There is a shift here from trying to *pull* language from a child via a question, to trying to encourage it collaboratively with a modelled choice. The choice often feels more comfortable for the child because there is less language load and pressure attached to it.

Make it affirming! Teaching 'no' and 'different'

As adults, we can be prepared and supportive of a child expressing 'no' or an option that is 'different' to the two choices we have suggested, and we can possibly explore a wider range of options together, if needed. If, in a play session, I say to a child, 'Let's play! Cars or bubbles?' and their response is to move away from me and towards building blocks, I can respond to that with the *adding language strategy,* by describing their actions – 'Something different? Let's play blocks!' I've added language to their actions that they may be able to copy at another time like this. This is to empower them to advocate for their own ideas when given a choice that restricts them. I've modelled language that they can use next time to express this. It wasn't my plan, but they have still learnt and been exposed to language. But more than that, it was naturally motivating and relevant to them because they chose it.

Teaching a child the word/sign/symbol for 'different' is a really powerful way to do this. It almost universally expresses that what is currently happening is not working for them and expresses the need for change in a single word. It is also a collaborative word for both adults and children to use, where sometimes 'no' and 'finished' feel very final and one-sided. A request for 'different' encourages us to go on a quest together to find a solution.

Combining these strategies with connection and collaboration at the heart of play therapy means that we move away from therapy and strategies that feel controlling of children, and towards strategies that support both language development and self-advocacy.

Always the last choice

You may notice when offering a choice that your child only ever repeats back the last thing you say to them, even when that isn't the item they actually want. This is an indication that the strategy needs adapting with visuals and props to make sure it is consistent, supportive, and doesn't become frustrating for the child. As the supporting adult, you need to add pictures, an AAC device, actions, real objects – or a combination of all of these things! To make sure that, when the child expresses themselves, it aligns with how they actually feel. In the snack example above, I would go and find a biscuit packet and a banana and hold both of these things out as I gave the verbal choice, so that the child could point/reach alongside their words. Or I might use an electronic or printed picture board with an image of both items, so there was the option to press the button or point to the symbol.

It's OK if they change their mind!

It goes without saying (but I'm going to say it anyway!) that if you offer a child a choice, they indicate what they want, verbally or through actions and then change their mind. This is OK. Even though we are using choices as a support for language learning, we do not need to stand by the first choice to make the language point. This actually presents us with an additional language learning opportunity as we can model and repeat the expressed change.

At snack time, this might look like the following example.

> I hold a banana and a packet of biscuits out, and verbally offer the choice: 'It's snack time! Let's have banana [showing them the item in one hand]... or biscuit [showing them the item in my other hand].' The child reaches for a banana and makes a 'ba' sound. I show them the AAC symbol and together we press the button for 'banana'. I confirm, 'You're choosing banana!' The child holds the banana for a second, drops it on the floor and cries out!

At this point, we might view this from different perspectives in terms of learning opportunities.

It could be argued that this child has expressed a choice and, for them to learn how choosing works, they need to now experience the item they have communicated to us. They asked for banana, they should have that choice. In my experience, this tends to lead to a wave of distress and I often see the child then process this communication experience as negative. I can almost imagine them thinking – I shared a message, I worked hard to express myself, but it didn't work out. I feel sad and unheard. This will not be an experience that then motivates them to try again another time.

Our alternative, neurodiversity-affirming learning opportunity is to acknowledge feelings, learn more about choices and model language again. We can do this by responding to the behaviour as communication. I can pick up the banana from the floor and describe what I see to them,

'Oh no! You feel sad...' I can model language as if I am them, saying, 'No, thank you, banana! Something different!' I can model the sign for 'different'. I can model the AAC for different. I can return to the choices and talk as if I am the child: 'Banana or biscuit – I choose biscuit.' I can model the word with my voice and the AAC again 'biscuit' as I hand a biscuit to them. This way, the child can see/hear the word 'biscuit' and experience the item at the same time, solidifying their understanding of the vocabulary.

Allowing a child to make a mistake with their choice or with their communication, and then guiding them and demonstrating how to request a change, is a powerful life skill. (Think of a time in a coffee shop where you maybe said no to sugar and then changed your mind and wanted some – imagine if the coffee shop owner said, 'I'm sorry, you said no first of all, so it's no longer an option for you!'). It is not as simple as giving them their own way. It is about empowering them to communicate a need with us in an appropriate way and showing them that we will respond to that communication. It is about understanding that they are learning and part of that process will involve getting it wrong and having big feelings about that. Walking through it with them and supporting them to try again will nurture future communication.

There will of course be times that boundaries need to be held – homes and education settings will develop these uniquely to mean there is consistency. This snack situation would not necessarily transfer to every choice-making situation. Some are harder to 'redo' and we would need to support the feeling without the resolution. However, it is important to consider your WHY, when upholding a boundary.

Consider: 'Am I upholding the boundary because it is important for safety and regulation of this child and others? OR am I upholding this boundary through fear that the shift away from it loses my position of power/status as the adult over this child?' Choosing collaboration over control will usually lead to connection, communication and learning a new skill in a state of calm.

Power of the pause

Having silences in play and conversations can feel quite uncomfortable for us as adults. Socially, we tend to associate these as 'gaps in conversation' or 'awkwardness'. We subconsciously fill them up with chit-chat, small talk, questions and thoughts. However, while children are learning language – and especially if language and communication is a struggle for them – these pauses are absolutely essential. Leaving silence and space within play and chats allows for *processing*. Children are learning and gaining information constantly. When you experience the world through a neurodivergent brain, you are often gaining even more information than others because of the amount of detail you access from your environment. Leaving pauses and having silent times in play provides much-needed time and space for this information to be organised, sorted and stored. It also gives time and space for children to set themselves up with what they might want to do or say next. If there is a consistent buzz of play, interaction and talking acting as *input* for a child, it is hard for them to filter out that buzz in order to make their own plan for their next *output*. It all becomes a jumble. Leaving pauses, silences and space, creates a relaxed environment for children to organise information we have *input* for them, and plan information for their next *output*.

Sentence set up

This is a simple strategy where the adult starts a sentence and leaves a space for the child to add to it at the end. The adult might point to a bird picture and say, 'Oh, look, it's a…' and wait for the child to said 'Bird!' This can work well because we have a natural human drive for completion. We enjoy the feeling of something being finished, so when a sentence is started, finishing it feels good. It is collaborative because both people are involved in the sentence. It models language. It encourages children to respond, but without adults using the pressure of a question. A question demands a response, whereas a sentence set up leads us to a response but if the child doesn't fill the gap, the adult can complete their own sentence without the conversation feeling like it has stopped and started over.

Useful sentence starters include:

- I can see…
- I can hear…
- Oh, look at this…
- Wow, it's a…
- This is a XX and this is a…

Video yourself

When I'm working with parents and staff who have been supporting, waiting and watching for communication skills for a long time, one of the things I recommend is for them to set up a camera and film themself playing with their child. Not to observe their child, but to observe your own play style and strategies in play. It can feel strange, but it's amazing what you notice about your style and how your child responds to it. Often, when we are anxious about our child's skills developing, we can change the way we interact by accident. Watching yourself back helps you spot these as well as notice strategies you are using and any you want to use more.

Watch your video at least twice. (The first time you may just feel awkward seeing yourself on camera so the second time is for real watching!)

Ask yourself when you watch it back, 'What am I doing that really keeps this play going?' and 'What seems to shift my child away from the play and communication?'

Note some ideas down as you watch it. Be kind to yourself. Keep your feedback to yourself balanced by choosing two things for each of those questions. Make sure you list your *play partner's strengths* as well as things you want to add or alter about your play style. You *will* be doing things to help. Notice them because then you can do those often.

A feedback list might look like this:

In this video, I notice...

- I'm right down on the floor so we can look at each other lots.
- We are both connected over the same play.
- I talk too fast. I'm so busy trying to squeeze in number work that I forget to follow his lead. He doesn't want the number song. He just wants to play 'ready go!'
- Linked to my speed, there aren't enough pauses for him to add in his own talking. I'm leading, when he could be.

I've always had to do this for student placements and through work observations. When I became a parent, I started to do this with my own children. I had the videos for my own watching and started sharing snippets to talk about communication development!

It might seem silly, and it might feel a bit awkward to start with, but watch it back two or times and it will do amazing things for your confidence and play style!

Chapter 5:
Play Patterns

The way children play tends to follow certain patterns and themes. These occur for all children and even adults. Some play patterns we associate more with younger children, while we tend to see others as children get older and their language, ideas and abstract thinking develops. However, as with all developmental theory, this is useful to know but not necessarily the step-by-step guide that your child will follow, especially if they are Autistic, because we know their pathway will tend to weave and flow in a way that is unique to them. Knowing these play patterns and systems is helpful because once we know about them, we can observe them in our children's play and communication and use these systems to make therapy ideas appealing. We can mirror how our children are playing and even anticipate a play sequence in order to then become part of it.

Play patterns

Let's explore some play patterns you might observe. This isn't an exhaustive list but lays a good foundation for understanding play patterns (also known as play schemas).

Trajectory

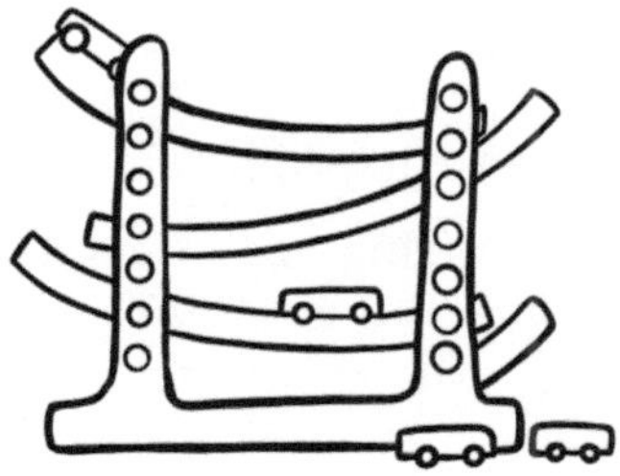

This type of play involves movement. The joy of this play comes from either moving themselves, and being in motion, or watching something in motion and tracking the way it moves.

This play pattern might be explored by a child moving by spinning themselves or sliding themselves on play equipment, going down the slide over and over again or wanting to move along the floor on their tummy.

It might be explored by a child moving other objects, such as pushing cars down a garage slide, rolling balls, throwing objects from their chair or buggy. They might enjoy watching toys fall out of their toy box, or emptying a container full of small parts.

If you notice this play pattern, here are some ways you could include it into your play therapy:

- Throwing, rolling and catching – balls, bean bags, sensory balls or bottles.
- Using a slide or ramp to drop cars or balls down.
- Blowing bubbles – watching them fall. Chasing them and popping them.
- Water play – watching water move between different pots, funnels and drip from containers.

Transformation

This type of play involves change. The joy of this play comes from observing or being part of how a toy or object changes and how we can control its change.

This play pattern might be explored by a child covering themselves or other objects in paint at the paint table. They might enjoy mixing colours together to see what new colour is created. They might enjoy creating and using sensory bottles that mix different textures or objects together.

If you notice this play pattern, here are some ways you could include it into your play therapy:

- Mixing with paint to see the colours change.
- Mixing coloured waters or making potions.

- Playing with different coloured play dough to mix the colours and see the change.
- Playing with chalk, smashing chalk, adding water, mixing it with cornflour or making it into dust with a grater or sandpaper to watch it change state.
- Playing with sand and water together.
- Baking activities or science experiments.

Transporting

This type of play involves gathering and carrying objects around in a space. This play pattern might be explored by a child picking up items from around the room and making collections. They might enjoy having a bag or basket to place items in and taking them to a new place. They might enjoy transporting items in different containers such as a toy shopping trolly, a dumper truck, handbag, or washing-up bowl.

If you notice this play pattern, here are some ways you could include it into your play therapy:

- Having small parts and containers for children to fill and carry.
- Using trucks and diggers with sand or gravel.
- Using a shopping troll/basket and play food items.
- Having collections of items that need taking to different parts of the room or organising my size or colour.
- Sensory play containers where items can be moved from one zone to another.

Rotation

This type of play involves the turning and rotating of objects or themselves. The joy here is found in the motion, movement and experience of change through movement.

This play pattern might be explored by a child moving themselves in a spinning or rolling motion. They might enjoy play where they can roll larger items like tyres or wheels. They might explore this play pattern by twisting buttons on toys or using wind-up/spinning top toys.

If you notice this play pattern, here are some ways you could include it into your play therapy:

- Exploring toys with wheels and cogs.
- Spinning tops and musical spinners.
- Rolling and spinning your own boy as part of songs and movement activities.
- Use silks and ribbons to swirl and spin.

Positioning

This type of play involves placing objects in carefully chosen positions or alignments of some kind. The joy here is in the precision and the pattern that is created as the end result of the order placement.

This play pattern might be explored by creating lines, stacks, circles or arches of toys or items. It might be explored by creating 'play scenes', where small world toys are organised to look like a scene from a TV show or still frame scene. Care will be taken to adjust where each object is placed, and enjoyment will be found in how this setup looks at the end of the arrangement. The motivation for this play is usually the precise placement of items rather than the traditional play function or story of the objects being used. For example, a line of cars is joyful because of the placement of each car, rather than the narrative of a traffic jam story being told. Or the setup of small character figures on a pirate ship is joyful because of where they stand in relation to each other, rather than each character being moved to speak to each other and tell a pirate story in play.

If you notice this play pattern, here are some ways you could include it into your play therapy:

- Blocks and building play.
- Loose parts play for making creations and patterns.

- Sorting and organising games – matching colours, making collections or themes like animal figures.

Orientation

This type of play involves looking at objects from different angles. The joy is found in viewing and observing the world or play items from a range of angles, noticing the difference and how it feels for them to see it that way.

This play pattern might be explored by laying down on the floor to look at toys from different angles. You might see children getting their body into different positions to view toys or objects from a range of angles. They might jump or swoosh their head from side to side as they look at a toy. They might move an object up to their face and move it around so they can view it carefully.

If you notice this play pattern, here are some ways you could include it into your play therapy:

- Playing movement games – gymnastics, yoga and balances.
- Playing with mirrors to explore the world at different angles.
- Having different surfaces for play – the floor, a table, a stool, a window ledge, for viewing items at different angles.
- Safe climbing and upside-down play – equipment that allows children to safely turn their body at different angles. Crash mats, pillows, climbing frames or trampolines.

Enveloping

This type of play involves placing things inside other things. The joy is found in hiding and revealing objects.

This type of play might be explored by a child posting picture cards into a bag or box. They might enjoy putting things into their pockets, or wrapping things in blankets. They might explore play that allows them to hide items away, for example pushing cars under the sofa, or posting toys down the back of the radiator.

If you notice this play pattern, here are some ways you could include it into your play therapy:

- Wrapping toys in tissue paper, newspaper or silk scarfs to be unwrapped and opened.
- Making a post box from a cardboard box with items to post.
- Swaddling dolls and teddies in play.
- Using tents, dens, blankets and baskets to envelope themselves.

Enclosure

This type of play involves creating barriers and systems to encase objects, often themselves. The joy is found in the visual separation of each collection.

This kind of play pattern might be explored by building dens and pillow caves to hide in. Using blankets to hide under. In small-world play, it might be explored by building a farm and creating lots of pens and fences with building blocks to section each type of animal. Or it might be explored by making collections items in themes and using bowls or pots to keep each collection separate.

If you notice this play pattern, here are some ways you could include it into your play therapy:

- Stacking cups or nesting toys.
- Hiding items under blankets and silk scarfs.
- Use tents and tunnels.
- Having blocks or sticks to create visual markers around other toys like toy animals or figures.

Connection

This type of play involves linking items together, the joy here is found by fixing and breaking items and exploring how the connection can be created or deconstructed.

This play is often explored using blocks and building toys, for example wooden blocks, Lego, magnetic tiles where you are able to explore creating different structures and then breaking them down again.

If you notice this play pattern, here are some ways you could include it into your play therapy:

- Playing with magnets and magnet tiles/ blocks.
- Construction blocks.
- Building train tracks.
- Toys with locks and doors that fasten together tin different ways – zips, buttons, padlocks.

Something completely different!

Although these are common play patterns we might observe children engaging in, our children will quite often use a combination of these patterns or even create a pattern completely unique to their own play style and joy-seeking combination. This is why it is important to watch and observe children in play to try and spot any patterns or links between what they do and why they do it.

Certain toys or themes

Very often, Autistic children's play will link to certain toys or themes that are currently comforting and pleasing for them. This may be certain programmes, shows, or songs that they currently enjoy, or specific characters that they currently have an interest in. This can shift and change depending on current interests and play stage for the child. It may be that you plan therapy activities for a few weeks based on a character that has been capturing their attention and things run successfully, however in the fourth week the child has entirely lost interest in this character and therefore the therapy activity is less engaging for them. This is OK and happens often when we lean in to current interests. It is then that we go back to observing and evaluating what shift has occurred and consider how we can add and adapt therapy to realign for that child's changing development.

Other times, a play theme will last for months and sometimes years! This is when we have an opportunity to be really creative in mixing and matching a 'favourite theme' with other skills to try and stretch and expand a child's learning opportunities through play. We are not trying to change what they love, but notice it as a play passion and use that strength to expand learning in other areas. When planning play session for children who have a long-lasting play passion, I tend to use a formula of:

- What they love + something new
- What they love + an extra play schema
- What they love + a sensory experience

This allows us to keep the play passion, while also exploring new language and play experiences.

For example, if a child loves numbers and their main play focus is to order and sequence numbers, I may gently extend our number play as follows:

- **What they love + something new:** Offering them number sets that vary in size, material and colour. As we sort through them together to organise them into an order, not only can we communicate about the letters themselves but also how they feel, what shape and colour they are and whether they match the same or are different.
- **What they love + an extra play schema:** Offering them numbers and a post box, with envelopes so we can post, envelope and retrieve the numbers. Exploring a new play schema of enveloping.
- **What they love + a sensory experience:** Offering them numbers as part of a water tray, offering them numbers to press into sand, offering them numbers hidden in play dough balls to dig out, offering them numbers on a light box.

Repetition and predictability

For children who are Autistic, there will often be an element of joy found in the repetition of play. This isn't an official 'play schema' but is certainly a key and dominant feature of how and why play becomes joyful for many of the children I support in therapy.

When an action or a play pattern occurs, there is natural comfort in experiencing the same thing each time we do it. We see this in adults too, and even when an adult claims to thrive on spontaneity, there will be clear markers of predictability and repetition built into their daily routine without them even realising. It is a natural part of human nature to enjoy the safety of a predictable outcome. It may only be small, like buying the same brand of coffee or driving to work the same route, but no matter how freely you live your life, there will be an element of repetition and predictability built in. The joy of predictability seems to be amplified for Autistic minds. The drive for repetition and known outcomes seems to offer a real moment of safety, connection and joy. Therefore, this is often seen in play and something that, as play partners, we can offer and nurture.

You might observe this in play, by a child exploring the same toys every time they arrive in your setting. Or they may create a sequence that they say or do at the start of play. It may be that they play in exactly the same way with a set of toys every time those toys are presented to them. Repetition may also occur within a play sequence itself, for example taking each car out of the toy basket, spinning the wheels one at a time and then placing it on the table edge, this exact sequence being done for all the cars in the basket.

This repetition should be treated with care and respect. It should be seen as a valid and intentional play type. It should be seen as a key system for a child regulating themselves and sending messages of safety to their nervous system. As they complete each sequence, they can experience the sense of completion, the joy of accomplishment and the safety and reassurance of seeing that, exactly as they expected, the toy reacted and responded to them in a predictable way. It is easy to see why this would be so motivating to children and adults who are so often misunderstood. The calm and safety of predictable outcomes are of huge value when the world around them frequently does not understand or react to them as they would like/predict.

Therefore, if you observe a repeated sequence of play, or you see that joy is found in the predictable, it is important not to disturb this. Historically, advice may have been given to engage in sabotaging this kind of play. (I discuss this further in 'Outdated advice' on p.241.)

This feels entirely counterproductive and unsupportive of a child's needs and play style, when we consider what this does to a child in terms of their nervous system, their regulation, their trust in communication partners. It means that we are teaching them that other people ruin play. It teaches them that allowing other people into your game or into your world leads to chaos and distress, when before it felt safe and predictable.

This is *not* the message we want to teach children in play. This is in fact the opposite message that we so desperately want to share with our children. When we play and communicate, our main focus and motivation should be connection. We should be driven to show them that we can be part of their play world *and enhance their experience*. Communication and play should be driven by connection, not control. Showing children that we are there to connect with them should be our main drive in communication therapy.

If we are supporting a child who prefers to play independently from us, and create safety and structure in their play, we don't want to give them more reasons to distrust our involvement. We want to show them that communication and collaboration in play brings additional joy, not stress and upset.

Play themes that lend themselves to repetition and predictability

These are not 'official' play schemas but play patterns I observe over again when supporting little ones who are Autistic and should be valued as play styles.

Numbers and letters

Numbers and letters aren't specifically named as part of the most common play patterns, however I have experienced that these are often a key feature in play for little ones who are Autistic. Often setting numbers or letters into shapes and sequences offers a real joy. There's a natural element of predictability about numbers and letters. They tend to be the same every time we experience them: 2 + 2 always equals 4. Although there is a small amount of flexibility in terms of font or formation for certain letters of numbers, they are otherwise consistently the same every time we experience them and they exist in a natural sequence that is known and accepted by everyone.

Rainbows

The same also seems true for colours in rainbow order. The visual sequence is very pleasing to experience, it exists in the same pattern every time we use it and it is easily predictable. Very often when observing play and watching patterns and sequences emerge, a rainbow pattern is created in play, whether its lining items in rainbow order, sequencing an activity in rainbow order, or having a preference to toys that feature a rainbow pattern.

Collections and categories

The other play patterns that feel closely linked to children and adults who are Autistic is a love of collections. Having many of the same or similar objects often seems to spark a real play joy. I believe this is down to a few factors, such as the repetition aspect of a collection – gaining the same thing over and over – as well as the satisfaction from task completion – seeing them all grouped together, it is complete, the job is done.

This can be with objects but also information. Collecting objects in play may involve searching the playroom/area for all the ducks and frogs is has to offer, and placing them on a window ledge in a line to admire. Collecting information may be wanting to know a lot of information or facts about cars, asking multiple questions, researching online, using books, information cards, learning and drawing the different logos.

Repeated sequences – of play, books, videos or songs

The safety and joy that comes from predictability is often seen in more extended play patterns too. A book read by the same person will contain the same words to match the same pictures every time it is read. A movie or video clip or theme song will play in the same way every single time. A song clip online or sung by the same adults will be sung the same way with the same actions, noises and reactions each time it is performed. These types of play lend themselves well to that feeling of predictability and are often a key part of how a child who is Autistic will play.

Celebrating Autistic play

Differences in play and interaction are, unfortunately, still seen as 'markers' or a 'red flag' for Autism. To be affirming, a shift is needed in our mindset when observing play and interaction styles that are commonly linked to Autistic ways of thinking. The way play presents itself is a wonderful insight into how a child views and processes information in the world. It gives us a peek at how they process and learn. Ultimately, it can give us key information about what neurotype they are. When we see these things, we don't need to perceive them as a warning or as something we need to encourage a child to stop. We need to notice them as a developmentally appropriate, or as expected parts of learning when someone is Autistic. These are the parts of play to *lean in to*, rather than move away from, because this type of play is chosen, it is what drives them, and it is a natural part of how that child is experiencing their world. Historically, there was often reference to a child 'being in their own world' and advice on how to shift them into interacting with others, but again, I see this as an upside-down perspective. We don't need to drag them out of their own world, we need find a way to safely be part of it *with* them. Leaning in towards their play passions, supporting their play patterns, sharing and copying the joy they create, means we are celebrating a child for exactly who they are. Our focus then becomes learning how to nurture and enhance their world, rather than change them to exist in ours.

Playing Autistically can often look like:

- Creating lines with similar shape/size items – lining up cars, figures, household items.
- Creating repeated patterns – putting numbers or letters in order.
- Creating collections – finding similar items, finding information.
- Collecting treasures or items that feel special to the individual. These will often fulfil a very particular criteria. These may be kept in a specially chosen safe place or placed on display.
- Creating sequences in play – wanting the same thing repeated many, many times.
- Exploring things with great sensory detail – holding items very close to the eyes, licking items, resting whole body on items.
- Creating repeated sensations – spinning, running, rolling, crashing on soft pillows.

- Feeling and expressing joy through the whole body – squealing with joy, tiny jumps on the spot, flapping hands, tip-toe leaps, teeth/jaw clenching.
- Being driven to manage the play idea themselves – a need to place items a certain way without help, re-doing parts of the play or sequence that other people have added, moving away from others in play, enjoying playing independently.
- Having very careful and specifically focused attention on one play/topic at a time.
- Having play that considers and includes small and specific details.
- Being very skilled at noticing patterns.
- Being very skilled at noticing details and remembering them.
- Being skilled at repeating and recreating play or language patterns.

This is not an exhaustive list and there will be many other ways that a child who is Autistic will play and find joy and connection through play. Keep a look out and watch for patterns so you can support and join them.

How do we use play pattern information in therapy?

Once you have noticed a pattern in a child's play, we can recreate it and incorporate it into the activities we complete in therapy play sessions. As we do this, we can then look for ways to layer in connection, shared joy and communication.

For example, we might notice a child is exploring a 'trajectory schema' – they are throwing items and watching how they travel. We may notice that they enjoy rainbow order, or that they play happily independently and are resourceful at meeting their own play needs (they climb and reach for the ball to recover it from wherever it bounces/travels too).

A therapy activity for this child may include the supporting adult preparing different coloured pom poms or ball-pit balls or scrunched up bits of paper into rainbow sections and placing them into tubs with lids on. A red one, and orange one, a yellow one etc. Once you are with the child, we help and work together to open each box and pour or throw the balls around the room. We can open the boxes in the rainbow sequence and enjoy the colours exploding as we tip them out. We can create some suspense if the child enjoys this by the adult lifting the box up high so the balls travel even more than if the child throws them without help. We can swoosh all the rainbow balls around in a mix on the floor. We can help collect the balls to repeat the activity if the child enjoys it. As the supporting adult, we can demonstrate language like 'more', 'let's play', 'go', 'help me' etc...

The reason this works is because it combines the child's play patterns and their play passions and creates an opportunity for collaborations. The supporting adults helps, facilitates and nurtures the child's play focus, rather than pulls them away from it. The connection and help builds trust and joined-up attention, which paves the way for communication.

therapeutic thought

There are different types of attention used within interaction: chosen attention and encouraged/ compliance-based attention

There is attention through compliance or task-completion focus. This might include saying something like, 'First sitting for circle time, and then we can do the bubbles'. This can have a helpful place, such as getting activity's done or following essential parts of routine. It also may be required at home for some daily tasks that aren't negotiable, like getting dressed to leave the house.

For me, within therapy, I want more. I want to encourage the attention and focus that connects us by choice. Not the means-to-an-end attention that is created by now and next boards. I want to create opportunities for communication where attention and focus are a choice. Where having me be part of their play and communication is interesting, intriguing, curious.

Not needed, but wanted.

To support this we can:

- Watch their play and discover what brings them joy. This is a crucial stage – invest time watching and learning what is motivating for them.

- Find ways to be 'a helper' in their play. Don't disrupt it, don't get in the way. Be there, and be available to support their play ideas.
- Talk a little but not a lot – make small comments about what they are doing but avoid asking questions or adding pressure. Too much talking can be an extra sensory load and spoil their play. Watch for the signs, children may turn their back to you in play if you become 'too involved'.
- Be available none verbally – lean forward with hands out ready to receive items of play.
- Look for moments to connect – what do they smile or laugh at, and can you become part of that? Allow this to happen fleetingly to start with – three seconds might be a good starting point.

Chapter 6:
Sensory play

Please note that sensory play needs to be carefully risk assessed. Make sure you have made things physically safe for yourself as the adult, for the child enjoying the play, and any other children in their environment. These are ideas that should be carefully considered and risk assessed by individuals and settings, thoroughly considering the skill set, behaviours and wellbeing of those involved.

Creating sensory play trays

A sensory play tray is a small or medium-sized tray, box or container filled with items that provide sensory feedback and stimulation. Usually, we explore these with our hands and play, but we can also set these up for children to walk through and experience the sensation through their feet. As well as adapt them for other physical needs.

Sensory play bases

From observing children in play, I consider there to be several different types of sensory play bases, and these lend themselves to different play styles and sensory needs. Noticing what sensory preferences a child has in play can really impact how successful your sensory play is. I've split these up into four sections to help *detect and discover* what preferences your children may show.

<table>
<tr><td>Dry sensory bases</td><td>
<ul>
<li>Sand</li>
<li>Kinetic sand</li>
<li>Salt</li>
<li>Rice</li>
<li>Cereal – cornflakes, rice pops, hoops</li>
<li>Pasta – different shapes and colours</li>
<li>Lentils</li>
<li>Oats</li>
<li>Dried couscous or quinoa</li>
</ul></td><td>
<ul>
<li>Popcorn kernels</li>
<li>Dried chickpeas</li>
<li>Dried beans – different shapes and colours</li>
<li>Chopped-up drinking straws</li>
<li>Shredded paper</li>
<li>Hole punch outs/ confetti</li>
<li>Cotton wool balls</li>
<li>Streamers – foil or paper</li>
</ul></td></tr>
<tr><td>Wet sensory bases</td><td>
<ul>
<li>Water</li>
<li>Paint</li>
<li>Frozen peas</li>
<li>Water beads</li>
<li>Tapioca pearls soaked in water</li>
<li>Cooked spaghetti or noodles</li>
</ul></td><td>
<ul>
<li>Ice cubes</li>
<li>Shaving foam</li>
<li>Squirty cream</li>
<li>Bubbles</li>
<li>Water with tea bags/ fruit tea bags</li>
<li>Water with food colouring</li>
</ul></td></tr>
<tr><td>Sticky sensory bases</td><td>
<ul>
<li>Play dough</li>
<li>Cloud dough</li>
<li>Slime</li>
<li>Chai seeds soaked in water</li>
<li>Jelly</li>
<li>Corn flour + water</li>
<li>Cooked couscous or quinoa</li>
</ul></td><td>
<ul>
<li>Hot chocolate powder + water</li>
<li>Fruits and seeds – pumpkin seeds and pulp, stewed apples, mashed banana</li>
<li>Baked beans</li>
<li>Mud play</li>
</ul></td></tr>
</table>

Loose/small part sensory bases	■ Tokens and discs – plastic game counters, wooden craft discs, buttons ■ Pompoms ■ Conkers ■ Leaves – real or play/silk leaves ■ Chopped-up wool ■ Lolly pop sticks ■ Craft sticks – match-stick size without the flame! ■ Wooden hoops – curtain pole hoops and loops	■ Beads ■ Bells ■ Pebbles/rocks/shells – shop-bought, polished, or from nature! ■ Gemstones – glass stones typically used for flower arranging or plastic stones typically used for fish tanks work well ■ Log slices

Tools and props list

To the above sensory bases, you can add any of the following tools and props to create a sensory play experience to explore. There are special kits and resources that you can buy but most of the items on the list below will hopefully be easy to find at your home or setting already:

- Stacking cups
- Scoops
- Spoons of different sizes and materials (metal, plastic, wooden)
- Picnic set or play tea set
- Plastic figures and characters that fit a theme or that are motivating. (cartoon characters from a favourite show, zoo animals/sea creatures to link to a book, fairies to create potions for)
- Transport toys – cars, diggers, trucks
- Rolling pin
- Pots and bowls of different shapes and sizes
- Tongs, tweezers or chopsticks
- Pipettes or medicine syringes
- Silicone baking equipment – cake cases, cake tray
- Baking tin, cupcake tin

- Paint brushes – different sizes and shapes
- Bottles and pots of different shapes and sizes

Combining a sensory base with one to three items from a props and tools list results in a play opportunity that lends itself to different play patterns. The play itself, containing sensory aspects, will be naturally regulating and engaging. This provides an opportunity for us as supporting adults to layer in language and communication strategies (described on p.67).

Table 6.1: Quick sensory play set up ideas

Rice crispies, stacking cups and spoons. Encourage your child to fill and pour. Say simple phrases like 'fill it up' and 'all gone now'.
Oats, toy diggers. Encourage your child to push the diggers through the oats. Say simple phrases like 'go', 'stop' and 'wheels go round'.
Hoop cereal and metal spoons. Encourage your child to crush the cereal with the spoon and mix the cereal with the spoon. Say simple phrases like 'crash' and 'mix mix'.
Baked beans, plastic pans and plates. Encourage your child to put their hands in the beans. Say simple phrases like 'splat', 'sticky' and 'drip drip drip'.
Instant mash (made thick) and play dough cutters. Encourage your child to place cutters onto the mash. Say simple phrases like 'on top' and 'down'
Dry pasta, baking tray. Encourage your child to drop pasta into the baking tray. Say simple phrases like 'noisy!', 'sprinkle' and 'bang'.
Bubbles/foam and sea creatures. Put a small amount of water and washing-up liquid in a bottle, shake it well to make foam, squirt it onto the tray and hide sea creature figures in it. Model words like 'hide it' and 'hello fish!'

Ice cubes and corn flour with polar bear/penguin figures.

Place ice cubes in a tray and sprinkle flour on the top. Model words like 'cold' and 'ice'.

Sensory play tray: Different reasons for play

Your sensory play tray may be used in different ways depending on your aim for the play activity. All of these reasons for sensory play are valid and can be used across the day to support children. It is important to decide *why* you are doing the sensory play activity because it will change how you, as the supporting adult, interact with the child as they play:

- It may be a chance for self-regulation – allow your child to play and chat to themselves, don't interrupt, leave them to enjoy the peace and regulate their bodies and mind.
- It may be an opportunity for language – copy what your child is saying, expand on their words and add ideas to their play.
- It may be an opportunity for them to learn through watching – get a tray for yourself and your child and play alongside them, this gives a non-intrusive play and language model for children to copy.
- It may be a chance for us to teach a new academic skill – put numbers of letters in the tray with the sensory base and teach as they play. This style of teaching exposes children to academic learning through play and helps build a foundation of knowledge.

BIG sensory play and SMALL sensory play

Sensory play trays usually condense our play into a relatively small and stationary type of sensory interaction (not always, but often). The tray itself acts as a visual marker for where the sensory experience needs to stay and the child tends to enjoy this play using their hands or maybe their feet. This type of play is not a whole-body experience, and so if your child is seeking bigger movement, we will need to adapt our sensory play to be bigger.

Bigger movement sensory play ideas

Sausage roll: Use a blanket to roll around the child and pretend they are a sausage roll. You can either wrap it around them as they stand up, or, if they enjoy it, lay them down and roll them along the blanket on the floor so they wrap up as they roll. Make up a song as you play. If they enjoy the feeling of weight, you can lay extra blankets, cushions or small bean bags on top of their legs and act out adding ketchup or toppings as you do.

Cushion slide: Encourage them to sit on a cushion and slide themselves across the surface of the floor, using their hands on the floor to pull themselves along. They may also enjoy you helping with this movement.

Basket boat: Sit them safely in a basket or box and sing 'Row, row, row the boat' as you slide the basket across the floor, away from you and back towards you.

Stepping stones: Use boxes or crates or cushions to set out stepping stones across the floor. Move from one to the next trying to balance. You can increase the sensory impact by adding different things to the surfaces so they feel different – a bathmat, fake grass mat, rubber mat, carpet mat.

Creating an obstacle course: Setting up a range of items to move between, around, over and under.

Taking sensory trays outside: Spreading the equipment and resources across an outside space means children naturally have bigger movement built into their play. Having the tray of rice in one part of the garden/ playground and needing to carry scoops of it across to a different sensory tray where the water and sieves are, creates an opportunity for movement as part of the play.

Acting out a story or song: Give children material, sensory scarfs or ribbons and encourage them to act out key parts of the song or story you read to them. Maybe there is a bird in the story and so they flap their arms and experience the sensory scarfs moving across them.

Pushing and pulling: Activities where children get to push or pull safely as part of play. This might be filling a cart with blocks and pulling it along, or putting heavier toys, like matchbox cars into a trolly and pushing it to the toybox. Placing beanbags or weighted teddies on a blanket and pulling them along them.

Carrying and moving: Activities where children can carry and transport things, allowing them to feel the weight in their own body and use their body strength to support it. This might be moving tyres or blocks in the garden/playground. Or carrying books to the bookshelf. Or carrying bottles of water to the kitchen.

Pretending to be different animals: Using picture cards or animal figures as a language prompt, act out how different animals may walk around the room. Change your body position, action and noise to allow for different body sensations. For a snake, lay on the floor and wiggle on your tummy. For a giraffe, stretch tall on your tip toes. For a flamingo, balance on one leg. For an owl, stretch your arms out as wide as you can.

Bubbles: Blow bubbles and encourage children to jump and stretch high to pop the high ones, stomp your feed to pop the low ones.

When designing therapy activities and sessions, we can use the sensory play information in this chapter to create engaging and naturally regulating play. We layer in the connection and language strategies described in Chapter 3, and the result is an activity that is motivating, regulating and engaging with the opportunity for adults to model language and communication skills as part of the play.

therapeutic thought

When children are overwhelmed – things to consider

When it gets chaotic in group play, I intervene considering these four things:

SEPARATE

Children may love being with each other, but I sometimes observe that they just can't manage being with each other safely in this moment. They need their own space. A simple solution is to set out trays or toy set ups so they can see each other but not touch each other. A tray gives a clear visual marker of what is in your zone for touching. There is a clear visual rule for where your hands, body and ideas need to stay.

SENSORY

Choose something that gives them a sensory outlet – kinetic sand, play dough, paint, water beads, clay. This type of play is naturally calming. It supports the body to focus inward on its own regulation. Without realising, we notice the feelings, the sensations and input, and it helps us to regulate that way. If you are concerned about your child eating sensory materials, keep it really simple with water play.

STIMULATION

I consider what external stimulation there is. Is music on? Is the TV on or the classroom big screen? What's in their view as they play? Can they see out the window or into the main hall where there is a lot of busyness? I try and clear this so they can focus better. A busy environment will make it difficult for them to become calm – imagine trying to concentrate on some work in the centre of a busy city street, compared to sat facing a still lake. Our surroundings matter and if we can take some of these pressures away from children it will really help.

STRUCTURE

I choose an activity with relative structure. It isn't free play, it isn't choosing, but it also isn't a work booklet with set answers. It's still child-led, but an adult-directed part of the play. I might phrase this with an invitation we can't say no to – 'Let's go and set up the kinetic sand together', then I'll add an element of choice: 'Would you like jungle animals with it, or hiding treasure?' A tray each gives the structure of a visual marker. Their own equipment gives structure for no transfer. This kind of play allows children to 'zone in'. This supports self-regulation and calm.

Chapter 7:

Total communication and supporting progress

We have mentioned total communication already, but because it is so important I'm going to mention it again!

Total communication is an approach to communication therapy that values all methods and forms of communication equally. Taking a total communication approach means we are nurturing all ways of sharing a message and not focusing only on verbal skills. We are encouraging all skills that support a child to be understood, to express their needs, share social messages, play, interact and engage with others.

Total communication skills may include:

- Using spoken words – single words, sentences, learnt phrases
- Using signs
- Using gestures
- Using looking – eye gazing or face gazing in the direction of the item that they want or are noticing
- Using body language and facial expressions
- Using noises
- Using stimming movements to share emotions

- Using photographs, pictures, picture boards or symbols
- Using drawing and writing
- Using objects to indicate needs – showing their shoes to indicate they want to go out to play
- Using technology – AAC devices, apps and buttons

Through valuing and modelling all these methods of communication, we can support children to embrace communication as they experience the empowering feeling of connecting, requesting or showing another person something. If we only focus on spoken words and talking words, we can often miss and overlook a child's attempts at these none-talking ways of communicating messages with us, and missing those means we miss an opportunity to celebrate connection and communication.

It is important to encourage, demonstrate and celebrate *all methods* of communication, because that is where the real joy in connection and empowerment of communication can start from and grow for our children.

With this in mind, it is important that our children have access to all of these methods of communication in their environment, in play therapy sessions and throughout their day. Within play-based therapy we can layer these different methods of communication into therapy.

For example, when exploring a storybook:

- Find real objects that match items and characters from the book.
- Create a core board of language to have on a device or a printout.
- Tell the story with spoken words.
- Use signs for some of the key words.
- Make symbolic noises to represent characters or actions in the book.
- Use facial expressions that link to the tone of the book.

Watch where the child's eyes are looking in the book and name the part of the picture you feel they may be looking at.

Consider the child's sensory load throughout the interaction and try to get a balance between empowering them to access all modes of communication, but without making the environment or play set up overstimulating or overwhelming. This will be different for each child, and is a consideration to observe and be mindful of.

Some parts of total communication happen so fleetingly and in such a small and delicate way that we can almost miss them. Be sure to actively decide to take a total communication approach and therefore look closely for all the tiny ways communication happens – fleeting eye gazes, gestures and small facial expression reactions can go unnoticed if we are not paying particular attention for them. Keep a close watch for these as you play and interact.

Different ways of using visuals

It is important to remember there are different reasons and ways of using visuals. These different visuals serve a different purpose for the child that needs them, and it is important that we offer both.

We may use visuals:

- To tell them something.
- For them to tell us something.

To tell them something, the message comes *from us*, to them:

- This is when we use visuals on a timetable, because we are letting them know what is happening on the schedule and across their day.
- This is when we use a now-and-next board to explain there is a sequence of activities.
- This is when we add symbols or photos to cupboard doors or toy boxes, to explain what is inside.
- This is when we use visual timers or countdown boards to show an activity is almost over.
- This is when we might have a sequence written down to help with part of a routine – 'Shoes off, bag on peg, carpet space'.
- This is when we, as adults, wear a lanyard of symbols so we can show children when activities are finished or to support behaviour.
- This is when we might use a photo to show whose peg it is, whose chair it is, whose drink bottle it is.

For them to tell us something: the messages come *from them*, to us:

- This is when children use a choosing board to indicate what they would like at snack time.
- This is when they may have a symbols folder to look through and express what they would like to play/eat.
- This is when they use a core board to share with us an emotion of ailment.
- This is when they use an AAC device to share a social message in play like 'I love it!', as you blow bubbles for them.
- This is when they take the 'I need help' symbol out of their coat pocket on the playground to let us know they need a sensory break from the noise.

When you are setting up visuals for your child, it is important to make sure you have considered the support you have created in *both* those categories. Make sure that at home, in therapy and in education settings, there are visual systems to support the adults to give messages to the children and that there are visual systems that support the children to give messages to the adults.

Different reasons/motivations to communication

When we communicate with each other, we do so for different reasons:

- Sometimes it is to express a want or a need and get it met, such as asking for help to open something or asking for a drink.
- Sometimes it is to share a social message, such as telling a friend about an activity we completed or to offer comfort when a friend is upset.
- Sometimes we communicate because we want to, and other times it is because we have to. We might ask someone to move their chair because we want to sit next to them, or we might have to ask someone to move their chair because it is trapping our toe. Our motivation and reason for the same request is different.

Within play therapy, it is important to plan interactions and communication opportunities that cover a range of reasons and motivations. We can model this with our total communication approach by considering key words and phrases that express needs and that share social joy.

For example, including an AAC button for the word 'help' and modelling the sign and the spoken word for 'help', which is an expression of need. But also including an AAC button for the phrase 'We did it!' and 'Look!', as well as modelling the sign and spoken words for these social phrases that can be used to share a social connection in play. If we want children to engage with us for more than just what they need, we need to offer opportunities, models and total communication systems that support this.

Different styles of language learning – zig-zag learning

Just like with their play patterns, the wonderful minds of Autistic children will very often learn language and communication in their own unique style, not necessarily following a step-by-step system. Their path to communication and language systems will zig-zag and wiggle, often with a huge range between strengths and needs. We often see that they may know a wide vocabulary linked to a play passion interest like sea creatures, numbers or dinosaurs, and can name or identify things way beyond their years, but may not be able to name household fruit to request a snack.

We may hear them use a long phrase from a favourite book or video clip, but see that it is tricky for them to generate a new phrase to describe part of their play or request a friend join their game.

This is where play-based speech, language and communication therapy thrives, because it is not focused on a structured target. Instead, we can meet the child where they are across their mixture of skills and support and enhance the skills they have while nurturing the skills they are yet to develop.

In Chapter 3, pp.51-52, there is a flow of step-by-step language learning to which we can refer to notice how our children are moving between language phases (but not feel the need to develop their skills exclusively in that order). Like a lot of theory about neurotypical development, this information helps us to know and understand how children who are Autistic acquire skills. This information helps us to plan how we can use their communication strengths to support areas of struggle.

Our aim is to meet them where their skills are. We do this by modelling and honouring current skills, while adding small extensions across each skill.

Zig-zag with them! In play therapy, this might look like:

Child's language strengths/skills:

- Advanced knowledge of dinosaur names at single-word level.
- Uses phrases from TV shows with up to five words.
- Sings entire songs.
- Knows and loves numbers.

Child's language struggles:

- Using vocabulary to describe.
- Using language to share a social meaning.

Therapy play to support strengths and struggles

Because of this mixture of skills, a mixture of language models and supports will need to be offered to match where the child is. This might include, for example, offering dinosaur figures in a sensory tray with dried rice and building blocks. The dinosaurs capture the child's attention because it's their play passion, the blocks have numbers on them which are curios to their love of numbers and the rice is a pleasing texture for the sensory profile, they enjoy the feel and love to watch it fall from their fingers. As they play, we model and honour each part of their current communication system while offering a small extension. They line up the dinosaurs and name them as they do. We can echo back the name of the dinosaurs (if that feels comfortable for the child) and extend it with an extra word that describes it. Such as 'Stegosaurus… is spiky!' 'Brontosaurus… is tall'. In this way, we are exposing the child to additional vocabulary and modelling how it fits to current play passion vocabulary.

We can create a small play story by building blocks and standing a dinosaur on the tower. Knowing that this child knows dinosaur vocabulary and knows numbers, we can model combining numbers and dinosaur vocabulary saying, 'Iguanodon is on number 3 block!' We can model social phrases to extend the reasons the child names dinosaurs. When he says 'Ankylosaurus', we can model, 'I love Ankylosaurus' or, 'Look! It's an Ankylosaurus!' Knowing their love and retention of songs and music we can create a play-based song for a play sequence, adding in new vocabulary and actions. It may sound like 'stomp stomp Tyrannosaurus is marching... chomp chomp Velociraptor is eating... flap flap pterodactyl is flying!' We might listen to a favourite song, repeating certain parts they love and blow bubbles and dance. Throughout the activities, total communication would be supported – such as core boards, signs, AAC an spoken words.

This therapy example is entirely child focused and child specific. It includes their play passions and their sensory needs. It considers their current language skills and offers a small extension in line with what they already enjoy and can achieve. It is play based, which keeps us connected and involves sensory play and movement, which supports regulation alongside learning. It leans into a topic of interest and facilitates new learning alongside that.

Support play passion + lean into strengths + gentle stretch of struggles

What is gestalt language processing?

This is when children/adults learn language as whole phrases or in chunks. The word 'gestalt' means an organised whole, that is more than the sum of its parts. Which fits perfectly with this style of language learning where entire phrases and sections of language are learnt as a whole, rather than by systematically adding together separate, single words.

The concept of 'gestalt language processing' was written about by researchers and therapists in the 1980s but has recently become more commonly used when describing, understanding and valuing this form of communication. Often in neurotypical language acquisition, we process language as single words or linked words and then create and generate our own sentences using grammar and vocab as and when we learn to. If you have a gestalt language learning style you will learn an entire phrase as a chunk and use that exact phrase at another time. Often the phrase is used at an appropriate time with key parts of the situation prompting the phrase to be repeated.

For example, a child goes to the zoo and sees a tiger and the parent says, 'Wow, that tiger is big and stripy!' The child may then lift that entire phrase, exactly, word for word, when looking at a book/toy at another time. These whole phrases often keep the intonation used by the adult who modelled it and can almost sound a little staged/acted in the way they are repeated, because they are an exact copy from another person. All language learners do this to some extent – think of when an early talker drops something and does a big sigh, saying, 'Oh, dear me' – they've learnt a phrase for a situation. But for some children, this will be their only or main way of learning language and processing.

Children learning language in this way will often find great joy in repeating phrases they have learnt. It becomes an important part of their language style and their interaction. The 'chunk/whole section' style of learning will also extend to their play. Children who are gestalt language processors will often enjoy watching the same video clips over and over again, finding joy in the completeness of the 'whole section'. They will often play or act out scenes from favourite shows or song videos and recreate these with incredible visual and audio accuracy. They may also enjoy repeating a play sequence many times and need supporting adults to say and act the same way every time the game is played. This is because they have processed it as a 'whole event' so to mix and switch within that whole feels confusing.

Impact on our play therapy

Knowing this about a child is really important and helpful for our play-based therapy because we can lean into this style of learning and provide children with play sequences that reflect this processing style:

- We can model phrases and sentences in their completion rather than stripping things back to single words.
- We can notice and be accepting of the range of accents and tones children may use as they borrow phrases from different people and characters.
- We can set up play that creates a simple and repeatable sequence.

- We can understand that repetition is going to be important for this child and ensure there is time, space and compassion for that.
- We can look out for repeated play sequences and try to detect what books or storytelling they link to, allowing us to become more in tune and part of the play and learning.
- We can add language to play sequences that we know features in their favourite shows and books because their processing style will be keen to store language sequences that way.

Pronouns, questions and tenses

Something to be mindful of when we model and support language learners who process information in whole phrases is that, when the phrase is repeated, the speaker won't change the tense or any of the pronouns from the way they first heard it. What this means is that, at times, the phrasing and grammar won't convert to support its meaning once the child is speaking it.

For example, children who learn in whole phrases may state the phrase 'Do you need the toilet?', when in fact they are expressing that *they* need go to the toilet. What they really mean is, 'I need to go to the toilet'. This has happened because, when they have experienced that need before, an adult has asked them that question. They have then stored the phrase with that situation and the associated feeling, all together as a whole. The next time they experience that feeling, the whole phrase they heard is used to represent the need.

This can be very confusing for supporting adults and can lead to frustration for our children. To support this we can:

- Work hard as a detective with the child to unpick what a repeated phrase means for them. Watch and observe any patterns you see linked to repeated phrases with needs/requests/play. If you work in a setting or home where many adults may support your child, it is helpful to write out key phrases that link to needs, to help educate everyone.

- Be mindful of what question phrases you model in key moments with your child. Swap questions for statements whenever possible, such as: 'Let's play together' instead of 'What are you playing?'
- Be mindful of what pronouns you model. This is really hard! Pronouns are a difficult and abstract concept for children to learn anyway because they change and shift depending on the speaker. I, me, you, your, mine, all change meaning depending on who is speaking at the time! To support children who are learning in phrases, try to model the language that will make sense if they copy it exactly. For example, if you see that they have sticky hands, model '*My* hands are sticky!' or 'Let's wash hands!' (avoiding *your* hands, or the question 'Do *you* have sticky hands?')
- Using these strategies in our own talking, but also being mindful of them when we programme AAC devices and create core boards.

Repeated stories and sequences – looking for hidden meaning

Very often a word or play phrase used by a child won't always make an exact match with the adult's perspective or expectation. This is usually because children will choose phrases that are significant and meaningful to them personally and uniquely, rather than what necessarily feels logical to others.

For example, a child might consistently come in from playtime saying, 'It's OK, look at the sky!' This feels unconnected to the current situation, but the root meaning may link to a previous experience – they may have been to see fireworks that were noisy and busy and a parent supported them by helping them focus on the patterns they made in the sky rather than the noises and the busyness of the other people at the show. This child has borrowed a soothing phrase to try and calm himself down after a similarly busy and noisy experience of running on the playground and coming inside to an echoing cloakroom. The phrase is not linked, but it *still holds meaning for them*.

When we notice these phrases being used, it is often helpful to echo them back to children so we are showing that we understand and acknowledge what they have said. Add this with your detective work and then model a new phrase. So, to the above example we can respond with: 'It's OK, look at the sky… I understand, it feels noisy in here – help, it's too loud!'

In order to respond appropriately, you can use this formula:

1. **Repeat their phrase** (this is validating).
2. **Explain it out loud** (this shows understanding and also explains it to others around them who may be unclear of the meaning).
3. **Model a phrase that matches for next time** (this gives a clear model that links more specifically for this situation, with the aim and hope that this model can be stored and borrowed another time).

Everything holds meaning

If a child has this processing style where they experience information as whole sequences, you will often see this style of learning in their play and life experiences, too. Chunks of play will be repeated, and chunks of life experience will be repeated and echoed. As with their language skills, this won't always be clear, but there will always be meaning. A wonderful way to validate and connect with our children is to spend time working out what and where the pattern has come from.

Let's look at some examples:

A child is visiting a setting with a narrow corridor with doorways either side. One doorway has a pink handle with a flamingo picture on it and the other doorway has a green handle. Each week, the child goes to the pink door and labels 'flamingo', then turns to the green door handle and labels 'and hippo'. For many weeks it is unclear why the green door handle is labelled 'hippo' – there are no hippo pictures, hippos aren't green. It's discussed with family and they don't own any soft toy animals that might explain it or have any posters with these animals opposite each other. We even look at the map of the zoo they visit to see if these animals are next to each other, but they aren't. Each week the child names the two doors and we acknowledge and accept the labelling. We decide to keep a look out for where this pattern may exist, and then one day it all became clear. The family visits the zoo and notices that there is a tunnel to walk through filled with a mural. Painted on one side is a flamingo and painted on the other side... is a hippo. This child had not made it up, or created his own pretend sequence. He was sharing an experience through repetition and borrowed sequencing. If this side is flamingo, then this side represents hippo. The following week this was acknowledged by adults – 'Yes, hippo on this side, like in the tunnel, flamingos one side and hippos on the other', and after that, the child didn't refer to it every week. His message had been shared and he could rest.

This example is so important to consider for our children. How they are constantly, through behaviour, sequences and play, trying to share important messages with us, and so often we might miss them. These are opportunities to connect with them and understand what feels meaningful to them. This is why it is so very important to continue and to strive to become part of their world and work out the root meaning of their behaviour and communications.

Something I have learnt through years of supporting children who are Autistic is that nothing is accidental. Every phrase, every play sequence, every look, every toy placement, holds significance. If we invest the time and care into detecting what that purpose is, we can create a very real and meaningful communication experience with our children.

> A child explores all the toys in the therapy room. His play joy is lining up, so he makes collections and starts to set them out in a line. When he discovers the play kitchen set, he stops. He picks items up individually. Any kitchenware, like spoons and whisks, is discarded, and any food item is brought to his mouth and then placed on his head. It is observed across the session that no other items get placed on his head, only the round food items. After the session, a little bit of research is done for nursery rhymes and songs where this might happen – and there is one! A funny song and video online about balancing apples on your head and counting how many are there before they wobble off! It's actually one of his favourites and he watches it often. It wasn't an accident. It wasn't a sensory difference, or a misbehaviour throwing things over his head. It was a repeated play sequence. A series of actions he had lifted exactly from a video and acted out for himself.

Because so often our children who are Autistic will learn and experience language skills in a different order to neurotypical children, it is hard for us to ever know exactly what internal language skills a child holds before they find a way to voice them. There are accounts from Autistic adults, sharing that, when they weren't talking out loud, they were talking inside to themselves. They were chatting away to us and wondering why we weren't replying! They were explaining things to us, answering, requesting, and we didn't always get it. I hold this thought close whenever I am supporting a child. Imagine how frustrating that must be, to not be heard but have the language processes happening internally. It is why it is important to assume a child's competence. Talk to them and about them with respect. Explain yourself to them – if you don't understand what a phrase in play means, be honest and hold yourself accountable. This might sound like, 'I hear you saying "Oh, Luna cat, what a mess!" I'm not sure what that means in our play dough game... I will keep trying!' Explore a few options that might link – is the 'mess' linked to the child having sticky hands from the play dough, is it a signal they want to wash them, or find a cloth? Does it mean they want the game to finish because it signals tidy up? Assume that there is a reason for that phrase and message being shared, and be honest and open if you aren't able to work it out straight away.

Having an open narrative with a child throughout the day and their play is a lovely gesture of care and respect for what they may be processing without us knowing. It will offer reassurance to uncertainty. It will show that we value their perspective.

Chapter 8:

Using play to support other skills

Play is naturally engaging for children, holding their focus and attention because they already want to be part of the activity. It is therefore the perfect way to encourage other skills that they may find harder. These ideas are for a range of skill sets – some will feel too difficult for your child, others will need adapting, and some will seem a perfect fit. Use these as a guide and as inspiration to create your own! Let's explore activity ideas for supporting new skills through play.

Playful ways to practice following instructions

Stickers and plasters on soft toys

What you'll need:

1. Stickers or plasters, depending on what the child will find the most exciting and enjoyable to use.
2. A soft toy that will capture their attention – a favourite animal or character from a show they love.
3. Additional props depending on the child. Some children will love having additional equipment like a fancy-dress doctor's kit to go with the plasters, or a special hat while they put stickers on.

How to play:

Explore the items together first and notice how the two link together – the stickers can be peeled off and added to the soft toy. Add in some role play if they enjoy this by pretending to be the doctor adding plasters or the teacher giving stickers. Slowly add some adult instructions that request the sticker to be placed on certain body parts of the soft toy, such as, 'Teddy needs a sticker on his tummy!' or 'Bunny needs a plaster on their foot'. Swap roles so you can sometimes offer the instructions and other times the child offers them to you.

Mix it up! Allow the play to extend and evolve, add stickers to yourselves, add stickers to furniture. Talk about what is happening and make suggestions. Among the fun and the connection, the verbal suggestions are instructions for the child to follow.

Finding items around the room

What you'll need:

1. Items of interest for the child – such as a set of toys they love to play with, photos of their friends or family, pieces of a favourite puzzle.
2. Optional props for looking such as binoculars or a magnifying glass, a bag or basket for collecting, a mat or tray to place the found items.

How to play:

Hide the items in plain sight to allow you to explore and discover where each item is together. Place some so they are easy to reach and others you will need to work together to get to. Show the child that the first item is hiding from us and we need to find them all. Create a space for the items to be placed once found that will be pleasing for the child (corresponding coloured spots, for example, or corresponding photos to match up, a tray to collect, a box to post them into). Explore together to find all the items. As you explore, give instructions using key location words – 'Let's look *under* the table', 'Let's look *behind* the chair'. Follow the instructions together. Find and collect all the items describing their location as you find them – 'We found Batman *on top* of the shelf!'

Get the balance right – make sure searching and discovering the items is enjoyable for the child. If they show distress at parts of their set being missing, make sure you recover them all quickly and reassure them.

Making potions with a visual sequence prompt

What you'll need:

1. Pots and bottles.
2. Water/coloured water and loose parts (this could be gems, rice, glitter, leaves, flowers, sticks. Choose items that will spark interest for your child.)
3. Scoops and syringes/pipettes.
4. Adult written symbol instructions – draw three or four pictures to represent potion ingredients. For example: pot + red water + three gems + one stick

How to play:

Explore the items together and notice the visual instruction prompts. Decode them together and describe the instructions to each other. Extend this activity by encouraging the child to make their own instruction cards for you to follow.

'Pass me the' activities

What you'll need:

1. Any play set up!
2. An adult as a play partner!

How to play:

We can sneak small instructions into our play by asking our children to pass us items as part of the game. Sometimes we can do this as ourselves – 'Can I have the cat stamper please?' – and other times we can do this as characters from the game – 'Oh no! Spiderman is stuck! Can you pass him the rope and pull him out?' Subtle instructions as part of play help our children to notice and respond to key words in spoken language.

Do not over use this though! Our children are so smart. If we do this too often the play will start to feel like a test, and our children will stop responding to us. So make sure you sprinkle this strategy in gently across your play and the day!

Baking and making

Any activity that involves baking or making will have instructions and language naturally built into it without even having to try. This kind of play is absolutely packed with language skills, so if your child enjoys crafts, creating, baking and making, these activities will be a natural source of speech and language therapy through play just by their very nature! Try and include visuals to make the instructions clear. For example, writing on a whiteboard or notepad the five steps involved in the making process, or drawing pictures that represent each of the items used, or demonstrating the signs for the different action words – mixing, baking cutting. This gives an extra layer of communication opportunity as we ask for items and give instructions throughout the play.

Playful ways to explore emotions

In order for children to understand and respond to their emotions, we need to explore the vocabulary that works alongside those feelings. At times of high emotion, children are not in their ready and learning state. Therefore, talking to them about 'feeling angry' or 'feeling sad' will not necessarily be taken and stored for use in the future. We wouldn't wait for a child to be crying before we taught them to count to ten or read or build a tower – it's not the right time! But most of the time we do wait to explain about emotions while children are in the middle of them.

To support children to learn about their emotions, we need to explore them and the vocabulary involved at times of play, calm and regulation. This skills them up with the pre-taught knowledge they need when they are in among that feeling and may hear adults using the words and phrases.

For all these activities it is absolutely essential that we make sure they are played in an affirming way. Always following the child's lead about how comfortable they are with the intensity of exploring emotions and faces. Monitor, notice and adapt the play accordingly. For learning to occur through play, children must feel safe and comfortable.

Play dough faces

What you'll need:

1. An outline drawing of a face, either laminated or in a plastic zip-bag to help the paper last longer.
2. Play dough, modelling clay or putty.
3. Cards with different expressions on – make these yourself or source a premade set.

How to play:

Choose a card from the pack and explore the facial expression. Notice the features of the mouth, eyes, eyebrows etc. Use the play dough to try and build the facial expression on the face outline mat. Talk about the emotion and what might have happened to make this person feel it.

Mirror play

What you'll need:

1. A mirror (one that is safe for play).
2. Whiteboard pens or chalk pens.
3. Clear plastic lids/trays/box.

How to play:

Make funny faces in the mirror and explore what emotion they may link to. You can draw on the mirror and try and match your face to the emotion you have drawn. Or you can hold a clear plastic lid up to your face and allow the child to trace the outline of your expression with a board pen on the plastic.

Characters in books

What you'll need:

1. Favourite books with characters and faces.
2. Searching props optional – like a magnifying glass.
3. Emotion picture cards optional.

How to play:

As you read the story, before you turn each page, notice one of the character's facial expressions and link it to a feeling. If they enjoy using a prop, they can place their magnifying glass on the key part of the page you are exploring. It might sound something like this: 'This little girl is making an oooooo face! I think she feels surprised!' When you notice the facial expression and the feeling, you may want to make the face to each other or match it to a picture card you have.

Using play props that link emotions to feelings inside the body

What you'll need:

1. Doctor's play kit.
2. Emotion cards – make these yourself or source a premade set.
3. A box of sensory toys that have different textures and features.

How to play:

Choose an emotions card and notice how that emotion might feel in your body. You can do this using the doctor's kit. For example, if you choose 'scared', you could use the toy stethoscope to pretend to listen to your heart beating fast. Look through your sensory box and choose an item that can represent this fast 'wooshy' feeling – you may have a spinning top. Use what you have to create concrete connections between the feelings we have and how it makes our body feel.

Here are just a few ideas to help get you started:

Emotion:	How it feels:	Toy that might link:
Happy	Warm and glowing	A light up toy
Sad	Heavy	Weighted blanket
Angry	Hot and busy	Rubbing hands together to make them feel hot
Worried	Fluttery	Wind-up toy that hops about
Excited	Bouncy	Balls or beads in a bottle to shake about

Linking emotions into other play patterns

It's a great idea to talk about emotions, even if you feel your child has a very early understanding of feelings. Try and link play that they already love to do with some resources that include different emotions. This will give you a chance to share with them the language and concepts we use to talk about our feelings, even when that isn't the main focus of their play. Exposing them to the language in a play-based way means that, in the intensity of the feeling, it is not the first time they have heard the vocabulary. As we have discussed before (p.132), during periods of high emotion our brains are not in a learning state. We need to do the learning and the play during periods of calm, so that we can then draw on these lessons in those difficult moments, rather than be starting from the beginning.

Table 7.1: Adding emotions to play

Their play passion	How we add emotions
Sorting and organising	Play with face/character counters and sort into colours or features. You can source premade items or use bottle tops/stickers to create your own.
Throwing	Play games with ball-pit balls but draw different faces on them, look at what emotion and facial expression you are throwing as you play.
Drawing, mark making and crafts	Draw on cupcake cases or blank circle shapes to make emotion shapes. Stick them onto lolly sticks or straws to make puppets.
Sensory exploring	Pushing counters into play dough to make the emotion prints. Hide characters in different sensory bases like rice or cornflour gloop and go on a mission to rescue them, looking at their emotions as you do.
Movement and weight	Use bean bags with faces on them (premade or homemade). Play a game of lifting them and splatting them to the ground. Or set out posters/boxes of different emotions and throw weighted bags/balls as target practice – name the emotion you hit.

Naming emotions throughout the day and how to respond to the need

When we teach children about emotions, it's important that we also teach them about how emotions signal needs. When we have feelings, they are a message to us and others that our body *feels* something and *needs* something:

- Sadness – we need comfort.
- Tired – we need rest.

- Excited – we need movement.
- Angry – we need a release.
- Overwhelmed – we need peace.
- Worried – we need more information/reassurance/a feeling of safety.

One of the most effective ways to teach children about their emotions is to name it when they feel it and when they see others feeling it, as well as explaining how our body reacts and what it needs. You can do this in accordance with the child's language levels and skill set.

When they are experiencing a feeling for themselves, you might use one of the following approaches:

- Exploring it very simply: 'Oh excited! A bouncy feeling!'
- Or in more detail with reasoning: 'What an excited jump! Your body feels so bouncy about this game!'

You can extend this by exploring what the person needs:

- Exploring it very simply: 'Excited energy is bursting out! You need to bounce!'
- Or in more detail with reasoning: 'Goodness! What a bouncy feeling you've got! You are so excited that you built the tower so high! Jumping about is helping your body feel steady again!'

Alternatively, when someone else is experiencing the emotion, you might use the following:

- Exploring it very simply: 'Oh crying! That is a sad feeling.'
- Or in more detail with reasoning: 'Oh no! The boy is crying, they feel sad. I can see they have dropped their ice cream, they are sad it is dirty now.'

You can extend this by exploring what the person needs:

- Exploring it very simply: 'They need a cuddle! Feel some love.'
- Or in more detail with reasoning: 'It's disappointing, they need some help. A cuddle to help them feel safe and loved. Maybe they can share their grown-ups?'

Playful ways to use books and storytelling to support communication

Books with props

When you read a story or explore a book with your child, try and find an object that links to a key feature of each page. It might be a sensory item, a prop to act out an action, a figure that matches a character or an item to represent a noise or texture in the book. This makes the book more hands on and more interactive. It can often give children more of a reason to interact with the book and motivate them to explore the language. Try not to make it over complicated – one simple item for each page is enough.

Borrow a book's theme

For this activity, we are going to borrow the narrative structure of a book but create our own toy and play-based story. A great example for this is the story book *Dear Zoo*. Rather than reading it in the usual order, collect several gift bags or pots and place an animal figure inside each one. Use the repeated story phrase 'I wrote to the zoo to send me a pet… they sent me a… X' and encourage your child to look inside a box or gift bag to reveal an animal. Use what you've got rather than be confined to the book's animal. You can find a tiger, hippo and tortoise rather than the animals named in the book itself.

The great thing about this is you can alter the vocabulary to fit with a child's interest. So, for example, if they love cars, write to the garage to send you a car. If they love dinosaurs, fill your bags with different dinosaur figures. If they love sea creatures, discover an octopus, a fish and a dolphin! This introduces a repeated narrative and keeps the play engaging and interactive for the children playing.

Another great source to borrow from is the 'that's not my…' style books. Make a collection of similar items and explore them together – 'That's not my car, the wheels are too small', 'That's not my car the roof is too shiny'. This is a great way to use a repeated phrase and also model a range of new descriptive vocabulary. You can use this activity idea to link to various themes in the curriculum too.

Books and adding movement

Our perception of reading together is often that we sit alongside each other and turn each page, reading all the words. But for some children, this won't be a motivating way to explore a book. Try instead adding action and movement to each page and allow children to act out part of the book. For example, if the story includes a dragon learning to fly, encourage children to fly around the room, the hall or the garden. On the next page, the dragon learns to breathe fire, so encourage them to jump up and down trying to puff flames. This is a great way to support children to learn different action words through play. This style of exploring books means we make the book active to match their play style. Rather than keeping the book stationary and enforcing stillness. What often happens with this style of storytelling is that children circle back to the pages ready, engaged and eager to find out what the next action is. They are then attending and listening through choice, which is an active learning state.

Books and adding order or sequencing

If your child enjoys sequencing and ordering in their play, they may enjoy adding it to storytelling. An easy way to do this is to find objects that match the sequence of the story so they can place them in a line as the story is being told. For example, if the story starts with an elephant, who goes into a jungle and meets a monkey, and they go to a river, you might have an elephant figure, a tree, a monkey figure and a bottle of water for the child to place in a sequential line. Alternatively, you could take pictures of part of each of the pages, for the child to match up as you read and place in a line or on number squares that match the page numbers.

Adding this kind of structure, sequence and matching element can make storytelling more motivating and meaningful for children who don't naturally find the creative parts of narrative appealing.

Books and adding sensory play

Adding a sensory play tray to a story is a great way to explore storytelling in a more hands-on and immersive way. Providing a child with a sensory tray to play with while a story is read can also support their focus and attention because they have a way of regulating themselves throughout the story. Here are a few ideas for making story themes sensory:

Story book theme	Sensory play tray idea
Farm animals	Hot chocolate powder mixed with water to make 'mud' and animal figures. Add paintbrushes for cleaning.
Pond/sea	Water tray or sensory bottles with glitter. Add green foam shapes for lily pads or seaweed.
Transport	play dough with vehicles to make tracks and marks on the dough.
Colours and shapes	Paper, card, confetti or tissue paper shapes in different colours with pots and tweezers.
Space	Black beans/dyed black rice with paper starts and gems. Pots and spoons for scooping.
Dinosaurs	Slime with dinosaur figures. Add plastic eggs and leaves for making nests.
Zoo/jungle animals	Green, chopped-up straws with animal figures. Add lolly sticks for building fences, caves and dens – use play dough to stand them up and stick them together.
Woods/nature	Loose parts – log slices, silk or real leaves, sticks, gemstones.

Playful ways to use music to support communication

Music can be a motivating and engaging way to practice language skills. Songs and nursery rhymes lend themselves to language learning naturally because they contain repeated phrases, repeated sequences and emphasise the natural rhythm and intonation of talking through song. It is important to notice that some children will not enjoy different adults singing their favourite songs. This is usually because they enjoy hearing it exactly the way they are expecting it – usually linked to the first time they heard it sung. This may mean that only a certain teacher can sing a song, or only a particular version of a song video can be played. If you notice this for a child, honour their preferences to help build your connection and show your understanding of what is important to them. You may also notice that children must complete a song sequence once it is started, so if they sing 'Ten in the Bed' they will need to complete the entire sequence from ten to zero in its entirety. This may be true of watching a song video, listening to a song on a music player or having it sung to them. It is important to be mindful of this and how failing to complete this song sequence may be distressing, so making time for its completion regardless of routines and schedules may be needed once the sequence has started.

Nursery rhymes with props – act out the story of the song

Here are a few ideas:

- Building blocks and egg toys for acting out Humpty Dumpty.
- Spider toy and marble run for acting out Incy Wincy Spider.
- Rolling play dough into shapes for current buns or sizzling sausages songs.
- Toy frogs and a tub of water for acting out speckled frogs on a log.
- Using a cosy blanket for Ten in the Bed.
- Using sensory bottles for Ten Green Bottles.
- Sensory scarfs for acting out different 'swooshy' shapes for Wheels on the Bus.
- Rainbow ribbons for dancing to songs about colours

Nursery rhymes with visuals for choice making

If you are supporting a child who loves music, it is a great opportunity to encourage them to make choices and express their interest. Try creating a basket of items that represent different songs so that they can hand you an item as a way of requesting a song they love. You can use real objects – like a toy bus, a gold star and a soft toy spider – or you can print pictures and make a flip book for choosing from.

Music bottles – explore different sounds

Collect differently shaped bottles and add different items inside. You can then explore how the sounds are different by shaking them. Try and choose different items that make a range of noises, such as: bells, beads, wool, small bricks, water, sticks, pompoms. Sing songs and shake the shakers exploring noise, music and volume.

Musical instruments for language concepts

You can use musical instruments to explore opposite concepts. Either make instrument shakers with your child or use instruments you have. With these, practice language concepts by:

- Shaking to the instructions stop and go.
- Playing music at different volumes – loud and quiet.
- Playing music of different strengths – soft and gentle.
- Playing music in different locations – up and down, behind and in front.
- Playing music at different speeds – fast and slow.
- Play music with different action words – tap, shake, push.

You could even link your music play to emotions and play in an angry way, a sad way and/or a happy way. Talk about how your body changes and how your music changes across each emotion.

Playful ways to explore social language, new experiences and advocating phrases

Play is a safe place for children to exist in. The wonderful thing about play is that, when a child creates it, it can't be done wrong. They are in control and there are very few rules. It is a freeing time for them. It makes it the perfect place to practice new skills, because even when the new skills are hard, we still have elements of enjoyment because they are baked into the play.

We can therefore use play to practice skills in a small, controlled way before we brave using them with the rest of the world. Some children will instinctively practice and experiment with their skills in play – pretend play or role play are brilliant examples of this. For some children who are Autistic, exploring socially and practising social skills in play with other children will be less appealing. It may not happen as often because these skills feel harder and less instinctive. Therefore, we, as adults, can create and enhance opportunities by setting up play to practice helpful scripts and phrases with them. This can be a low-pressured approach to supporting children to learn about complicated social skills, to rehearse new experiences, or to learn scripts for advocating, that they can then transfer to other play or life interactions. Using figures and characters to act out sequences provides the supporting adults with a brilliant opportunity to practice *social use of language* through play.

I have included below some examples created by merging real therapy play I have explored with children over the years. These examples depict play in which we explored social skills, new experiences or practiced phrases that would help the child advocate for their needs outside of the therapy session. This play gave children an opportunity to rehearse actions and phrases in play that could be transferred to their life. Because these are specific, the resources and play ideas themselves may not be directly transferable for your own children., But my hope is that they will inspire you to use play in a similar way for unique and specific learning opportunities for the children that you support.

Making a magnetic tiles fairground

In a play session, you could make a fairground ride out of magnetic tiles – the characters line up and wait for a turn, then they go and get an ice cream. As the adult in play, we can model practical, useful phrases for our children such as 'Hello! Can I join your game?', 'I'm waiting for my turn next, let me know when you're ready', 'Hello, please can I have an ice cream from your shop?' or 'Here's the money'. Because our children are playing, engaged and enjoying the interaction, they are very likely to store and remember these phrases. The phrases can be modelled so that children can copy and use them exactly as they are in real-life situations, with friends or at a shop etc.

A Play Dough tray that practises birthday assemblies

Sometimes a play opportunity that explores a new skill may present unexpectedly. This happens often in my therapy sessions and below I will describe a reoccurring theme that I support frequently through play – assemblies and school events. The activity presented is a play dough tray which includes play dough, plastic insect figures, buttons and candles, with the aim to explore the sensory textures and allow for story telling with the props as we play. As we start pressing the plastic insects into the play dough all in a line and exploring the shape the prints make. The adult says, 'Look, they are in a row like when it is assembly time'. The child responds with a set phrase, such as 'It's not a happy birthday today'. The two statements seem unconnected, however after further discussion with staff it is described that this child dislikes the Friday celebration assembly where the school sings happy birthday to any children who have celebrated that week. We now have an unplanned opportunity through play to explore this child's worry and develop strategies to support them.

Returning to the play dough tray, the adult talks as one of the plastic insects, modelling key phrases such as: 'It's too loud', 'I don't like it', 'I need help', 'My ears hurt' or 'I need to go'.

As part of the play, we can explore volume by whispering the happy birthday song, or making the character shout the happy birthday song.

(Following the child's lead and comfort must be the guide for this – they must feel in control as part of this play and find the volume change playful. Any request to stop or signs of even low-level discomfort, need responding to immediately.)

We can explore covering our ears with our hands, the hood of our jumper, or using ear defenders or earphones.

We can explore emotions, comfort and regulation through our play characters – an insect figure can become upset by the signing and we can show them kindness and comfort and we can practice regulating as part of the play – by covering them in a play dough blanket, giving them a play dough snack and helping them take some breaths after their upset.

Fairy peg dolls playing pass the parcel

Set out some peg dolls in a circle and make them little pompom cakes to eat. Take a small box/wooden brick and pretend it is a present. Sing a song together and pass the present around the circle, and when the music stops each fairy pretends to have a turn. Not everyone wins a prize. As part of the play, you can rehearse different reactions to this. Some fairies just say 'Never mind', while others may get really cross and leave the party! You can practice scripts for self-soothing like, 'Oh, I wish I had won the big prize. I will take a breath and feel OK soon', or 'It's hard when you don't win, but I did like the music part', or, 'I'm sad to lose I need a hug'.

Remember to adapt this to use favourite and preferred characters to keep the activity motivating – using cartoon character figures, dinosaurs or even cars to act out this situation would work well too.

Wind-up toys being used in a small group

You can explore wind-up toys together as a small group and practice key phrases for collaborative play with peers. An adult can support the children through the emotions involved in waiting, responding to others and, when peers behave less predictably than adults, support can be given to use key social phrases like 'Can I have a turn?', 'I need help', 'I'm not finished my turn yet' or 'I can pass it to you after one more go'. We can talk about and explore long and short turns and how that feels for the different people in the play – having the long turn feels great, but waiting for someone to finish a long turn feels tricky.

Cars crashing into each other

As you play cars, they can crash into each other and you can rehearse different reactions. Sometimes the car will keep driving and say, 'I'm OK', and the game carries on. Sometimes the car can say, 'Ow! That hurt!' and the other car can respond 'I'm sorry' or 'Do you need help?' Other times the cars can almost crash and use a phrase like, 'Ooo, that was close! Are you OK?' Sometimes the cars might go slowly and tell a car friend, 'I need a quiet game today'. These are transferable play phrases that can be stored away for busy play situations on the playground or with peers playing cars too. The idea is that practising them in play allows the brain to learn the skill in a state of calm.

For all the examples shown in this chapter, these are often skills that we assume children will learn through merely living their lives and existing with other children and adults. However, very often for neurodivergent individuals, we will need to actively teach and practice these skills. The instinctive exploration and experience of these skills will not be enough. Even if they do experience them, the 'take away message' may not be a positive one and this can feed into a sense of social anxiety or confusion. By exploring these skills through play, we take the pressure away from the child and away from the moments of distress during which the new skills will be needed. As the child is in control of the play and the characters, they are often filled with a sense of empowerment as they guide the story and support the characters. We are giving them the skills and strategies at a time that they feel safe, regulated and playful. This is when the brain is best equipped to learn. Children will need support to transfer these skills to the real moments. This will take time and practice, however starting this practice in play will support the child's success.

Playful ways to use sensory elements to extend skills

A simple way to encourage new play patterns or skill is by merging new play ideas with a familiar or preferred sensory play elements. The sensory addition adds an element of curiosity and more motivation for the child to explore and extend from their usual play sequence. For example, if they love to throw pom poms and watch them fall but are not motivated or engaging in pretend play. We can combine the two by placing pompoms in mixing bowl and stir in big movements to make the pompoms fly out the bowl. The child gets the same sensory joy of watching the pompom fly around the room, but we have gently extended their play to involve a new action. It gives them a chance to experience something new because they want to rather than because they are being asked to. Once they have chosen it, we are then in a position to model language, play ideas and sequences that may not have been relevant in their previous play. In this example, when scooping and throwing pompoms we can use phrases like "ready steady go" "lets find them" "pick them up". But by simply adding the mixing bowl and spoon, we can now extend our language models to – "let's mix it" "mix it fast, mix it slow" "the bowl is full / empty", as well as singing nursery rhymes about baking and mixing. As their play partner, combining these play types opens up more play and language opportunities for us, but keeping it playful and linked to the child's preferred play patterns keeps it motivating and joyful

This might look like:

- Adding letter counters to slime to encourage letter naming.
- Finger writing in cornflour and water gloop to encourage mark making.
- Adding pompoms and feathers to a play kitchen to encourage pretend play sequences.
- Adding water and bubbles to a car track to encourage a longer play story: The cars don't just drive round and round the track, they now go to the car wash, use bubbles, rinse off, dry off... And then go round the track. The sensory element makes the story longer, which offers more language opportunities.

There many more sensory play ideas and resources listen in Chapter 6, p.112.

Playful ways to redirect behaviour

Swap 'no!' for 'let's go!'

Sometimes our little ones send us a play message that they feel the need to move or play in a certain way. Remembering that *all behaviour is communication*, this play message is a signal that they are searching for feedback or play that fulfils a sensory or stimulation need.

In these moments, it's almost pointless telling them 'no' or 'stop' or 'don't throw that/jump on that/ eat that' because there's a pull within them telling them that the sensory or stimulation need must be filled. In these moments, meeting them with a negative statement will often set off a 'fight, flight, freeze' response and often escalate a behaviour rather than support it. (Read more on this on p.10.) As their supporting adults, we can notice a pattern of behaviour that isn't safe and we can try to *swap the no for a let's go*, sometimes referred to as a 'creative yes'.

This means we want to try and find a way to fulfil the need but in a safe or appropriate way.

It is dangerous to throw heavy wooden blocks, but we can throw a bean bag, ball, or petals and felt shapes. It is dangerous to jump on the top bunk, but we can go on the trampoline. It is dangerous to eat and crunch the sand, but we can go get a crunchy snack of crisps, a carrot or dry cereal.

The best way to make a *creative yes solution* is to consider, 'What does my child get from that behaviour?' 'What feeling are they craving?'... Once you've spotted that you can find a safe alternative for them, you can offer it with a 'let's go' phrasing:

- 'You are trying to do big jumps – let's go jump on the trampoline!'
- 'You are feeling that sand crunch in your mouth – let's go get a drink and some crisps to crunch.'
- 'You want to throw something – lets grab some bean bags and throw in the hall.'

This phrasing acknowledges the need and feeling, links it to the behaviour and presents a safe alternative. This phrasing can also help children to become more aware of the messages their body is sending them, and advocate for these in the future. In an ideal world, they may show a card for 'crunchy snack' rather than eating the sand. Or they may say, 'My legs feel busy, can we go jump somewhere?'

Here are some more *creative yes solutions* you can try:

- **Throwing box:** Teach your child to recognise what is safe to throw in play. Notice the different materials and noise things make when we squeeze or tap them gently on the floor. Wooden blocks: feel hard, make a big tap noise = not OK to throw. Sponge ball: feels soft, quiet when we tap it = OK to throw. Work together to create a 'throwing box' full of items that are safe and fun to throw. When you see your child in a throwing mood, help them to find items from the box and encourage safe throwing.
- **Obstacle course:** Notice with your child that they are climbing and moving their body across people and furniture. Maybe they need time to climb in their play. Work together to create an obstacle course or climbing space for safe climbing and clambering.
- **Cushion or trampoline for jumping:** Redirect jumping and launching from things to a more controlled jumping motion. On a cushion, across stepping stones or a mini trampoline works well. Try adding a jumping song so that the jumping has purpose and rhythm and a clear end point to avoid escalation – Five Little Monkeys Jumping on the Bed, Sleeping Bunnies Hopping Bunnies. Alternatively, count down from ten jumps, nine jumps and so on.
- **Big page or chalk scribbles:** If children are mark-making or scribbling on the walls or floors it may be that they are looking for larger motions for mark-making in their play. We can create this using chalk in outside spaces. Placing big rolls of paper on the floor. Using washable paint on screens or patio windows.
- **Squashing dough/putty:** Some children may scrunch up their work when they make mistakes, or swoosh across other children's desks with their arms in a moment of upset. Helping children release frustration through squashing putty or dough in their hands, rather than squashing their worksheets, can help release the burst of energy linked to that emotion. Follow this up by soothing and then exploring the process of learning through doing, making mistakes and trying again.

therapeutic thought

A child's energy cannot be lessened or contained, but it can be directed and guided

Imagine a handful of marbles being thrown across the room; the energy stored in them as they are released makes them spread chaotically across the floor in all directions and under furniture. Now picture these same marbles, with the same energy and force, released into a marble run flow with purpose, direction and focus; guided to the end destination in triumph.

The same marbles, the same energy, but two very different outcomes.

At school, so many of the children I support present with what are termed 'challenging behaviours', but so often it is that their energy has been left untapped and unused by us adults. Carpet times are long, tabletop work is under stimulating, and there is a surplus of undirected energy left over buzzing about inside them. This can be physical or mental energy. It has nowhere to go, so they find their own ways to release it. The problem is, the ideas developed by a six year old are not always safe. They aren't always appropriate for inside. They aren't always small and steady, but explosively chaotic.

These are often children who have energy to spare and maybe do not as much social restraint or impulse control as their peers. That's a tricky combination! It means that common classroom tasks don't use enough of the stocked-up energy. Sitting to wait for the class doesn't use enough. Standing in the line doesn't use enough. Writing one sentence doesn't use enough. Watching the video doesn't use enough. There's lots of movement and ideas left over! When it's left, this spare energy goes into flicking the person in front of them. Or rolling up their work sheet to make a sword. Or sneaking some maths blocks to make a stick that pokes the ceiling.

What I find, though, is that if children are given enough to keep their energy focused, it becomes a real strength. They achieve quickly and the buzz of success motivates them even further. A positive cycle begins where this surplus of energy helps them thrive.

If we don't *give* children enough stimulation for their energy levels, they will find ways to use it up by themselves. So, if you need their energy to be productive, make sure they have enough accessible and motivating activities to channel that energy in to.

therapeutic thought

Social survival strategies

It occurred to me recently that I have been teaching my children 'social survival skills' for a while, as an alternative to teaching the neurotypical social skills to 'copy'. I teach these not with the motive to change their personality or teach them how to fit in, but instead to explain that there are some things that socially lots of other people will 'get' or 'understand' that might not make instant sense to them - and that is not their fault and there is no need for them to change, but it helps them to notice and be aware of these differences.

For example:

- Not everyone cares very deeply about winning. That doesn't mean they aren't a good team player, or are a bad friend, or not trying their best. It just means their motive for play isn't to win. It might be they just like the play, togetherness, or giggles of the game. All motives are ok.
- Sometimes we say "sorry" to help the other person feel better - I've labelled this "a social sorry". Such as if we accidentally hurt someone (e.g. by dropping our book and it lands on their foot) we say "sorry" because it helps our friendship heal, not because we did something wrong by choice and need to feel a deep remorse (e.g. throwing a book at someone on purpose).

- Not everyone will be able to talk for a long time about the same topics as you. That doesn't mean they don't care, it just means they might need a rest or a change of topic. Your passion and knowledge for that topic is greater than theirs. They still value you and your knowledge.

Ideally, we pair this explanation with lessons for our Neurotypical children about accepting that some people find winning and losing very emotional and that we support them through this, rather than adding to their upset. Or that some people feel passionately about certain topics and will want to share this with you; if you need a break, let them know politely.

My hope is that these 'social survival skills' give children the knowledge about how people experience the world differently, without insisting that they need to adhere to a certain way of existing. I'm not asking them to change, or learn how to adapt. I fully accept their way of experiencing the world. You do you, and let's understand that when others may do it differently, that

Chapter 9:

Neurodiversity-affirming considerations

Task completion and attention

Task completion can be a really strong urge for children who are Autistic (as it can be for adults too!). The need and desire to finish something in its entirety will sometimes override all other needs. This is difficult within many settings as other pressures such as time, focus, activities or social requests can interfere with this process. The easiest way to explain this is with an example.

> A four-year-old boy is playing at the junk box modelling table. He has made a plan of what he wants to make, he has carefully selected pieces of card, small straw pieces, the tape that he likes, and he's waited (as requested by an adult) for the particular scissors he likes (there is only one pair that have an old golden star sticker on them and those are the only ones he is willing to cut with, but another child had them). He starts to stick and cut, and his creation is coming to life. He has planned the order and sequence and end result in his mind almost meticulously, and the joy and anticipation of it being real builds in his mind as he builds with his hands. But then

> the 'tidy up' wind chime jingles. He feels instant panic. The brain is flooded with all those panic hormones and his body goes into fight, flight or freeze mode, heart racing. He isn't finished and he knows what the rule is. The chime means tidy up and he likes to follow the rules, he doesn't like to make mistakes and he definitely doesn't like key adults to be upset with him. But his model is unfinished. He's noticed by a staff member who tells him, 'Don't worry, you can finish it later, let's leave it on the table and have to sit on the carpet'... 'But I need to finish it!' comes the child's response, and he's right, it's a real need for him, the unfinished-ness of the task almost hurts... 'Play is finished, it's carpet time'. He's presented with a now-and-next board and he knows the rules so walks to his space and sits down. His body is now sat on the carpet, but his mind is not. In his head, he goes over and over the next steps needed for completion of his model. He imagines someone moving those three pieces of perfectly chosen straw – what if another child gets to the table before him? What if someone thinks it's rubbish and they put it in the bin... a rustle in the background of the teaching assistant setting up the next activity... panic! Has she moved the box he needs? The rustle sounded like the bin, what's going on back there? 'Eyes at the front, please!' the teacher prompts... his mind continues to race, and he tells himself what to do – 'OK, keep your eyes looking forward but listen carefully for any movement in the junk box corner, the phonics song is finishing so its nearly time to go, if I start getting up now I'll get there first, OK get ready.... It's finished the teacher has said it's OK, so go go go!!!!'

In this example, to the outside world, the child has 'successfully transitioned from a preferred activity to carpet time, using a visual'. You may have seen targets like this on reports. Technically, the child and staff have achieved this target here using strategies and visuals to support the child. However, with a closer look, we can see that their body has moved, but their mind wasn't there with them. Their mind was so preoccupied with the possible threat to their previous task that they were unable to access any learning. They won't have had capacity to absorb any phonics, to notice any social cues, to engage with any learning. They will have *looked* like they were there, but that doesn't feel enough. In this example, it would have been useful to notice that this child is mid-project and understand that task completion is important to them. Our job as the supporting adults is to then weigh up the timings and the attention and the regulation. This is true inclusion because we are considering the child's perspective and needs alongside the systems and routines in place within the setting.

Possible options may look like this:

- We know the child is able to continue their project calmly at the junk box modelling table, and access the phonics lesson simultaneously so we can facilitate them to do that. This allows task completion and includes them in the lesson that's planned for the class. They sit and finish their project and sing the phonics song to themselves as they do, glancing up at the teacher with a little prompt every now and then. (Other children may ask why, and we can be honest – letting them know there is a special job X needs to get done but he is still learning while he finishes).
- We know that they will not be able to multitask, it will be too difficult for their learning style, but we also know that pulling them away mid-project will be distracting (internally, if not externally). So instead, we set them up a 'keep it safe box'. We place all the important things and his favourite scissors into a tray and put the tray in an agreed safe space. If possible, we include the child in this process so they can help pack the items away (taking ownership of their project and keeping a sense of autonomy while following the school routine). We use an empathetic narrative with connection, explaining to them, 'I know you wish you could finish this straight away, we have phonics now. Let's keep this stuff super safe so we know for sure it will be here for you. We will make time for you to do this afterwards, so you can get a nice, finished feeling.'

Both these solutions do take time and adult energy, however the investment of that time will mean that a connected understanding and feeling of safety is developed for that child in their learning environment. Instead of spending the phonics lesson in fight or flight mode, unable to learn. Their brain will be calm, settled and in the perfect space for acquiring new skills.

This is an example of a really transferable scenario that I have often observed in schools, homes and nurseries. As adults, we often have so many time pressures, schedules, targets and plans to fulfil that we can really miss the importance of task completion for the child and how that might impact them. How frustrating and disempowering it is to be whisked away from something before it feels fully finished. If you are working with a child who is struggling with transitions, this is a really important place to start exploring – do they need more opportunities to complete tasks in their entirety?

Other examples of task completion for home and school include:

- Needing a certain number of turns on a set activity (lots of children who are Autistic will have a favourite number or sequences that link to this).
- Needing to order things by certain colours, like rainbow order.
- Needing to be the one who closes the lid or zips up the bag, as this gives that feeling of completion and finish.
- Needing to complete a certain level on a video game.
- Needing to leave a pattern of food items on their plate.
- Needing toys or objects to be left in a particular pattern after play.
- Needing songs/films/theme music to be completed in their entirety.

Explore this by observing their play style and what kind of sequences they might be creating for themselves. This often means that, as supporting adults, we need to go against the structure and routine a little bit to allow the child's process to shine through – perhaps they like to always do five tries of a game, so if you stop at four, the task will feel incomplete and the transition will be a fight. If we insist on the finish at four, because of the time, the routine and the structure of the day, we will never get to observe that, actually, after that fifth turn, the child's attention naturally fades and the transition occurs smoothly. Perhaps they like to be the one that closes the zip, or put the box lid on, so when you have done it for them, they grab and reach for the box, but aren't taking it off to have another turn, they are taking it off so that they can be the one to put it on again.

Make time to watch and observe in order to learn what it is about a task that makes it feel finished. This will often be slightly different for every child.

Children will of course let you know in different ways – some children will be able to explain this to you verbally – 'I just need to finish!' – and others will show you with behaviour, crying or even breaking what they are in the middle of creating. Breaking it takes away the need to finish it, but the upset over it being broken is just as big, so that is a heavy emotion to then carry into the next part of their routine. *Remember – all behaviour is communication*. Knowing this about our children will support them across their entire day. Think of how many things we start and finish across all the tasks we do in a day, the impact can be huge.

Like all strategies, theory and knowledge, there are going to be times when we know something about a child, but we physically can't allow them to keep going with a task. This may be due to safety or the impact it will have on their environment. For example, if they throw a basketball once, inside the classroom – we can't allow them to throw it another four times to give themselves a feeling of task completion, because this isn't safe for them, others or the classroom. In this instance, we need to find a way to *acknowledge* their need and offer an *alternative* with direction.

This might look like saying, 'Wow, that made a big crash – I understand you want to throw it another time. That's not safe. We can't throw it inside, I can take you to the playground, let's go! Ball, playground [pointing to the door], let's go!'

I would suggest using this level of language even if the child you are supporting is not using spoken language to communicate themselves. It is important to assume competence, assume that this child understands more than they are sharing with us. My sentence is broken down into sections:

1. A sentence where I understand their need.
2. A sentence where I state it can't happen, even though I know they want it to (add empathy).
3. A sentence where I offer a safe alternative.

If, at sentence three, your child continues to find things difficult and expresses this loudly and with dysregulation, we need to invest time in calming them with more empathy – a 'You wish it was different' statement is helpful here. So, in this instance, 'You wish you could throw it more, that feels important for you, I understand', and then go back to your safe alternative.

This also works for scenarios where completion isn't physically possible – for example, you have a set of animal toys that has been made in different colours but there isn't an orange one. The child attempts to line them up in rainbow order as a pleasing play sequence, but the task remains unfinished because the orange item physically doesn't exist. First, we need to acknowledge an understanding of the situation – 'Oh no! There isn't an orange, and you wanted to make a rainbow, how frustrating.' We can then create an attempt at a *compromised task completion* by offering a different way to complete. In this example, it might be finding an orange toy of a similar shape and size that can be slotted into the sequence. Or by shifting the focus of completion to a different theme – so we can't make the rainbow but, we have stacking cups, and we can put each animal into a pot that corresponds to its colour. The rainbow task is incomplete, but the task of matching and putting them in the cups is complete. Here we have attempted to offer a compromise where the feeling of completion is still gained to some extent.

Later, on p.189, we will consider how task completion may impact transitioning.

Zig-zag skills

One of the amazing parts of a neurodiverse brain is its ability to learn in a different style and system to a neurotypical brain. Often, this has been seen as a struggle and that it can lead to a 'lack of skills'. If we re-address this, what we often see is that the skill set of a neurodiverse child is simply different and less linear in progress than their peers' because of the way they absorb, process and store information. Once we understand and embrace this about children, we can gain a much better understanding of their skills and really notice where they are thriving. What this also does is give us a better understanding that the appearance of strengths and needs in one area doesn't necessarily correlate with strengths and needs in others. For example, a child may have extremely advanced maths and number recognition skills for their chronological age, but need considerable support for their emotional understanding. A child may present with exceptional language and verbal reasoning skills for a child of their chronological age, but need considerable support for peer interaction and social activities. It may mean that they are able to read by sight, but not break down phonological processes. It may mean they are able to tell you many facts and figures about favourite subjects but are unable to hold their pencil or complete mark-making activities.

Understanding that this zig-zag of skills is very likely to exist supports us as adults when we are looking at what support children need to succeed in our settings, because a skill in one area does not necessarily translate to a corresponding or existing skill in another area. It can also support our expectations when helping children, for example a child who is able to express in detail what happened in an incident on the playground may not have the social, emotional or empathy skills to interpret and act in a way that repairs this with their peers. A child who plays with numbers and seeks them out throughout their day may not achieve a high score in a maths assessment because these rely on social compliance for completion.

Notice and accept the way a child learns skills in a zig-zag. Celebrate their success and support the development of areas that are more difficult. Know that the zig-zag means that they won't always present in assessments with their true level of knowledge. Know and understand that this zig-zag of skills may mean your expectations need adjusting because knowledge of one skill won't necessarily mean knowledge of a corresponding skill.

What listening looks like with Autism or other neurodiversity

There is a very 'traditional' view of what listening, attending and responding looks like in communication, particularly for us as adults. Our expectations about what a responsive communication partner looks like is fairly set. We want to see someone looking at us, making eye contact, their body facing us or orientated towards us. We might expect to see a nod or a gesture to indicate they have heard us so far. And often we expect them to echo back part of what we have said or to say something linked to what we have just discussed as an indication they have absorbed and processed our side of the conversation. When it comes to our children (and adults too) who are Autistic, this expectation and picture of an 'active listener' needs completely rewriting.

Quite often, almost the opposite of that needs to happen in order for an Autistic brain to have the capacity to absorb and attend to the new information it's being offered. Very often, if attention, focus and energy are given to conforming their body and face to give the appearance of listening, they have less energy to process the new ideas being presented verbally/through pictures/play.

Movement will often mean their brain and body feels more settled and ready for information. So pacing and looking at the floor may mean they are at their very best for listening. Small hand gestures or movements can often help steady their nervous system, so fidgeting with a toy, or carrying on playing or stimming may be what means they are at their most ready for listening.

Often looking at someone's face can be distracting and even painful or uncomfortable, so if we insist on it, we are actually adding a distraction and detracting from our message. Their focus will be on forcing that face gaze and getting the appearance of listening just right, rather than actually tuning in to the key words we are saying.

'Why do I need to look with my eyes, when it's my ears that hear you?'

When we can be more flexible about our expectations of what listening looks like, we actually increase our chances of creating connection and gaining the child's attention.

I once attended a meeting with a child and a teacher at which we were discussing how he could feel more independent at school. The teacher was discussing options and asking for his suggestions and how he felt about it all. It was a really collaborative discussion, but there was also a lot of pressure for this young child. I watched him swing on his chair and place the chair leg on the edge of his shoe, then swing off and on the rubber part of his shoe (I assume enjoying the swing of the chair and then the pressure of their weight of his body concentrated down the chair leg on to his shoe). In between, he twiddled at his hair and pulled at his jumper sleeve. We were in a conservatory classroom and he gazed up a at the glass and I saw him noticing patterns and shadows created by the sun and the window frames. The teacher spoke for a while and at the end of her sentence, she asked, 'Are you listening? Put your chair down properly on the floor, let's tuck you in so you can get steady here' – a seemingly helpful gesture, but I noticed for the second half of the meeting the child did not talk as much, he didn't contribute ideas, he just agreed and nodded. You see, he *had* been listening while wiggling away, but as soon as he was 'still and listening', all his energy went into looking still and like he was listening and the only thing he had capacity for was to agree and try and get the meeting over.

So, the takeaway point here is to really question what expectations are truly *needed* for listening.

What boundaries, rules and expectations are keeping that child safe? We can't swing ourselves backwards onto the hard floor, of course! But can we have a meeting and allow the child to pace? Yes. That may be tricky for us, as the adults, who aren't used to it, but it does work for the child, who is the person we want to hear from and do the listening. It's an important shift in perspective and has such a significant impact on the child's capacity to fulfil other requirements and achieve their learning objectives within an education setting.

When we set up therapy, activities or learning, consider how movements, toys and body position may not need to be as traditional or structured (these are often referred to as neurotypical expectations/standards). Spend time watching how your child moves when they are given total freedom. Catch yourself, before you prompt them to sit still or put their hands down so they can listen. If you forget and find yourself prompting them and then see their focus deteriorate, it's OK to acknowledge it. I call this a 'do-over'. Be open and honest with the child and explain you think you've made a mistake.

This might sound like this: 'I asked you to stop walking while you were chatting to me then because I'm used to being still when I chat. You know what I've noticed though? Walking seems to help your thoughts flow more easily. Would you like to go back to moving while we talk? I'm sorry, let's find a way that works for you.' This is a very early stage of both repairing a connection with a child when we haven't quite managed to be neurodiversity affirming, and also models how they can politely advocate for themselves in the future. We've helped them to notice what their body needs, and then we've voiced that on their behalf and encouraged them to go ahead and do what they need. We've also owned the mistake, apologised, and then narrated to them the process of working that out. This will hopefully mean they can voice this for themselves another time.

Masking, collapse and inclusion

Masking is the process that neurodivergent individuals will go through to feel a sense of belonging. It may be a series of skills and strategies that is put in place in order to meet standards set within settings and to meet social expectations. An example of masking is an Autistic child not stimming by flapping their hands because they don't want their friends to see them and notice the different way they feel their joy. Masking might be using extra energy and strategies to not call out in class when their natural impulse control levels are different to their peers. Masking might be using a lot of energy to internally process and monitor whose turn it is within the conversation to make sure they speak at a socially appropriate moment. Masking might be not talking for a long time about something they are very passionate about because they have been told it is boring for other people even when it brings them great joy.

Masking, simply, is the use of energy to implement strategies, skills and processes, that don't feel a natural part of a person's personality, communication or interaction style, in order to seem more neurotypical or meet a neurotypical standard.

For a long time, therapy and support almost 'taught' masking. Teaching children the rules of conversations, play and interaction to make them fit in with peers and to meet the expectations of those around them. When a child or adult was good at masking they were often referred to as being 'high functioning'. This is not a term we use or strive for as part of neurodiversity-affirming therapy because it takes away a lot of the unique and wonderful parts of Autism and other conditions that create diversity and uniqueness. We can equate high functioning with high masking, and this isn't something to teach in therapy or aspire to. Not only does it suggest that Autistic play and behaviours are something to hide, it also fails to acknowledge the immense load that masking places on an individual. This load is carried around like a pile of rocks. Each skill a child tries to use or hide, that isn't a natural part of them, is like an extra rock on their pile. This load gets heavier and heavier and usually when they move to a space that feels safe, they drop their load and collapse. This can happen daily when a child arrives home from school/nursery/a party/event, and we often see a great crash of emotions. Sometimes, this is in an uncontrollable explosion of anger or sadness (often referred to as a meltdown) and sometimes it is in an uncontrollable flop of exhaustion (often referred to as burn out).

If a child is showing signs of high masking in one setting, and episodes of collapse in another, it is important to work collaboratively across both settings. This makes sure that the child can be true to themselves and their needs across them both, in order to reduce their masking load and eventual collapse in these two extremes. Being high masking and 'coping with everything' at school, but having a daily collapse, burn out or meltdown once home, is not a healthy or sustainable way to live. Both settings need to take responsibility for this balance regardless of where the collapse is happening. (i.e. just because the collapse happens at home, it does not exempt the education setting from setting up strategies and support systems. The 'coping' at school adds to the child's load and therefore needs to be part of the solution.)

This might look like creating safe spaces within school to allow the child to rest across the day, rather than carry the load for their entire day. It might look like offering support and education for peers to ensure they understand the different ways a child plays and enjoys activities, allowing them to be more included as their true self. This might look like adding sensory play for regulation or high-energy/movement activities across the day so that there isn't a build up of restraint ready to burst come the end of the school day.

We don't want to teach zebras to be horses!

There's an analogy among late-diagnosed adults, that describes the life-long effort to fit in and be among others as being like a horse among a herd but knowing deep down that you were somehow different. That being 'horse-like' didn't feel natural to you. You had to try harder. Notice and learn skills and hide other skills, you couldn't just be a horse, you had to try really hard to be 'horse-like', unlike your fellow horses. But then you discover your diagnosis and accept your neurodiversity and allow the masking to fade away. What's left is not a horse, it's an amazingly unique zebra. You have spent a lifetime, altering your mane and covering your stripes and always felt like a slightly rubbish horse. But you weren't. You weren't a rubbish horse at all, you were actually an absolutely perfect zebra. Unique and exactly how you were meant to be.

It's so important we celebrate children for who they are. It's so important we raise a generation of children who are proud of their unique stripes and don't feel the need to cover them up. We don't want to teach zebras how to be horses, we want to nurture zebras to be the best, most stripy and magnificent zebras that they can be!

What is real inclusion?

Inclusion doesn't mean making everyone seem the same. Inclusion isn't about developing enough strategies that the child is able to conform and appear the same as their peers. Inclusion is about opportunity, understanding and acceptance. It is not changing things to make all children access exactly the same tasks or activities.

If inclusion doesn't mean the same for everyone, how can we make sure our neurodivergent children feel included and accepted? It's about considering what the experience provides them with as an individual.

Let's explore how we might make a school show/performance inclusive as an example:

> Inclusion is *not* including them in the show regardless.
>
> It is *not* including them in the show and holding them to the same expectations as their peers.
>
> It is *not* removing them from the show entirely because it may be too overwhelming or too much.
>
> Being inclusive is about *giving choices* and *exploring adaptations*.

This might look like:

- Creating roles specifically for the child and their skill set. Using a child's strengths and passion, write a part especially for them that considers their skills, communication style and strengths.
- Adding in and including total communication across the performance – use signs, symbols, pictures and AAC across the show or for a number of scenes.
- Creating sensory props that link to the show and will offer 'on theme' regulation throughout the show.
- Allowing and encouraging the use of comfort items like plush/soft toys or blankets.

- Scheduling in quieter shows with fewer audience members.
- Recording a show with no audience and extra adult support, to be sent home, allowing the child to be part of the show and practices, but able to opt out of the main performance. (This allows the family to see them in the show, but removes pressure for them to be in the show on the performance night.)
- Recording a key song or part of the show with the child and a few friends for parents to view.
- Sending home music and videos of the performance, to watch at home and become familiar with in a safe environment.
- Using visuals for the child to help their understanding and motivation to participate, such as adding symbols to the song sheets, creating a flipbook of photos that link to the song lyrics for the child to hold and look at, or making a basket of props that link to the story being told.
- Sensory adaptations with regards to costumes, lights, noises and proximity to others.
- Offering ear defenders at the start and end of the show when clapping happens and a chance to take them off in between if wanted.
- Offering flexibility about how much of the show the child will be part of, need to watch or be backstage for.
- Collaborating with parents from the early planning stages. Have open conversations about how inclusion will look and feel for this child and their family. What are the families' expectations and hopes? What are the benefits and possible upsets for the child? Discuss openly the choice to opt in with adaptations and support or the choice to opt out if the wellbeing of the child will be the cost of participation.

If opting out feels the most inclusive for a child, consider if there are inclusive alternatives that are separate and more appropriate, such as:

- A sensory play tray in the theme of the show.
- An interactive story in the theme of the show.
- Listening to the music from the show and dancing.
- Small group work with peers in the theme of the show.

Consider whether it is appropriate to take short videos or photos of the child enjoying and participating in these activities to send home to the family as an inclusive alternative to attending the performance.

Terms to be aware of

PDA – What is it and how can we offer support?

The term PDA stands for Pathologic Demand Avoidance, or more recently as a Persistent Drive for Autonomy. Autonomy means a person's sense of self-governance – their feeling of being in control of themselves, their choices and their own being. Very simply, this is when a person perceives demands as threats and they have a physical nervous system reaction to them by being flung into fight, flight, freeze or fawn response. When children are neurodivergent (Autistic, ADHD and many other conditions), they are much more likely to present with this nervous system reaction to instructions and directions from persons of authority – for children, these are demands from parents and teachers. As adults, these might be demands from colleagues, partners and bosses.

What this means is that every demand placed on the child is perceived by their nervous system as a low- or high-level threat. It throws their nervous system into action and immediately dysregulates them. Even a simple instruction like 'put on your coat' can elicit an uncontrollable physical surge in their nervous system that they will react to as a threat to their autonomy. These can either build up across the day until the child runs out of capacity and a small request is met with a huge reaction. Or if the child already has a low capacity for demands, it means they have a high reaction to all requests. Unfortunately, meeting this reaction with more authority, punishments, rules and consequences will only further prove the child's nervous system correct – that demands equal threats – and the cycle escalates rapidly and dramatically.

You may notice that a child is often refusing to participate in activities or follow instructions, or is often opting out even when you think they may enjoy the task or activity. It might be that there is a strong drive for them to feel autonomous, and that drive is stronger than their desire to complete an activity. For these children, we want to evoke a feeling of safety and connection through the language that we use. We want to offer comfort to their nervous system that lights up and gets ready every time it hears a request. (This must be so exhausting for children! Imagine hearing 'put your shoes on' and your body reacting like it was being chased by a lion?) It's about how things are present. It's all about the words we choose and the tone we use. For these children, it's all about making it a partnership rather than a battle.

Big trigger words for children with this drive might be:

'No.'

'Stop.'

'Do it.'

'You must…'

'It's X and then Y.'

'If you do X we can do Y.'

'If you don't do X, Y will happen…'

These phrases are 'power phrases' – the person using them holds all the power and it is intended that the person receiving them should respond with compliance. A brain that perceives demands as danger will have an explosive reaction to these.

WH questions are high-demand statements – what are you doing? Why did you do that? Where are you going? What happened here? All of these will likely get a 'whoosh' reaction full of defence, anger and fear. We can try curiosity instead to sidestep the demand, for example saying, 'Goodness, there seems to be a lot going on here', pause and wait gently for an answer (even though you haven't directly asked for one).

Helpful alternatives include phrases starting:

'Let's…'

'I wonder what it would be like to….'

'We could…'

'Maybe we can…'

'Would you prefer X or y?'

'Together we could…'

'Let's be a team and…'

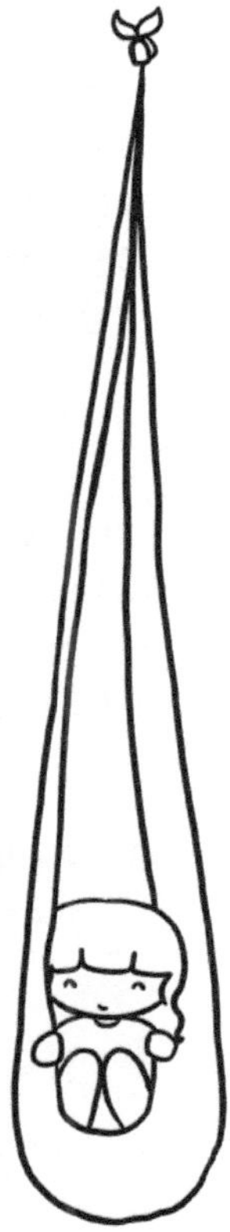

These are collaborative phrases; they offer connection with the child. Although the adult is still leading, there is choice and partnership.

Other strategies to support a PDA profile

The psychology of language helps here.

- **Ask for help:** 'I've started this picture, but I haven't managed to draw all the spots on this ladybird.'
- **Be ready to help:** 'Your shoes are here – I'm happy to help.'
- **Make statements:** 'Here's your lunch box' (rather than 'eat your lunch').
- **Make logical prompts:** 'It's so cold outside today!', handing them their coat.
- **Talk to others or toys:** 'Pink fairy can you find the number 7 on the number chart' (child holds pink fairy and follows instruction as this character).
- **Create phrasing that shows benefit to the child:** Imagine when you give an instruction that the child thinks, 'Why should I?', not in a rude way, but from a curious need to motivate themselves. With this in mind, we can give them as much motivation to collaborate with us as possible. For example, 'I can see it's super sunny outside today so let's get these maths books tidied up so we can get out to play…' is much more motivating than, 'It's tidy-up time, hurry up everyone'.
- **Offer a chance for self-discovery rather than demand:** Rather than 'Stop shoving all of that into that draw', say, 'Mmm that doesn't seem to be working, I *wonder* what else *we* can try…'
- **Create a chance for them to lead:** Play games that allow them to take control and lead you. Let them teach you their favourite game, telling you all the rules you need to follow. Let them teach you about their favourite topic/show/character when you know nothing about it. Play games where it is OK for them to knock over your tower, or move the pieces you've set out (make boundaries clear for when they are playing with peers and siblings). This role reversal helps connect you through play and can rebalance a history of fighting for autonomy the child may have felt.

There will be times when this feels like a long and winding road, and simply telling the child what to do, and them doing it, would be much quicker and easier. But our children aren't robots and we can't programme them to respond that way, so very often if we attempt the 'quicker' version of this, we end up in a cycle of: power statement > refusal > dysregulation > upset > calm > readiness.

Once back at readiness, we then have to choose whether to offer the power statement again to restart the cycle or try something different. Usually, the cycle of dysregulation and calming has taken much longer than offering a more collaborative statement would have done in the first place! There is also the added benefit that the child stays feeling safe and regulated with the adult, the relationship and bond is maintained and connection is created.

It feels like an easy choice when it's laid out like that! – connection and collaboration!

Impulse control

Children (and adults) who are Autistic and/or ADHD often have a delayed impulse control system. What this means is that, when they have a thought, they often act before considering the consequence.

This may look like:

- Speaking when it isn't their turn.
- Shouting out.
- Reacting in a big way to a seemingly small problem.
- Becoming physical when upset.

This delay in skills doesn't automatically make the behaviour acceptable, but it is helpful to know that, when a child calls out in class, for example, they are often not in control of that response. It is not a choice to break the rules, they are acting impulsively because of a delayed system. Children with delayed impulse control systems benefit from additional prompts to wait, layered with compassion statements: 'It's great you have so many ideas, I'm going to listen to X's idea this time', or, 'I can see everyone is bursting with ideas. I know, it's hard to keep them inside. Let's try to wait and listen for a few more moments.'

Executive function

Executive function is the set of skills involved in planning, organising coordinating and controlling our thoughts and actions. Planning and predicting is a skill that needs support for many neurodivergent individuals. It is often a struggle to order and sequence events keeping time and other routines or systems in mind. This often leads them to stay with one activity for longer than needed and then having to rush the next. Time management and the ability to predict a sequence can be impacted because of this skill difference.

In school, this translates to:

- Difficulty planning work.
- Difficulty organising resources needed for each lesson.
- Planning what order to collect belongings.
- Processing verbal instructions and then following them.
- Decision-making within play and friendships.

Using phrases that prompt children to consider their planning is helpful and supportive: for example, 'XX, what's your plan here?' or, 'XX, what might happen next here?' or, 'I'm wondering whether the next thing that happens will be positive or negative'. Using phrases that incite retrospective shame are unhelpful, for example, 'What were you thinking? That was silly, wasn't it? Look at what has happened now.'

Using visuals is helpful as it takes away the verbal processing load and memory load. It will be helpful to write lists for children to follow, either in words or pictures. Create short visual sequences or prompt cards for key parts of their routine.

It would also be helpful after giving a long verbal instruction, to repeat back four key words that will support the steps you want to be taken. For example, if you give a long description of an activity, finish of with 'Here are the key things to remember: purple pen, talking partners, carpet spot… Go!' We can encourage children to repeat these to themselves as a checklist if it feels playful and appropriate.

RSD

RSD stands for 'Rejection Sensitivity Disorder', which commonly co-occurs with ADHD and other neurodivergent conditions. It is a sensitivity to negative feedback. An extreme nervous system reaction to making mistakes and the perception of a person thinking negatively of them. As you can imagine, this occurs regularly when you have ADHD because you often break rules or make mistakes through the nature of the other features of your personality and skill set. It is worth being mindful that school behaviour policies have a significant impact on this as they often involve naming in public, being sent to another teacher to describe their behaviour or being sent away from the class. These are all a gesture of rejection from the class social group.

Negative feedback and ADHD

Research estimates that by the age of ten, children with ADHD will have been given 20,000 more negative messages and critiques than their peers without ADHD (this figure is commonly attributed to psychologist Dr William Dodson). Twenty-thousand more 'stop thats', 'get downs' and 'leave the classrooms'... The sad fact is that most children with ADHD are trying their best to follow all the rules all the time, in a world that isn't designed for the type of brain and body they have. It's exhausting for them, and being told they still aren't getting it right can have a significant impact on their wellbeing.

We can support a change here by:

- Finding ways to 'catch' our children getting it right and celebrating these times.
- Noticing when they need to move and encourage them to do so safely.
- Giving them yes statements instead of no statements wherever possible to redirect their energy into positive missions/tasks. For example, rather than saying, 'X, move away from Y child', you might say, 'X, I see you have loads of energy and I need the bookshelf organising – please sort it out for me!'
- Believe in their goodness – believe that if a child had the skills and capacity to meet the expectations placed on them, then they would. The struggle and behaviour is a message they need help.

- Make connections – tell them that you believe in them, identify key personality traits to celebrate with them, encourage them to do the same in themselves.
- Make sure you are more than just an 'instruction-giver' – go out of your way to say things to children that are purely for connection and social enjoyment. Make sure there is a balance between the number of times you instruct, and the number of times you connect.

Supporting perfectionism

Perfectionism and communication difficulties often come hand in hand. Not exclusively, but often children with Autism, children who stammer and children with language delays/conditions can all have perfectionist character traits. They may want things to be just a certain way, setting themselves very high standards and feeling incredibly frustrated and disappointed when it doesn't go to their plan exactly.

If you have a child who finds it hard to make mistakes, here are a few ideas to help them:

- **Talk about your own mistakes:** When you lose your keys, drop something, trip over, forget what you're saying, label it and self-soothe! 'Ooops, I dropped that, not to worry!', 'I really can't find those, but I can keep looking!', 'Oh no, I made it wrong! Try again, it's part of learning'. Model imperfection and how to cope with it. Show children that we all make mistakes.
- **Make little mistakes on purpose:** Depending on the child you are supporting this can help, but some children will find it distressing to see you make certain mistakes, so be mindful that distress is not a learning state to be in. If this strategy causes anxiety, it is not a good fit for supporting that particular child. A good example of a small mistake you can make on purpose is, when colouring or drawing or writing, go out the lines a bit or make a spelling mistake (on your own page) so that you can demonstrate to them how to notice, manage and move forward from the mistake.
- **Play games about winning and losing** in a calm and safe place – perhaps a board game or something simple like musical statues. Allow the child to choose whether they want to participate – we do not need to force practising these skills. Exposure to

unpleasant experiences doesn't lessen how unpleasant they are, it merely gives us a chance to rehearse them. Therefore, practising winning and losing won't make the losing feel less intense. But for a child who has the skills and capacity, they may gain recovery strategies, they may gain some social phrases to use, they may gain a feeling and sense of control for how they want to react in the moment when it happens with their peers. While you play, model what happens if you lose, and support the child if they lose, talk about how it is tough and it can feel difficult to lose. Explain that you can have another try and playing the game can still feel positive in different ways – explore this with the child. Allow the feelings to feel big, offer comfort and support and suggest strategies for calming and soothing their body afterwards.

- **Have a set phrase** that helps soothe them, like, 'Making a mistake is how we learn for next time', 'Uh-oh moments happen to everyone' or, 'Oh, that's frustrating, let's take a breath'. These can offer language for the child to reassure themselves in your absence.
- **Comment on your own speech mistakes or struggles.** If you forget what you're saying, notice and share this with the child lightly. 'Oops, I lost my words then!'... Or, if you stammer/trip over your words, comment on it: 'I couldn't get those words out then, but I got there in the end!' Telling a story of resilience by sharing your own speech and language mistakes shows that 'perfect talking' doesn't exist and this may teach your child to give themselves self-compassion when they find it difficult.
- **Exploring books about mistakes, resilience and trying again.** There are some wonderful children's books about emotions, making mistakes, building resilience and determination. Looking through picture books and listening to the words and phrases in the narrative can really help support a child to feel less isolated in their struggle. If a child finds talking about their own struggles difficult, it can also provide a way to talk indirectly about it because the focus is on the character and their story rather than a real-life experience for the child. Toys can be used as props and activities when reading books to make them more engaging (see p.138 for more ideas of using books in play).

Strategies to support change

Periods of change (especially sudden change) or unexpected events can feel very unsettling for children who are Autistic. As discussed previously, there is often a joy in the repetition and predictability of activities and change strips this away leaving uncertainty and the unknown. Change can feel very debilitating because any plans and predictions previously made will no longer be possible. Change often means adaptations are needed to lessen a child's sensory load. Change often signals new and unknown activities which feel impossible to plan for. Change often occurs with additional demands.

We will explore 'transitions' in more detail Chapter 10 as these tend to span across our everyday routines, however here are some key strategies for those bigger episodes of change.

Strategies to support times of change

Different individuals will respond differently to change and strategies will therefore need adapting according to their unique needs.

Give notice: If a new activity or change of routine is anticipated in plans, we can help children to prepare for this by giving them notice. We can use a total communication approach here (see p.115) to make sure that the information is understood and supported. This may be done by creating a Calendar or visual board to show an event is coming up. You may use key signs like 'next' or a number to represent a countdown t when the event is happening. This allows you and the child to understand that the change is on its way and do any activities that help prepare for this. For example, if starting nursery, you can try on the uniform, go and look at the entrance gates, practice the walk from home to nursery, hang their nursery jumper up in sight so they can become familiar with its colour and fabric texture.

But don't give too much notice: Here's where we need to be child specific, because there are some children who won't benefit from a long countdown to prepare for change. The anticipation stretched over too long a period will actually make things a lot worse and have a greater impact on their wellbeing. It will be a case of learning through experience, learning with the child what works for them. Some children will need three weeks to prepare for school photo day and other children will need to be told the day before, some will need telling on the morning of the event.

Practice and prepare: There will be some events and changes that you can prepare for through rehearsal and practice. If you are visiting the dentist, you can watch videos, read books or watch cartoons that involve this activity. You can explore items like surgical gloves, toothbrushes and mirrors. You can talk about different smells and lighting that might be present.

Notice the change outright: The change will sometimes happen and there won't be a chance to prepare for it. Maybe their preferred crisps are no longer sold in the local shops, maybe the tablet/computer didn't charge overnight as expected, maybe the road is shut and we have to drive a different way to nursery. These are unexpected and we couldn't plan or prepare for them. When this happens, we will have to follow the child's lead in terms of what regulation and emotional support they need. We can use the strategies discussed on p.11 for emotional regulation, calling out the change and the feeling it brings. This might sound like: 'That's different! We can't go left at the roundabout, the road is shut. Oh no, I love it when we always go left. That feels cross for me. I wanted to go the usual way'. We can then practise calming and soothing regulation in a way that is specific for that child.

Make it slow and steady: If you, as the adult, have an element of control over the change, you can try and introduce the new thing or event slowly. For example, when decorating your home at certain times of year, complete the process in stages to ease the feeling of sudden change. You could bring the decorations into the room to explore in the box. Put the tree up but not lights, add the lights the next day, add the decorations a few days later. The change evolves across and number of days to help the child acclimatise to each part that is new in their environment.

Create a calming self-soothing phrase: 'It is different today, I will be ok': If you know you have to change a system or routine, try adding as much comfort to it as possible. Allow the child to take comfort items, favourite toys or blankets with them to help make the change feel less 'unsafe' because it is layered with comfort and reassurance. Try adding a soothing phrase that they can use to regulate as they complete the new/changed activity.

Notice positive change too: Don't forget to actively notice when change brings your child joy. Celebrate this and name it as change so that words like 'surprise' and 'change' and 'different' don't become negative or upsetting for them. This might be noticing that the café changed the pudding from biscuits to sponge cake and that is good because cake is our favourite. It might be noticing that they used chalks instead of pens and enjoyed the task even more than usual – what a lovely change! It might be that a spinning toy has new batteries and now flashes again, what a wonderful, unexpected change!

Create extra periods of low demand for rest and recovery: Be mindful that changes, surprises and shifts in routine, environments and systems will use extra energy and capacity for the child. Notice the energy they use and make time for them to rest and recover. Adapt your expectations for them, knowing that their resources will be low. For example, if there is a substitute teacher for the afternoon because the regular teacher goes home unwell at lunchtime, you may know that this will take energy for your child to process, and that by 2pm in the afternoon they are likely to need respite from all the adapting they have done. They may not have usually needed this, but on a day of change, they may need time in a sensory tent, with favourite books, with a calming tray of kinetic sand or with a weighted blanket.

Staged change in play: As always, play can be used to help us experience change in a safe play environment. We can use different play to support different changes. For example, at Christmas we may create sensory baskets that include the different textures and colours of decorations around us, allowing our children to explore these close up in a quiet and safe way. We might play a small world activity where the superhero characters hear a fire bell and need to line up to leave the building. As supporting adults, we could also model change happening to ourselves in play: for example, we could change what character we are and model soothing phrases – 'There's no Spiderman in the box today! That's different... Mmm, it's different today and that's OK... I will choose Batman instead.'

therapeutic thought

Verbal instructions and executive function

'Put your sock on…' Something we all call out to our kids. But have you ever stopped to consider why this seems to be such a large cognitive load for little people? I've broken it down for us...

1. Pick up socks.
2. Make pincer grip.
3. Squeeze end of sock.
4. Pull hard.
5. Open sock roll.
6. Pick one of two socks.
7. Coordinate both thumbs and both pincer grips to clasp the open seam.
8. Bend leg at the knee.
9. Balance using core strength now leg is bent.
10. Balance and coordinate leg to direct toe-end of foot towards sock.
11. During this time, maintain pincer grip on sock seam and stretch it over the top of toes.
    - Restart should any toes pop out the sides.
    - Restart should you core strength falter, and you wobble your leg the wrong direction.
12. Use fingertips to claw at sock to move the fabric further down foot
    - Restart if foot moves and sock pops the wrong direction.
13. Use thumb and fingertips in a tight pincer grip to hold seam and pull with strength over heal.
14. Make sure thumb is tucked inside seam and fingertips outside for best grip
15. Make sure balance is maintained while leg is bent towards body
16. Make sure leg remains bent so arms can reach foot.

17. Maintain strong grip and pull sock fabric up over ankle.
18. Identify if sock heal is correct, if not go back to step 12.
19. Check toes within the sock, is the fabric bunched, is it in between toes, is it stiff or threads loose.
20. Use fingertip to adjust accordingly. Consider returning to the start if uncomfortable.

One sock is on!

- Return to step 6 and repeat for second sock.

Total steps for two socks = 36 steps, but that is with zero errors, zero restarts or repeats and zero distractions.

A distraction may be a sibling, a noise on the TV, being asked a question, noticing a toy, having a thought or a worry about the day, feeling hungry, the sun getting in your eyes, a cough. Anything that shifts your focus from these instructions and requires you to reconsider which step you are at.

It's one verbal instruction, it seems simple, but there are A LOT of steps!

therapeutic thought

Find out what they love, and love it too!

One of the easiest ways to connect with your neurodivergent children is to find out what they love, and to love it too. Find out what their play passion is. Find out what their special topic of joys is. Find out what programme they adore. And then throw yourself into learning all about it. Learn the character names, learn the rules of the game, learn the specialist vocab that links to it. Learn the catch phrase or the theme music.

It is such an amazing signal to a child that you want to connect. It's a clear demonstration that we long to be part of what brings them happiness!

It would be easy to brush it off with 'Oh, I don't know this new stuff they do/watch' or, 'It's all a different language to me?'... But when my work children love Minecraft, I learn the vocab so I can chat blocks and creepers with them. When they love Octonauts, I learn the character names and theme songs. Because it means I can show in a very real way that I care about what's important to them. It's about them, not me. I'm not dragging them into my world, but asking to be part of theirs.

This is particularly important when our children have a very focused attention on one topic or theme because it shows that we value their choices and interests. It means that when they are very focused and their attention is zoned into a single topic, we can become part of that with them, rather than trying to shift them to something different. It is also very supportive for our children with a PDA profile, because you can ask them questions, get their advice and hand over all that power of knowledge to them: we can say, 'You are the expert here, teach me! Tell me all about it!' It's not very often our children get to do that to adults. It is such an empowering shift in status and it does wonders for your rapport and connection.

If you can respond with questions, knowledge or a genuine interest, you build an instant connection and send the message that your priority is connection and understanding the world that they are passionate about.

Chapter 10:
Strategies for transitions

What is a transition?

'Transitions' refer to the *movement and shift* from one activity/event/place/time to another.

Transitions are hard. There is no getting around it – most of us find change and shifts in time take more of our energy. Some of us enjoy using our energy this way and others don't.

For children who are Autistic, movement between activities and periods of transition can be unsettling and difficult. They are often when a child will feel over-stimulated by their environment. They may feel unsure what to expect and what will happen next. Generally, times of transition feel very 'floaty' and abstract. They can also often be times of busyness, with both noise and movement, and this often leads to children feeling unsafe and unsure.

Movement and transition of any kind is difficult because there is always an element of unknown:

- Even if you are going from one nice activity to another nice activity, there is still an element of uncertainty about how the change and movement will impact you.

- Transitioning from one thing to another means that the first thing has to come to an end and this can feel uncomfortable.
- An Autistic mind often finds real joy in completion, a task being finished in just the right way, but often 'just the right way' can be hard to find and they might be asked to stop before they have achieved that feeling. (See p.153 for more on task completion.)
- Time concepts are abstract and unclear, and this means that the span of time feels like too much of a risk, but staying with what is known and what is currently happening feels safer and steadier.
- Transitions are often periods of uncertainty, and they are usually periods of unstructured busyness. For example, within the classroom, transitional times will involve lots of children moving around to try and organise themselves, leaving the house involves shoes on, coats and bag organisation.

I observe there to be two types of transition:

1. Large transitions that tend to occur at key times in the year, for example, going back to school, going on holiday or to an appointment. These are often linked to a 'change' (see strategies to support change on p.132).
2. Micro transitions, which are all the tiny transitions we have to do throughout the day, for example, brushing teeth, putting shoes on, leaving the house, getting out the car, tidying up, going out for lunch/break, sitting on the carpet.

If you think your child is struggling with transitions because these periods feel 'floaty' and uncertain, the easiest thing we can do as supporting adults is to make them as concrete and consistent as possible. Look at how you can take away as much of the 'unknown aspect' of a transition as possible. Giving certainty, consistency and concrete reassurance, at uncertain times, gets to the root of why the transition is difficult for the child and makes it easier. If we don't put things in place to support this, our children will often develop their own strategies and these are often not as safe or appropriate as an adult-supported strategy – they may run out of the classroom, look to hide, push other children out the way to be first in the line. These are self-developed strategies to support themselves feel safer and more in control during a time that feels chaotic for them. The behaviour is communication. We can use this as a signal that we need to layer in strategies and support.

Making transitions playful

Here are a few practical suggestions to help soothe micro transitions:

- **Missions and tasks:** Create very specific missions for children not only gives them a sense of purpose and achievement, it can also make a very large and daunting task seem much smaller. At school, this might look like setting a child a 'tidy-up time mission'. Tidy-up time is a huge and open task instruction. Tidy up the cars, although a little narrower, is still a large unspecific task. Setting up a child with a 'mission to put ten cars in the box', is small, specific and measurable. It reduces ambiguity and allows a sense of ownership during a very fluid part of routine. At home, this might look like a 'Let's-get-going mission'. Get dressed is a huge and open task, but breaking it down into smaller chunks 'socks on... check!' 'jumper on... check!' etc, provides small measurable movements towards a larger transition. Not to mention, calling it a mission creates a sense of playfulness that can make a less-appealing instruction feel more like a game to connect over.
- **Visual schedules:** Create a visual routine with picture cards or photos can allow children to see the process and movement of their day. Having a knowledge of what is coming can remove some of the worry and anticipation. You can scale this up and down depending on the child and what they need. Some children will benefit from a timetable for their whole day, whereas others will need less detail. It is also worth monitoring whether a visual schedule supports or upsets your child. Some children may see a schedule as too structured/demanding and may actually become more anxious with its introduction. As always, follow your child's lead to create holistic, child-centred practice.
- **Visual prompts:** Use simple activity cards to hold or view while the activity is happening. For example, if you are transitioning from the carpet to the garden time, you may hand the child a picture card of their welly boots (photo or carton image) so that they have the visual prompt themselves to walk with and match the object and the picture together. Having the card to go and match with the real object can almost act as a matching game, making the transition feel more playful and more appealing – 'Here's the picture of welly boots, but where are the real ones? Let's go and find them!'

- **Adding flexibility within structure:** This is where we look at transitions and find a way to give routine and structure as reassurance, but with the option of flexibility. A common transition through which I support children at school is lining up time. Many of the children I support who are Autistic are keen to be number one in the line, or they jump past the line and go straight into the classroom. I believe this happens because lining up time is quite a noisy, chaotic and busy part of the day. Cleverly, these children who dislike a chaotic time have found a way to make it consistent for themselves. Being the first in line means they always know their role, their place, their view and their purpose, at a period of time that is unknown for others. It's a self-created strategy. Socially, however, it can cause difficulties with teachers and peers. Different settings will want different solutions depending on their systems and ethos. It may feel appropriate and manageable to allow that child to always be first because it gives them that sense of safety, but it may be that it isn't possible to allow one child to be first in the line every time and we need therefore to offer the same structure for that child but with an element of flexibility. For example, we can create a 'standing in the line' card for our child to hold and each day we write a number on the card to help them find their place in the line. The number changes, which adds flexibility, but the system of getting a card, counting along the line and standing in a set numbered spot gives the feeling of safety and structure that supports the child to succeed. This would also work if multiple children needed the same level of support in one class.
- **Objects to mark transition:** This very simply involves showing where you are going next through the presentation of a linked object. The same object is used each time and represents the transition in some way. Showing objects becomes a consistent signal and acts as a marker for the change. So, when it is time for lunch, we show a plate, to indicate that movement to the lunch hall will happen soon. Or, if it is time to go home, we show them their coat to initiate the transition of getting ready with all our belongings. You can also do this when moving from one play activity/therapy activity to another. While the child is still playing with one item, get the next item out to show them what will be next. For example: as they finish their drawing, get the box of trains out and hold a train up to show them " tidy up drawring, it's time for trains". It reassures

them that, when the current activity finishes, they aren't going into a time of nothingness, they are going straight into a time of different play. It reassures them that there is more to come and the next thing is also good!

- **Objects to hold during a transition.** This is about providing an object that the child is going to take from one place to the next place. With the aim of making the movement from one thing to the next feel less abrupt and more like a continuation of play. At school you may do this by allowing a child to hold a favourite car as they put on their coat and move outside for playtime. At home you may do this by allowing them to carry an action figure from downstairs up to the bathroom to help turn the taps on for bathtime The item itself is not instructing them of the transition. But it is helpful because it adds an element of playfulness to the transitions. The object also gives them something concrete and consistent during a period of change. Even though they are changing from being inside the classroom to outside the classroom, they have something with them that is staying the same The object goes with you as you journey from activity one to activity two, which gives you something that bridges the gap between these two. That consistency in a time of change can be very reassuring and act as a comfort.
- **Slowing it down by telling the story of the transition.** Sometimes as adults we anticipate that a change in routine is approaching and we will warn children about it using pictures or words – we may suggest that they can have one more turn and then it's time for change, or say, 'Now that X is finished, it's time for Y…' or use a visual timetable – although this appears to be a warning, it still offers a very quick shift and change to the activity. The sudden change being announced can trigger a 'fight or flight response' for some children and lead to upset and resistance to the change. As an alternative, try telling a *transition story*, so they can follow along and anticipate the change more gently. Start with what's happening with their current activity, then state what might happen next in the current activity, and then state how the current activity can travel along to the new one with them.

- For example, 'Wow, X, you've built such a wonderful train track here, I can see all the trains are driving around in a big circle. The yellow train has had a turn, let's ask the green train to have a turn next. Then, let's drive it all the way over to your shoes so we can get ready for play time outside.' You can hear how this is different to, 'One more turn with trains, trains is finished and next is garden time'. It's softer, slower and allows time for children to process the transition as part of their play.
- **Try singing.** Turn the instruction into a song – use any well-known nursery rhyme tune and add your instruction into it. For example, the tune for 'Happy and you know it' can turn into 'Oh, it's time to put your shoes on your feet! It's time to put your shoes on your feet! It's time to put your shoes on to your feeeeeeet, yes it's time to put your shoes on your feet!' This feels silly and simple, but it works for a few reasons:
    - The instruction is no longer a demand, it's a song that the child can choose to be part of.
    - The words are cheerful in tone and our facial expressions and body language will naturally shift as we sing to be more playful, open and engaging than when we typically give instructions.
    - Singing activates a different part of the brain.
    - If your child likes to learn language in chunks and sections (I'll talk about this more on page X), they will find the phrasing and intonation of the song more appealing than a sentence.
    - You will very likely, accidentally, add movement while you sing, clapping your hands, waving or tapping the shoes together. This all adds to a more playful instruction, reduces demand and makes the instruction more appealing.

The transition itself is then motivating because there is an element of play and connection built into it.

Transitions and sensory load

It's worth considering the *sensory load* during these micro transitions, and whether there are simple strategies you can introduce to soothe this.

For example:

- Moving from inside to outside leads to a big change in lighting – consider the impact that has on your child, and perhaps offer them sunglasses, hats/caps.
- Tidy-up time can be extremely noisy – consider offering ear defenders or suggesting they tidy up in the book corner where it is quieter.
- Lining up can be visually stimulating – consider whether their behaviour or choices are for stimulation and joy. Consider whether they are seeking joy from running up and down the line to view everyone, or whether being at the front means they can count all their peers. Can you create a play sequence where they run up and down once and then join the line? This way, we recognise their joy through stimming and honour the class routine with some structure. Rather than a power struggle, it becomes a strategy of collaboration.
- Collecting coats from the cloakroom might be too hot and busy – consider whether they can go before everyone else or after everyone else so the area is more still and breathable.

Top tips for transitions

Making transitions *connected and playful* can also be helpful because it takes away the power struggle:

- Using phrases like: 'Let's go and get your shoes' rather than 'It's time to put your shoes on now' will support children to feel like the transition is a collaborative activity.
- Using humour also creates a collaborative connection – for example, putting shoes on their hands rather than their feet and then laughing about it while putting them on their feet.

Make transitions *motivational:*

- Help children to see why the transition helps or benefits them. Children are much more likely to collaborate with us if we share the motivation. I like the phrasing 'Let's get X done, and next we can Y'. This avoids getting into a power struggle – 'If you don't…' or, 'You have to do this'.
- So we avoid saying things like, 'If you don't put your boots on you can't go outside', and instead find a child-focused motivation – 'Let's put your boots on, and then next we can jump in puddles!'

Give reassurance that transition *doesn't mean the end, forever:*

- Some children will need reassuring that the thing they are playing with or activity they are transitioning away from will still be available another time. As adults, we have this assumed knowledge. We know that the garden will still be there tomorrow, or that trains will come out again after lunch. But children don't have this knowledge, control or power. This can make them anxious to leave the activity, with the possibility it may be 'finished' forever! So, very simply explaining this can be really supportive in transitions.
- This might look like:
    - Stating it verbally to them: 'Trains are finished now, but more after lunch!'
    - Giving them a safe space to leave an item: 'We can leave that on my desk to keep it safe for after. It will be safe and waiting here for you.'

- Adding an extra symbol to your timetable after home time to show 'back to school tomorrow' or after bedtime to show 'morning + iPad time'.

Things being 'finished' and timetables being completely empty may feel unsettling and finite, so adding this reassurance can soothe the worry of a 'forever' feeling and make giving up an item or moving away from an activity more manageable.

Consider whether *task completion is impacting your transition:*

Most individuals who are Autistic will have a strong drive for task completion (discussed previously on p.153). This means they have a need for ideas to be fulfilled, completed and finished in a specific way which they have planned, and this brings them great joy. It also means that being interrupted can bring great distress. As adults, we often use the clock as an indicator of when we need to shift from one thing to the next, but our children don't do this. It is not always important to them that 10am means assembly time. They may be at number eight of lining up ten cars. Or on the blue item of their rainbow sequence. Or about to write their seventh sentence because seven is their favourite number and that will make their brain feel nice. What this means is that our transition shift is going to be received as an extreme threat to their play sequence and the element of task completion that will bring them satisfaction. Some children will have the skill set and capacity to express this and others will react through behaviour. It is helpful for us, as supporting adults, to know and understand a child's play passions and look at how these may be impacting other times of their routine. Sometimes we can pre-empt this, and other times it isn't possible, and we have to act with flexibility in response to a behaviour.

For example, at school we may see a child in reception ordering things in a rainbow sequence and we know that tidy-up time will begin shortly. We can therefore advise them in advance: 'It's almost tidy-up time, build one more rainbow, but don't start anymore because there won't be time to finish them'. This validates the task and the completion, as well as upholds the boundary.

Using the same example, if we don't spot the play in advance and tidy-up time starts, the child becomes distressed and refuses to tidy up, our attention is drawn to them as they start taking coloured blocks out of the box instead of putting them in. This is a time for us to look beyond the behaviour and seek connection and communication. Label what you see – 'Tidying up feels so bad for you right now, I see that. You weren't ready. Show me…' the child grabs a red block and an orange block and a yellow block. We see the pattern and we have a chance for (what I call) a *transition do-over*. Make the statement as before: 'I understand, you need to make a rainbow before we tidy it up. It's OK, I'm here to help. One rainbow and then, next, we put the blocks away.' Be a calm and affirming presence. Watch them complete their task and celebrate the rainbow, enjoy the task completion with them: 'Aww! Did it! A rainbow! All the colours!' Now is the time to reinstate the boundary: 'Let's tidy up now, all the blocks away, shall we tidy up in rainbow order? All the red ones first!' There may still be resistance, there may still be a desire to continue, but because there has been an element of task completion and acknowledgement of that need, the chances for success will be greater and more regulated.

Adding play to the transition itself

One of my favourite additions to these strategies is to *make the transition itself more playful*. Make the journey from one thing to the next part of the activity. Adding play and joy to anything will make it more motivating, more appealing, and harder to resist. It will also help keep your child's brain in its safe and steady state rather than triggered into its fight, flight, freeze, fawn state.

Therapy examples

At the end of a therapy session, children need to put their shoes on ready to go. This signals the end of playing and the big transition of leaving the playroom. As well as offering notice that we need to transition, using a visual on a whiteboard, offering task completion support, I will also *add play* into the transition – so, for example, the figures we are using in the water tray will hide in the child's shoes!

This will be a surprise and a shock, and we can be in a commotion about it together! Pour them out and notice together that that is not the proper way to use a shoe – it lives on your foot! Shoes are placed on to make sure no other water tray animals creep inside! The play spreads itself across to the next activity acting as a *play bridge* from one transition to the next.

At school, I often ask a child if they want to take a toy from the session to show their teacher, which helps us journey back to the classroom. Or we see how many jumps it takes us to get from the hall to the door. Or you sing a favourite song for as long as it takes to tidy up.

I will sometimes choose to add an element of play that I know can stretch across and cover all aspects of the transition. For example, we will blow bubbles as our last activity of play, and I can then blow some for them while they put their shoes on, while we open the clinic door, and then they can chase them as they head out to the car. The transition feels smoother because the movement has been eased by an arch of play.

That's a lot of extra work! Who has the time?
Who has the staff? Can't we just teach them to stop and do the thing we are asking them to do?

These are common and understandable worries and I'm going to give a little bit of theory and share my thoughts on this, just in case as you read all the adaptations you start to have these worries...

It's important to notice that, yes, this does take more time and energy to start with. It would be really easy for us as adults if, when we said, 'the end', that felt OK for everyone and everyone slowly and carefully moved to the next thing. It would also be a little bit worrying and robotic if children worked like this! It's an unrealistic expectation, and we therefore have to make a choice about where our adult time and energy is going to go.

We can invest time and energy into embedding inclusive strategies into our classrooms and homes. We can invest time and energy into making boring instructions more appealing and playful so children choose to them with us.

Or, the alternative, is that our energy must go into fighting children who resist us. Our energy has to go into soothing and calming dysregulated or dangerous behaviour as a result of transitions. Our energy has to go into firefighting surface-level behaviour rather than into the strategies that solve the root of them. *Because behaviour is the communication of a need.*

It is also important to notice and understand that neurodivergent children are responding to their needs and their bodies. They are working within their capacity and skill set. It is not a choice to become distressed when that task can't be completed, or that the movement between tasks feels overwhelming; it's a body and brain reaction. Adults pushing against it won't change that, but working alongside it will. By adding these strategies, we are meeting a child where they are, developmentally and emotionally.

These strategies are an investment of time and resources and staffing at the beginning, but once they are embedded, the level of regulation, inclusion and capacity it brings for children means you don't need to use your energy supporting the distress that was there before you invested in them.

What we know from neuroscience and child development research is that children don't and can't learn new skills in a state of fear or stress. So getting louder, getting stricter, creating more behaviour rewards, insisting a routine is met exactly or having overly rigid systems will not help a child to grow and learn. The opposite in fact occurs. *Holistic, child-centred, neurodiversity-affirming strategies are an investment that is worth making.*

My hope and experience is that children make progress because they feel safe, understood and connected to trusted adults. They develop their skills through safe experiences, rather than as a reaction to trauma as a means to survive their experiences.

therapeutic thought

Sometimes we have to choose between being on time/maintaining our schedule or maintaining a child's regulation...

We've all been there. They need one more turn, they need an extra five minutes, they need to complete one more sequence, or to ask one more question...

But as the adult, you look at the clock and know that the 'one more' will make you late. It will mean it's a rush to the car. Or the session will over run. Or phonics will start late. It puts us in a really hard position because we are faced with a choice and a gamble – do we rush through/refuse the extra turn and maintain the schedule of events, or do we offer the needed time up to the child and maintain their regulation?

I will almost always choose to maintain regulation – here is why...

- Often, the dysregulation of rushing, leaving something unfinished, or not having adequate notice takes so much energy and time to recover from that we end up being 'off the schedule' anyway.
- Often, arriving on time but arriving dysregulated/distressed means we are on time but not ready to learn/engage, so it's counterproductive.
- I am not willing to create possible trauma/upset for the sake of time keeping and schedules.
- The cost to wellbeing is too great compared to the gain of maintain systems/schedules.
- Being the cause of dysregulation damages the connection and feeling of safety that I create as an adult, which will eventually result in a breakdown in our relationship.

There are of course things that are out of our control – there are times where being late feels like it isn't an option. Missing a train, the cinema start time, the impact it may have on another person who also has needs... But, also, there will be another train, we can sign in late at the office, we can reschedule or catch up in some of those instances... My current mindset is to *consider the cost*... I ask myself, I'll be on time, but at what cost to this child and their nervous system? At what cost to our connection? At what cost to the rest of their day? Sometimes, then, we still need to rush, but almost always we don't – the cost would be too great and the gain too small.

therapeutic thought

'It's OK, I'm listening.'

This is my favourite phrase in therapy and parenting.

I use this along with a connecting touch – a hand hold, a hair stroke, a back rub – as well as leaning my body in and gently nodding my head. It works because its sub-text is, 'I see it's hard, let's calm, let's slow, tell me all about it, I'm not going anywhere, I'm here to help and sort this…' But it's simpler and has zero pressure attached to it.

I use this for my little ones who are stammering if a word is very stuck. It almost interprets the anxiety and takes away the urgency.

I use this when a little one is trying hard to find a word or sound after I've asked them a question or set a bit of a therapy challenge.

I use this when a child has been talking for a long time about something and I want to show I am still paying attention and remain part of their world.

I do this in play if a play pattern goes wrong and we need to repair it.

I use this when a child is upset and trying to explain why.

I use this when kids are tired or confused and can't find the words they need.

I use this to find out more when there's a scuffle between children and everyone is in a rage and a kerfuffle!

Our ability to process information, produce words and make sounds is significantly impacted by what's known as 'emotional arousal' and the urgency of the message. This is how we feel about what we are saying and how fast we feel we need to say it. As soon as there's pressure, as soon as there's emotion – excitement, upset, worry, distress, our brain has to work extra hard to produce words and sentences. So this phrase and gesture of connection helps soothe that, which in turn helps children find their words/communication tools and let us know their message.

Chapter 11:

Supporting progress without overwhelm

Demand, capacity, comfort and gentle stretch.

Within therapy and learning environments, I have found that these four things need to be simultaneously balanced in order for a child to make progress *and* remain regulated. So often, these four things being off balance is why we hear stories of trauma from neurodivergent adults. When a child is out of capacity and in a state of discomfort, allocating more demand or persisting with stretching skills will become harmful to their wellbeing. These four elements link closely to the theory I've shared in earlier chapters about sensory regulation, emotional regulation and physical regulation (see p.26). Although these areas interlink and crossover, I observe them to extend beyond this and include *all input from an individual's life*, to then settle themselves into this overview. Let's explore each of these, considering how they interact and what our role can be as a supporting adult to nurture children to thrive.

Demand: Very simply, this is any request, demand or expectation – physical, sensory, emotional, language or social that is placed on a child. A demand can be as simple as a request to pass an object or as complicated as completing a written assessment. It may be the demand of a social expectation that they won't interrupt when you are mid-sentence. It may be an emotional demand that they need to process feeling disappointed that they didn't win at a game. It may be a sensory demand like having the lights on or accepting background noises. It may be a self-chosen demand like taking part in a football match. It may be an externally placed demand like going on a school trip. It may be an environmental demand like experiencing festive decorations. Our lives are full of demands and we constantly process them and manage them.

Capacity: This is how many demands we are able to cope with before it feels overwhelming and unmanageable. Our capacity will often change and shift depending on how our physical needs have been met, such as how tired we are and how much sleep we have had, how hungry we are, how thirsty we are, how hot or cold we are or how safe we feel.

If we are hungry, tired, cold and in a new place, so unsure of our environment, our capacity will shrink, making any additional demand feel unbearable.

Comfort: This refers to how comfortable an activity makes us feel, physically and emotionally. This can often relate to how familiar it is. It can also link to what level of sensory feedback we get from it and how our body and mind react when completing it.

Gentle stretch: This refers to gently stretching outside of what feels comfortable and well-known, in order to keep and maintain interest and motivation. It is what keeps an activity feeling wanted. For example, if a child lines up a set of animal figures, they may go on a search for more to add to their line and make it longer. They want to stretch their current interest a little further to keep it motivating. For example, a child might be spinning in a circle, and gradually they want to spin faster or for a longer period of time. They are gently stretching themselves beyond that initial comfort, to try and keep the comfort feeling and joy going. It also refers to external gentle stretches suggested by others, for example trying a new game or skill. Sometimes a gentle stretch will be child-led and sometimes it will be adult-led/collaborative.

- *Example for a child-led gentle stretch*: Trying the trampoline/bouncy castle for the first time. The child is motivated to try, they want to try it because it looks appealing, they choose it themselves, but it is new and stretches them outside of what they usually feel comfortable in.

- *Example of an adult-led gentle stretch*: A child is encouraged to attend a school trip. The adults anticipate that the child will enjoy the activities but are aware there will be parts of the day that feel new and stretch the child. The adult and child work collaboratively to prepare for the stretch, but the idea has come from the adult.

As supporting adults, we often have our hearts set on the gentle stretch – we want to nurture our child's skills and extend what they are able to do. Whether that's regarding communication, play, exploring the world around them, connection with others, turn-taking, reading, writing. We will often be keen for our child to try new things or extend what they can currently do to support their progress and development.

How can we use this concept to support progress and develop new skills and a love of learning?

I once read someone describing how we should never push a neurodivergent person out of their comfort zone because it only ever leads to trauma. They described that they felt the idea of learning only happening when you were out of your comfort zone was a very neurotypical concept. They described that they had spent a lifetime never feeling comfortable, and this discomfort hadn't led to great things and new skills, it had only led to burn out, exhaustion, mental health and wellbeing issues.

But I think this is a tricky concept to apply universally because, if we never leave our comfort zone, and we never try anything that feels new or unknown, whether we are neurotypical or neurodivergent, we would remain exactly the same always. It feels like it may be impossible to make progress and remain always the same simultaneously.

It made me reflect on this person's viewpoint, reflect on this for my work families, my children and my own experience as a late-diagnosed neurodivergent adult and what I considered was this:

Perhaps, as a neurodivergent individual, it is possible to step outside of your comfort zone in order to learn and experience new things – BUT only if there is time and space allocated to you to return to a zone of comfort in order to process and grow from the experience.

I reflected that if you are undiagnosed and/or unaccommodated for long periods of your life, you exist in a world where there is no comfort zone. All your experiences are uncomfortable, and you move from one high-alert learning experience into another. This is not a sustainable way to learn or live. You are above your capacity always.

I also considered that for neurodivergent individuals there can often be little choice involved, regarding when new experiences or activities out of the usual comfort occurs. This in itself makes a huge difference and may go overlooked. *Choosing* to try something outside of your usual comfort, is entirely different to being pushed or forced outside of your comfort zone. Developing a collaborative plan for how to make a new experience work for you is empowering. Being told you must try something no matter how it makes you feel, is not.

I observe that moving out of your comfort zone to learn a new skill can be OK, as long as it is the individuals *choice*, there is support during the stretch and as long as you can return safely to somewhere to *recover*. As long as you have a comfort zone, as it were, to return back to. As long as it is understood and acknowledged that there will be a need to recharge, and to regain capacity, process and make space for the next demand or load that presents itself. Without that chance, your entire life experience is out of your comfort zone, and consequently uncomfortable.

Let's add this concept to our understanding of neurodiverse experiences being higher in frequency, intensity and impact (see p.11). Let's add into this the knowledge we have about our neurodivergent individuals' sensory and regulation needs and how much these vary, how differently their imaginary balloons fill, float, inflate and explode (see p.27). It is suddenly easy to see how often our beautiful neurodivergent children are nudged, pushed or encouraged to exist in discomfort. How many demands they absorb for neurotypical expectation, leaving them with very little capacity for gentle stretches at other times.

As part of our mission to be neurodiversity affirming, we need to be proactive and look at where we can make accommodations to meet them where their needs are. Reduce unnecessary demands in order to free up capacity, which then allows for choosing new experiences, a gentle stretch and comfort-based recovery.

With all of this in mind, it is important that in all our child's environments – school, home, after school clubs, family and friends' houses – we create comfort zones for our children. That way they can choose, and they can listen to what their body needs. We can encourage and nurture them to bravely step out of that comfort zone and try new things, confident in the knowledge that they can step back into comfort to recover and to grow.

If we want children to choose to try new things, to experience new feelings and stretch the skills they already have, we also need to plan and to schedule times of real comfort and safety for them to return to.

What if worries...

Sometimes we are able to plan, pre-empt and soothe this balance. At other times we can't, and this leads to us needing to react and respond to communicative behaviours. Neurotypical and outdated psychology teaching can leave us with a lot of worries about how to respond in these times. So often we know what our child needs but we worry about the lesson we are teaching them in these highly emotive moments.

What if worries might sound like...

- What if they learn the that behaviour gets them the thing they want?
- What if they learn that screaming gets them out the classroom?
- What if they learn that throwing gets them a sensory break?
- What if they learn that they can manipulate us?
- What if they don't try because they are never stretched?

But let's challenge those so they sound like...

- What if they learn that you are a grown up that understands them?
- What if they learn that you will facilitate their body to regulate when it feels out of control?
- What if they learn that, when they feel chaotic, you offer something calming?

- What if they create attachment with you as a safe adult?
- What if they learn that we can work together to find a way to make this work, feel easier, understand ourselves?

I talk to teachers and parents a lot about those first 'what ifs'. Genuine worries that we are storing up problems for the future. So often we can see the need, we understand that the capacity has gone, but the 'what ifs' stop us in our tracks.

Remember: all behaviour is communication of a need, feeling or experience.

Let your only *'what if'* be:

> ***What if we communicate back to children that we see the struggle, they aren't alone, they don't need to fight, we are here WITH them.***

Visualise the concept

Let's imagine that, alongside holding their sensory balloon (discussed on p.27), our children are also carrying a test tube – they've got a lot to hold onto – you can see why we need to help them out! Each time they receive a demand, a pompom or a marble is slotted in, and the tube gradually fills. Some demands feel softer and lighter, other demands are heavy and hard. Each one takes up space in the tube. Some demands a child chooses and places in there themselves, and others are given to them by adults, peers and their environment. Children have a set of test tubes of different sizes and how many of their basic needs have been met will determine what size test tube they have access to.

On a day that child is tired, hungry and with an unknown teacher, their tube will be small.

On a day that a child is well rested and sat with their parent/regular teacher, their tube will be large.

Let's envisage a day when they have a large test tube – it can fit six items in it:

They come into therapy and take off their shoes = demand.

They see their favourite toy and choose to interact with it = chosen play demand.

They want the adult to wind up a spinning toy so they pass it to them to request collaboration = chosen social demand.

At this point, we know that the child is well within their capacity and demand limit – as an adult, I can suggest a gentle stretch by modelling the word and AAC use for the word 'go' – I pause as I place the spinning toy on the floor, creating anticipation and an opportunity for them to copy if they can.

This adult demand is a gentle stretch within the child's current capacity. It is the chance to practice a new skill in the knowledge that they have capacity to try, as well as the option to opt out. That's what makes it gentle, but it's still a stretch. Whether they respond to the opportunity or not, the demand has still been placed and lands a hard marble into their tube, filling it further.

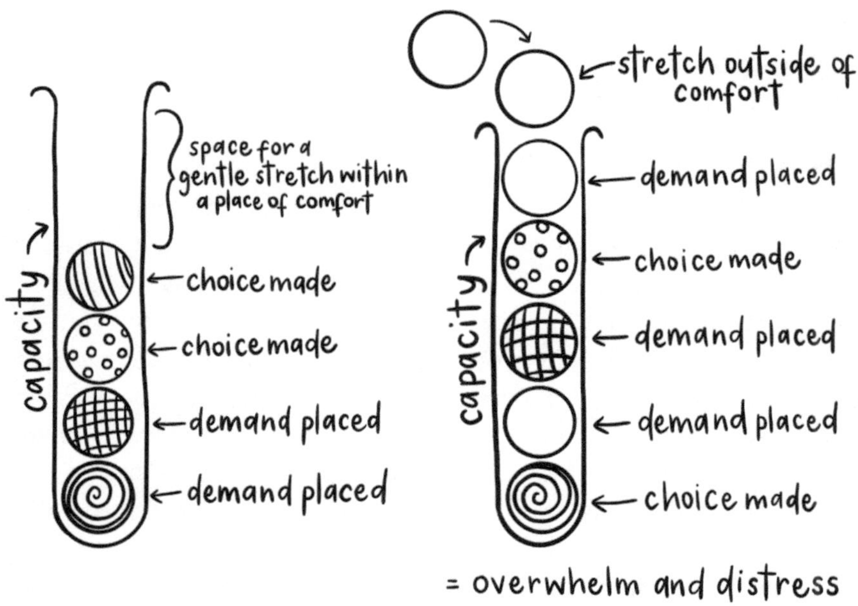

There are now only two slots left. If this play sequence happens again, the capacity tube will be full. The demands following this will not feel like a gentle stretch, they will feel like an unmanageable demand, leading to possible distress and overwhelm.

This can sometimes be confusing to us as adults in play based therapy because what we do, how we've played and interacted hasn't changed, but the response and ability to cope from the child does change. This is because of their capacity and how they are constantly having to manage what is in there.

At this point, children need support and an opportunity to unload some of the demands, recharge and return to a feeling of comfort. This means they then have capacity to receive and choose demands again.

Communication environments to support comfort and recharge

Being a neurodiverse individual in a neurotypical world can place an already heavy load of demand on a person's body and mind. In their home and education setting, they can create pockets of play that will lend themselves to recharging and creating capacity. Having these available and encouraging children to explore them as and when they need them will gently support their self-awareness as well as support them to advocate for their needs as they grow older.

Environmental stimulus

Consider the parts of your environment that may place demands on your child. We can link these to the senses (see p.21). In homes and education settings, we can often overlook how visually busy environments can be. We may be keen to have bright posters, key words, numbers and alphabets available for children to support their learning. We may want to have toys set out on open shelves or transparent boxes to support independence and choosing. However, for some children. Existing in visually stimulating settings can use a lot of their capacity and mean that there is less left for our gentle stretch of new skills. It is not necessarily that we need to alter our entire home or classroom, but we should have an awareness of the impact these environments may have on different individuals. You may discover that a child enjoys therapy sessions more in the hallway, because the walls and floor are empty and there are no shelves. You may discover that they dislike sensory play in the classroom where it is already stimulating, but enjoy taking the tray into a pop-up tent where they can be alone and feel enclosed.

There will be demands linked to every environment simply by the nature of how it is set up. The dining hall at school will be echoey, loud and contain a lot of smells. The play park will be visually stimulating with the movement of other children, unpredictable, and offer a range of tactile experiences in terms of the equipment's materials (the slides metal is cold in the winter and hot in the summer), and how the equipment affects the body's systems (swinging, sliding and zooming). These will impact our children's ability to play, learn and grow within them. If we want to present activities that will offer children a gentle stretch to their skills, we must make sure that the environment provides them with the capacity for this demand.

Create quiet dens/zones/safe spaces

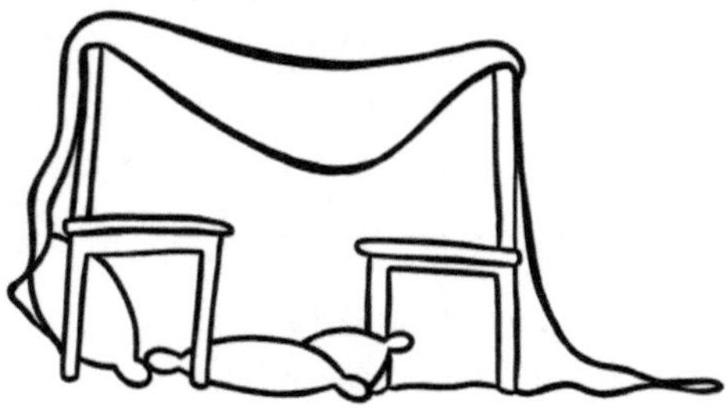

Building areas for restoration of capacity around your home and setting is a wonderfully inclusive and affirming action of care for children. These don't need to be separate sensory rooms full of equipment, or playrooms converted into perfect play spaces. They can be created using the space you've got and the resources you've got. Here are a few ideas:

- A pop-up tent with cushions and favourite books/music.
- A bean bag with a blanket and ear defenders.
- A high-backed armchair or rocking chair with a blanket draped over the top to create coverage.
- Cushions and teddies under a spare table with light-up toys/ fairy lights.

- Sheets/material fixed from the ceiling that hang to create a teepee, add a basket of preferred sensory items.
- Sitting with an adult for quiet play – board game, cards, drawing.
- Sitting on the swing in the garden.
- Creating an inviting calm corner and offering a sensory play tray.

It is tempting to fill these areas with resources that teach children about emotions. Posters that name emotions and reactions, sensory bottles that feature emotions, books that explain emotions… but the teaching needs to happen at other times. If a child is out of capacity and needs a safe space to rest, the very nature of the space means they don't have capacity to learn new skills. The learning about emotions must happen separately at other times when there is capacity and readiness for a gentle stretch. The zones you create for recovery must be calm and low on environmental stimulation and demand (see p.132 for separate activities that support teaching emotions).

NOTE: Having a core board for communication that includes symbols/ pictures to communicate emotions feelings and needs is different to what is described above. Communication devices and systems should be available for children at all times and should travel with them to safe/quiet zones to encourage them to express themselves at all times.

Have regulating resources available

Free access to resources and play that regulates a child's emotions, sensory load and reduces demand is a really simple and effective way to encourage children to listen and respond to their needs.

To set this up, consider what kind of play seems to soothe and regulate your child when they are out of capacity – this will be different for different children, observe them and notice the patterns in their play and behaviour to unpick what it is they are searching for.

If they like to calm and soothe themselves with small, quiet organising and sorting sensory play, you can create tubs/trays that are ready to go whenever they need something to help them recharge. These are not large interactive sensory trays, they are smaller, for one individual to use at a time. (You can use the trays/draws children keep their book bags in at school, or A4 paper stationery trays work well too.) Create these collections and keep them in a set place so that children can be shown how to take you there to ask for them or help themselves (depending on the setting and the skill set you are supporting).

Play trays/tubs might include:

- Sand.
- Play dough.
- Collections of animal figures.
- Small connecting toys like Lego, cog toys, stick/click together bricks.
- Buttons or counters of different shapes, colours and sizes.
- Collection of different materials /textures to explore – a wooden toy, a soft toy, a mental toy, a spiky toy, a smooth toy.
- Science exploring, like a big magnet and mix of items that are magnetic and not magnetic.
- Stretchy fidget toys.
- Suction toys and sticky toys.
- Peel and stick toys or stickers.

If they seem to need bigger movements and stretches for their body, you could create a space and resources for that too. If you are in a classroom, you can use a small doormat/floor sticker or masking tape to mark out a 'movement zone'. Having a clear marker like this will keep the movement manageable for the rest of the class. This may also work at home, but you may also have more flexibility for how big and how far the movement can happen!

Create a box of movement resources to be used in this zone.
This might include:

- Different textured mats or bath nonslip spots that can be used to stand and tip toe on.
- A resistance band for stretching across your legs (don't use these in your hands as they can be pinged across the room!)
- Some sponges for standing on and squeezing in your hands.
- A yoga block to balance on.

- Handprint pictures. Place these on the floor, table or wall and ask the child to press against them as hard as they can. Make it fun by asking them to push the floor lower, or push the school walls over – this deep-pressure feedback can be very soothing.
- Create or print some action prompt cards that state a number and an action – five star jumps or stretch to the sky three times or scrunch into a hedgehog ball for six seconds.

To start with, children will need full adult support for this concept and how to use it. They will need you to narrate the process and guide them through how this play supports their body. When you introduce these ideas, it should ***not*** be 'in the moment of crisis'. In this moment, a child will be in turmoil and out of capacity to absorb the boundaries that keep this kind of regulation safe and helpful. These activities will need to be demonstrated carefully, boundaries will need to be supported, and a lot of supportive praise offered to help create a positive association with regulating through play.

Once these ideas and activities have been demonstrated and supported, you can suggest them *before* children become completely dysregulated, in that moment when you can feel a shift happening for them and you can tell their capacity is becoming low. Make sure you use simple advocating phrases and provide these in a full range of communication options – words, on devices, as printed symbols, as an action or a sign. This will encourage children to copy them for themselves.

Phrases or symbols may include:

'I need a break.'

'I don't feel OK.'

'I need something different.'

'My body feels X.'

'My mind feels X.'

Our aim for this set up should be to guide our children with the resources and teach them skills in the hope that, eventually, they will notice across their day when their capacity is low, when they need support to recharge and regulate from the demands being placed on their body and mind, and either source it for themselves – taking themselves to a quiet den, sensory tray or movement zone – or use an advocate phrase to request support to regulate.

This system will ideally help children to recharge, gain back some capacity and settle them back into a feeling of comfort, so that they are ready for the gentle stretch of learning again.

Use low demand communication

When a child has limited capacity, our communication can become a load that they cannot process. Here are a few ways you can reduce your communication capacity:

- Ask zero WH questions, not a single one. As tempting as it might be to ask, 'What's the matter?', 'Where does it hurt?', 'What can I do to help?', even though these are offered as support, the nature of such questions is a demand because there is an expectation to respond. This accidental pressure and request for output could end up exacerbating the feeling of overwhelm.
- Offer a visual board as optional communication, without expectation. Present a core board so that, if the child is able to point and express their needs, they can do this without relying on verbal skills.
- Provide a calm presence. If their reaction to low capacity is becoming big and loud, our own energy needs to soothe and calm them – slowing our rate of speech, using a gentle tone and a quieter volume. Matching their energy with loud animated responses will likely drain their resources leading to distress.
- Touch and contact. Consider for the individual what physical contact offers them. For some children, a hug will offer the deep pressure and emotional support they crave to increase their capacity and recharge themselves. For others, physical contact will be unpleasant and actually reduce their capacity further. Having symbol cards, or including this language on core boards that express this will encourage children to advocate for their needs. For example, a symbol that represents 'I need space'.
- Adapt your play style. Shift your play style to be parallel or distanced rather than collaborative (see p.65). This presents you as available but reduces the demand for including you. This will provide a chance for social recharging.

Watch for signs and signal

Follow your child's lead as often as you can and watch for signs and signals that they are seeking a break from demands to create capacity for themselves. Watch for patterns in behaviour and in play that indicate these needs and help facilitate them. As you facilitate the need, narrate to the child what you see and how the support will help. For example, you notice your child sitting under the table in a café/classroom, and so you notice the demand with them and how they have resolved it – 'It's noisy in here, you've looked for a quiet space to sit'. If the action they have taken is safe, allow them to continue. If it isn't, facilitate an alternative – 'I understand, you need a quiet, safe space, but we can't wait here – let's go outside for some fresh air/to the sensory tent/to the sofa with the weighted blanket.'

Creating opportunities for a *gentle stretch* in play therapy

The possibility for a gentle stretch – and therefore progress onto a new skill – will very much depend on the coordination and correspondence between the demand and the capacity and comfort of the child. These factors will be changing from day to day and even within days. It's really helpful for us to be evaluating and monitoring these factors for our children because it allows us to notice the optimum time for progress without distress.

We must consider their capacity – thinking about where they are starting from on that particular day. For example, in the lead up to Christmas, when there are lights flashing, busy play rehearsals, extra decorations, new aspects of their routine, it's just before lunchtime, and they didn't sleep well the night before, a child will have a very low capacity for a gentle stretch. Things are too big for them, and any additional expectations presented to them will be met with a feeling of overwhelm. The same child on a Monday morning after a restful weekend, on a day that they have walked to school to regulate their body, had solid rest and breakfast followed by their favourite snack, will be in an entirely different place. Their capacity to try new things and experience a gentle stretch in a positive way may be in the optimum position. Their capacity isn't full and there is room for us to add a gentle stretch of demand.

This works at home and at school, and can play a crucial part in how successful therapy and activities are when presented to children. It is why we should always plan flexible play activities that allow us to adapt and to change according to the child in front of us. If you have a very narrow plan with minimal wiggle room, it means you cannot adapt to the child's individual capacity, demand, comfort and stretch levels.

Play therapy: planning for a gentle stretch

In Chapter 7 we described how, when planning a play activity, we aim to combine several key factors for its success and allow for shifts in demand, capacity and create a gentle stretch:

1. Include the child's interests and passions so that they have a reason to be engaged with it.
2. Include an element of sensory exploration or movement so that the activity fills their sensory needs and supports their regulation.
3. Include something familiar and predictable, so that they gain a feeling of safety and reassurance for engaging with it.
4. Include an opportunity for a gentle stretch – consider how you predict they may play with it and plan for how you may stretch them to try a new skill as part of the play.
5. Include an opportunity to reduce the demand – consider how you predict they may play with it and plan for how you can remove demands in case the child does not have the capacity to engage or be stretched.

Often, this ebb and flow of engagement, along with the increase and decrease of demand, stretch and capacity, will occur across the activity time. There are very few times I have played and the play has remained the same for the duration. You will need to adapt and slide the gentle stretch and level of comfort up and down accordingly while you play. The result of this is often increased attention and listening, sustained attention and focus for longer periods of time, and an increased level of enjoyment and connection. The child doesn't need to exit the activity when they begin to feel overwhelmed by the demand because we actively reduce the demand to allow them to recover and remain comfortable. Equally, the child doesn't get bored of the activity and seek other engagement because, at this point, we increase the demand and stimulation. This sliding up and down on the 'play volume controls' results in regulated, engaged children.

This doesn't happen easily to start with, so do not get disheartened if this feels difficult and clunky to start with. You may need to actively plan and write out what your ups and downs and demand shifts are going to include for children to start with. You may need to have an internally planned structure for a period of time. However, over time, this starts to become more natural. You will notice yourself observing the signs and signals that your child gives you, and that you become more and more creative in the way that you adapt the play to meet them where they are.

Play therapy: layering play types to optimise success

When designing a therapy activity, it is helpful to combine our knowledge of different play types and layer these together. This works because it allows children to explore a set of toys in several different ways, which extends their attention. It means we have more opportunities to extend and gently stretch play ideas and skills, as well as collaborate and communicate as part of the play.

This may look like:

- Choosing a number and letter insert puzzle because their current play passion is the alphabet. By including letters as part of the play, the aim is that the child will *actively choose* to play. It's appealing to them, and they will find joy here. Their attention is already obtained by their own choosing, which will mean they are already in a place where they have capacity to learn and extend skills.
- We can layer this simple play activity with a sensory element that is appealing to the child. Placing the puzzle on a tray and adding a cup full of rice pops. Now the puzzle is not just a puzzle, we can also use the pieces to squash and crush the rice pops. We can explore the sound, texture and change that occurs when we break them.
- We can layer this further by adding a teaspoon and some stacking cups. Now we have the added play opportunity to fill, scoop, pour and empty the cups. We have the play opportunity to hide the numbers under the cups. To watch the rice pops fall or sprinkle out of different containers.

- We can layer this further by offering a number/letter storybook to match with or singing a song that includes rain as we pour the rice pops and hear them pitter-patter.

By adding extra layers to the puzzle, we have extended the types of play that the activity lends itself to.

The puzzle by itself = a logic academic activity, sorting with an element of enveloping (because the puzzle piece sits snug into the puzzle board).

The puzzle + rice pops + cups and spoons + story/song = a logic academic activity, sorting with an element of enveloping… PLUS:

- A tactile experience of feeling the rice pops.
- Trajectory watching rice pops and puzzle pieces fall from the cups.
- Enveloping, by placing items into and under cups.
- Transporting, by scooping and moving with the spoons.
- Transformation, by watching the rice pops change consistency, shape and size when squashed by fingers or puzzle pieces.
- Object picture matching from book to toy.
- Song sequence and noisy play.
- And more! Depending on what your child ends up doing to explore this combination!

Layering play types together offers children an opportunity to explore and create their own way to play. The knock-on effect of this is that their attention and engagement progress and this gives us a longer opportunity as communication partners to then become part of the play and to model language and communication skills throughout.

Remember to get it 'just right' in terms of stimulation when layering play – too many layers may create an activity that is overstimulating and overwhelming, because the demands are too high. This will often lead to the play idea being rejected. Not enough layers will create a restrictive activity that may be under-stimulating and finished with very quickly. As a general rule, I tend to add two layers when I initially present an activity, and keep two more hidden away to add in if they are needed later.

For the example above, I may present the puzzle with the rice pops and spoons, and see how the child responds to this. Then, once we've played a while, or if they seem under-stimulated, or if focus is wavering, I may add the stacking cups and matching picture book to increase stimulation when needed. Equally, it's OK to clear space and move items out of the play space if things seem too busy. The layers mean you can increase and decrease according to what the child needs.

Planning for low demand

Within therapy and across your day, plan for pockets of low demand. Make it part of your plan that children will get the opportunity to recover from the episodes of high demand in their day or as part of their therapy. We can do this alongside responding to the behaviour and requests our children will give us, letting us know it is what they need. We may plan for this by scheduling in time with a sensory tray after assembly. We may do this by expecting our children to need time with their tablet/device under a blanket after a trip to the shops or to the park. We may do this by planning in light toys and spinning tops after a more collaborative therapy task, to allow children to zone into their own senses rather than the people in their environment. Planning in periods of low demand shows a deep understanding of the load that Autistic and neurodivergent children carry. It provides them with the opportunity they deserve to recharge, rest and create space for the next part of their day. It means that they are given a chance to return to a place of comfort, which in turn allows them to do more than just cope with the demands in their life. They are able to create capacity for new skills, learning and joy. They are given the capacity to progress and thrive.

Example of a demand and capacity plan when a child's hours increase in a setting

- Schedule in 'low demand time' in the afternoons for X. These are play periods where adults will use minimal questions and minimal direction to XX and allow him to play in his own way without key learning objectives being scaffolded in. This is really helpful for self-regulating as it gives X time and space away from the layers of demand within school.

- Create low sensory input areas for X. These may be particularly useful for the afternoon when X will be more tired and his resilience to stimulation will be lower. This may look like extra cushions and blankets on the sofa area, a pop-up tent with soft toys and books in, a homemade den or tent with soft lights (not sensory spinning flashing lights though! These create high input, and we want to lower and calm things).
- Increase sensory play time – particularly in the afternoons when XX will be working extra hard to access the classroom environment. Scheduling a sensory tray activity for XX will really support his regulation. XX enjoys an adult supporting him with this activity, however this is also an excellent 'low demand' activity where XX can focus on the feeling of the playdough/sensations/his thoughts and play ideas.
- Plan for it to be tough to start with – this sounds strange, but it is sometimes worth expecting it to be tricky, the days are longer and XX will feel more tired, his capacity will be full and things he can manage on Monday morning will be harder by Thursday afternoon. If we plan for this, it can help transitions and support to work more smoothly. The above strategies will help with this.
- It is worth being mindful that XX may ask more questions to soothe his anxiety, he may stim more or need more movement/garden time to regulate himself. He may be less tolerant of his peers, mistakes and the unexpected. He may also need more support with basic care needs – reminders to have a drink/snack/use the toilet, as his ability to self-monitor these needs will decrease when he is tired and busy.

therapeutic thought

Thriving - coping - collapse

'They coped in maths today', 'They cope with playtime now', 'We use a timetable and they cope with change'...

Let's really think about the word and concept of 'coping'. Coping means that an individual is at full capacity but not outwardly collapsing. We so often seem to aim for this for our high support needs children. But for many others, most others, this wouldn't be our target.

If I asked a friend how their Christmas holiday was and they answered, 'I coped with it...' I'd be worried! If I checked in with a friend how work was going and they answered, 'just about coping', I'd be worried! And yet we use the word 'coping' as a triumph for neurodivergent children. We use it as a mark of accomplishment, and I don't think it's enough.

Coping should be the very bare minimum because it's only a trip away from collapse.

As soon as we aren't coping, we slip into collapse, burn out, meltdown, spiralling out of control, high emotions, big behaviours. So if we aim for 'coping', it's no wonder that, in a blink of an eye, our children fall and crash. Coping shouldn't be our end goal, it should only be the beginning, a stepping stone for thriving, enjoying, connecting, creating and more!

So if you have a little one who has just started coping with something, don't settle for that. Look for more for them. Keep working. Keep finding ways to make it better, easier happier for them.

Coping isn't the job done, it's only the very start of the process.

therapeutic thought

Low demand life

When there have been periods of high demand placed on our children, it is important to create a safe place of low demand for them to recover in. After a busy day, a school is an excellent example. As a parent, here are a few things I set up to support a low demand life after school pick up:

- Not rushing home; we walk and wander and stop to look at things here and there. When I do drive, I park down the road away from the manic school-road parking so we still get a short wander.
- Reducing questions; I don't ask too much about their day or request info about what has happened straight away.
- Offer minimal verbal choices; for example, with their snacks, I take two for each child that I know they like. I hold out both without saying anything and let them take what they want. This meets the need for food to regulate, but takes away the demand for verbal choices and decision making. (This may seem small but can make a big difference!)
- Lower demand for play and interaction; we come home and the boys will often sit separately and watch TV, do gaming, play with fidgets or sensory items. Relax and rest.
- Keep food and drinks familiar in favourite cups/plates. No demand to tolerate new flavours or textures.
- Keep things as predictable as possible. No demand to tolerate the unexpected.
- Consider the amount of after school clubs, activities and events we attend. Space them out across the week with clear rest days of nothing in between.

Adapting demands and reducing them wherever possible allows their capacity to reboot and replenish after their school day. Gradually, over time, I can readjust these, and as their capacity increases, I can increase the small demands – like the expectation to do activities after school, to try new things, or to complete activities.

Chapter 12:

Bringing play and communication into the classroom

Let's start by noticing the types of attention children engage in at school:

- **Passive attention:** When information is presented to them (e.g. watching a screen, being talked at/lesson presented to by one person). This is the hardest and often the quickest to deteriorate.
- **Joint attention:** When two people are focusing on the same item of interest and sharing joy in that item. This is when our brain is most engaged, 'lit up', and ready to receive information. You might see this when a child waits and anticipates bubbles being blown from a bubble wand – both the adult and the child are watching the wand, excited for the next thing to happen.
- **Self-chosen attention:** When an activity captivates a child's own unique interest and they become 'lost' in an activity – this is usually a child's favourite type of play. It can be achieved alone or with another and lasts a really long time because it is a choice. In play, this might be a child creating a castle out of blocks, collecting the blocks, designing the structure of the castle, discussing the look and function of the towers with a peer/adult.
- **Deep attention:** When a child has worked hard to create focus and manages to settle into a task and seeks task completion.

- **Attention shifts:** When a child is engaged with an activity and someone or something encourages them to shift their attention away from it – this can be very frustrating for a child when they are focusing on something that is motivating, or there is a drive for them to finish. In class, we are often asking children to shift – from worksheets, to routines, to the windchime noise, for movement to the carpet, from the board, to their pairs. This can be both a blessing and a curse for a child. Some shifts will help keep things 'snappy' for them, other shifts will disrupt them just as they were settling into a task and achieving deep attention.
- **Fleeting attention/overstimulation:** This is when an environment is busy and a child's skill set means they cannot filter out environmental distractions. It results in a child moving quickly from one activity or item to another very quickly, as they search for a way to feel more settled.

Why does knowing this help us as supporting adults?

As adults, we don't always look at the child's attention type – we often have to look at the clock and be guided by timings and routines. This means we can sometimes overlook an opportunity to allow children at school or at home to truly settle into a deep focus. Sometimes this cannot be helped, but it is helpful to understand and be mindful of these different attention types as they can hold the solution to resolving upset/dysregulation during transitions in class, as well as supporting task completion and engagement with lesson-based tasks.

Using play for attention and focus in the classroom

More and more children are being given access to *fidget toys* in the classroom. In order for these to do a good job at supporting attention and engagement rather than add to distraction and discomfort, there are a few things to consider.

What movement does this child crave the most?

We need to spend time observing children and looking for the play patterns in how they fidget and find stimulation/regulation that way. This way we can choose a fidget toy that best matches their play.

For example, a child who is swinging back on their chair is unlikely to settle when given sticky tack or play dough to fidget with because the play patterns are different. The information and the play stimulation they receive from these two actions/items are not a match. Giving them a resistance band on their chair legs or a wobble board for their feet to press against may have more success because the play styles match – they both involve pressure, leg movement and balance.

We have talked about play patterns in Chapter 5 and the senses in Chapter 2, which should help us match together play styles and sensory needs. Ultimately, though, the official name of the play style doesn't matter – what matters is that the two styles match up. We can work this out by watching and making a list of what we see, evaluating what feeling the child is seeking and then offering toys and play that give the child the same feeling and feedback but in a way that is appropriate for a school/educational setting.

Table 12.1: What we see + what the feeling is = what we offer...

What we see...	What's the feeling they get?
Leg swinging and leaning back on chair.	Leg movement and push back in your feet/legs.

What play solution we offer...

- Resistance band on the chair legs to push onto.
- Time on a wobble board before sitting down.
- Regular stretch breaks that involve leg movement – marching on the spot, jumping on the spot, star stretch, touching their toes for a gentle inverse.

Remember to make this playful: Offer it as a time challenge, or use 'magic' to turn the child into a frog to make them jump. We want children to *want* to regulate themselves and engage with this! Doing it as a chore or a consequence will not be as effective.

What we see...	What's the feeling they get?
Pen, jumper and nail chewing.	A chew sensation in their mouth.

What play solution we offer...

- Request crunchy snacks from home – carrots/crackers/crisps/apple (if this is safe for the child).
- Chew buddy, safe chew jewellery.
- A chew-safe pen topper.
- A cold drink with a rubber straw.
- Fidget toys that are safe for the mouth.

What we see...	What's the feeling they get?
Constantly asking to get up to get a drink or use the toilet.	Bigger movements – a chance to walk around/a break from being still. It is also worth checking that there is not an underlying physical need here and to consult a doctor if these symptoms persist, as these can also indicate a UTI.

What play solution we offer...

Create chances within the learning for them to move naturally:

Rotate children from table to table within the lesson.

Have periods of the lesson where children can stand rather than sit.

Stand up and stretch half-way through carpet time.

Offer a movement break sequence: for example – five star jumps, stand on one leg for ten seconds and then toe touch three times.

What we see…	What's the feeling they get?
Pushing other children on the carpet or in the line. (These children often, also swing themselves between two tables and lean on the edge of desks kicking their legs up!)	Something to do with their hands. Push back and resistance into their upper body.
What play solution we offer…	
Create a 'wall push zone' – this is simply having two handprints on the wall somewhere for the child to push against. Make this playful by challenging them to try and push the school over! Show them that when sitting on the floor, they can put their hands either side of them flat on the floor and push downwards to slightly lift their own body weight. Place a blob of play dough on the table and encourage them to stand over it and press down with flat hands to squash the blob to a pancake – guidance on how to push down, not pat or slap will be needed here to make sure they get the right feeling.	

What we see…	What's the feeling they get?
Leaning on others at carpet time or laying down on the floor or head on the desk.	Warmth and comfort of another person. Body surface contact – are they trying to get as much of their body in contact with something else? It is also worth checking that there is not a physical need here and to consult a doctor to further investigate if this persists – occasionally, this behaviour can be linked to muscle tone, strength or fatigue.
What play solution we offer…	
Weighted blanket for legs or shoulders. A bean bag chair to sit in, so they can safely sink into sitting. Time when they can explore or play with a Lycra cloth/sensory sock blanket. Time when they can be in a 'cosy corner' with blankets, pillows and cushions to enclose themselves in softness and warmth.	

How to use fidget toys instinctively?

When given a fidget item, can a child instinctively play/fidget with it safely and appropriately? When we choose a fidget item for our classroom, we need to spend time exploring it ourselves to make sure it can be used in a way that works for you and your class. Consider natural and instinctive ways a child may interact with an item when it is presented to them.

For example, if we give a child a 'stress ball' or 'squishy bead ball', the nature of a ball encourages them to roll and throw it. If this is not going to work for your child and your class, then this item is not a good fit for the setting. We cannot present this kind of item to a child and then expect them to *not* throw it between their hands or roll it across their table. This is a natural way to play and engage with any ball. We need to set children up to succeed with their fidget items. We need to offer tools that will be played with instinctively in a way that matches your classroom expectations.

Teach the boundaries of play for a fidget item

Children are naturally playful and curious. If they are left to their own playful and exploratory devices, they are likely to come up with all sorts of creative ways to fidget, especially when presented with a new toy. It is important to invest time in explaining *why* you are presenting them with a fidget toy. Talk to them about its function and purpose. Explore the item together at a separate time to when you need them to use it, to see how it moves, feels and makes us feel. Set clear play boundaries for when it is in use.

Depending on your child's language skills, this might sound like:

> 'I've noticed that carpet time can feel a bit tricky, and maybe uncomfortable for you? [Allow response and discussion.] I'd love to help you feel happier and more settled when we all sit together. Sometimes when we need our body to be really still it can help if we give our hands/feet something quietly to do. I've got this twist toy that you can move about with both your hands, give it a go. [Time to explore the toy, observe what the child does.] This toy isn't like other toys! It's actually got a really important job to do, it helps our body and our brain be ready for learning. So we can't swing it about, or bash it on the table because then it's not doing

its job. It does its job best when you hold it in both hands and twist it and click it. Can you show me how you use this? [Playful way to check the boundary is understood.] Yes! That's exactly right, it's doing its job perfectly there!'

This demonstration sets a clear boundary. It uses demonstration. It gives reason and purpose to the fidget and it starts to educate the child about how their learning system works, which will support them as they get older to reflect, notice and advocate for what they need. This demonstration also gives you a chance to connect with the child about a struggle rather than giving them the item in order to 'fix them being the problem'. It is a collaboration in which the child and teacher and working together to make school accessible. The teacher can also check in with the child over carpet time with a phrase like, 'Make sure that twist toy is doing his job!' rather than, 'Stop swinging that twist toy around'. Giving the toy itself an identity allows us to redirect our behaviour prompts so that reminders don't feel like criticisms.

Consistency and a fair trial

When you introduce a fidget toy, in order for it be successful, there needs to be a period of embedding the strategy into the classroom and the child's routine. It needs to be available at consistent times, and the adult and the child need to work together to take responsibility for remembering to use it. If it is introduced in a patchy way, where at times it's there and others it's not, the boundaries and systems around it will be much harder for the child to learn and to benefit from. New systems take time, and they need to be given a fair trial. I usually recommend a new system is given at least two weeks of being consistently used before changing it dramatically.

We are often supporting children who thrive on consistency and routine. When we add a new system, we are asking them to adapt to change and learn new boundaries. Altering things too quickly after they have been introduced will mean children are never able to recover from the initial phase of adapting to the change. This can often lead us to feel that no system ever works because it has never had chance to embed. Obviously, if there is clear distress and clear flaws that can be adapted and amended along the way, we need to respond to these – the child's wellbeing should always be at the centre of our decision making. For example, if after three days you still need to offer behaviour boundaries for the fidget toy, this is something that we need to calmly and consistently persevere with as the supporting adults. This is the phase of adjustment for the child, they need to be given time to absorb and settle into the 'new'. They need help and time, not additional change.

Expect prompts to be needed

Although fidget toys and sensory systems are a supportive measure to include in your classroom, they are not magic! As adults, we cannot expect a single introduction and explanation to set us up for ongoing success. We will need to recap the boundaries and refresh the demonstration on a regular basis. This doesn't mean that the tool isn't working. It just means that a child's skill set and capacity for boundaries will be ever-changing and therefore need updated support.

Never use fidget toys as an incentive or punishment

These are often an essential lifeline for children, and to take them away for behaviour is both unfair and emotionally damaging. Phrases such as 'If you don't stop swinging that fidget I will take it away' or 'If you sit nicely for two more minutes you can have your fidget toy' are not acceptable and are not affirming or inclusive.

Is there a universal way we can use play that will benefit the whole class rather than a single child?

An inclusive and reflective way to support fidgets in the classroom is to consider how movement and regulation may be naturally incorporated into your lesson. Not just for a specific child but to benefit all the children in your class. Consider how long your carpet times or teaching times are. Can movement be naturally integrated, such as encouraging children to swap chairs or spaces or collect things from around the room? Or include stretch and movements as part of your teaching, almost like a call and response but for movement – you do an action, and they copy it back. Or schedule movement and music for one or two minutes after a five-minute teaching set to give an opportunity to shake all the 'wiggles' out and help reset body systems.

What if they keep using it in an unsafe way?

If you have done all of the above and your child is still not able to fidget with their fidget toy in a safe and appropriate way in the classroom, this is a message from the child that we haven't managed to find the right support for them yet. In terms of sensory input and stimulation to support attention and focus, this is either too much, or not quite enough. It is at this point that we must start this sequence again, evaluating their play, evaluating *how* they are interacting with the current fidget toy they have and what this tells us about their play.

It is also worth considering at this point other aspects of their sensory and emotional regulation systems throughout the day – we discussed sensory capacity earlier (see p.25) and it might be that this child needs bigger input across the day to mean they can sustain their attention for learning. Or it may mean they need more grounding work to steady their system before learning.

If you have explored the above, we can then try to find a safe alternative for them. Ideally, this can be done collaboratively with the child. Depending on their language skills, it may sound like this:

'I can see you really love having the twist toy in your hands at carpet time. What I've noticed is that often you start to use it like a spinning top and it bumps into the other children. I'm wondering if there is a different toy we can try that is going to do an even better job at helping you enjoy carpet time more?'

You can hear how this is very different to, 'I'm taking this away because you aren't using it properly'.

What if they all want one?

Making adaptations for children can often lead to questions from other children in the class. This also happens at home, when boundaries are adapted for one child and upheld for another, depending on the needs between the siblings. This can feel really challenging as a supporting adult, here are a few suggestions for how to approach this:

- Carefully consider whether an adaptation can be generalised and benefit the whole class/family. There are many adjustments that we make for children who display their needs more clearly to us that would actually support children across our class or home who may also be struggling quietly without us realising it. When you develop a strategy for one child, take a moment to explore whether it could be integrated more widely into your classroom or home and teaching style holistically for universal benefit.

- If it's possible, have times when all children can explore resources – this takes away their mystery. Set up time where they can come and ask questions about resources, have a feel of fidgets and sensory toys and experiment with them. If possible/appropriate, include the child they are intended for in this, and encourage them to show and tell their peers what they use and how it helps them.
- Have books on your classroom bookshelf about diversity, and read them as your class books so that children experience and understand diversity and inclusion.
- Talk to children openly about how we all learn in different ways and therefore need different things to help us be successful. Let children feel safe enough to complain to you and tell you it feels unfair, so that you can explore that with them in detail.

This might sound like:

> 'You've spotted that X has a heavy blanket for carpet time and you wish you had one too… I can see why you would like one, it does look snug! The thing is, we all grow and learn in different ways. I've given the blanket to X because, for his brain to be ready for learning at carpet time, he needs a heavy cosy feeling on his legs. It helps his brain feel awake and ready to learn… You know what, though, if I had a cosy blanket on my legs I think I would feel sleepy and ready for a rest! My brain needs different things to X to make sure it's ready for learning. We all need different things sometimes. So even though we don't have the *same* things, it is still *fair* because everyone is getting a chance to learn in the *best way for them* at school.'

You might also talk about:

> 'Having exactly the *same* things as someone else is not quite the same, as things being *fair*. X wears glasses to help her see more clearly – if she doesn't wear them, things are blurry and fuzzy. If we give everyone the same, that would mean the whole class has to wear glasses! But that's not fair because now everyone else's

> eyes feel fuzzy and blurry. It's not the *same*, but it is *fair*, because it is helping give everyone their best chance at learning and feeling comfortable.'

You might need to keep it really simple:

> 'Everyone needs different things to help them learn, feel comfortable and happy at school. I can't give everyone an X, but I will make sure I'm doing lots of other things to make sure school is a lovely place for you to be and learn.'

Using play to differentiate your lesson for motivation

Motivation can be a really big factor in whether a child completes an activity. When we support and teach neurotypical children, one of the skills that often underpins success is the natural, inbuilt drive to socially please others around us. Very often, instructions and requests are met with an eagerness to comply, because there is a social drive to be part of the group, to please the instruction-giver, and there is a social interest in what might be coming next.

Not always, but often, this dive to comply 'just because' seems a lot less for our wonderful neurodivergent children. A child who is Autistic will often need more of a reason or more of a personal drive in order for them to complete a task or follow an instruction.

Historically, this observation may have been met with the viewpoint that 'they need to learn' or 'that's not the real world' or 'they'll need these skills when they are adults'. But this is outdated and leads to compliance-based therapy and activities, which result in children achieving tasks and behaviours but at the cost of their mental health and at the cost of their trust in other people. (We explore this more in Chapter 13.)

Through working with children for many years, I have found the most successful way to support a child through learning tasks and daily routine instructions is to *make them*

motivating and playful for that individual. When presenting an activity or an instruction, I often imagine the child thinking to themselves, 'But why? What's interesting for me about this?' Not in a rude way, in a genuinely curious way. I have observed children and adults who are Autistic to have the most wonderful way of prioritising their own playful joy if they are allowed to. And therefore, if we want or need to encourage them to complete a different task or move to a different part of the daily routine, we need to show them that the new phase will bring them joy and benefit. For example, 'It's time to line up to go inside' holds very little motivation, but often children will comply because they understand and appreciate it is what is expected. But 'It's time to go inside for singing! Your favourite!' holds more intrinsic motivation – there is reason and drive to complete the task.

For example, a seven-year-old child who is Autistic is presented with a worksheet after carpet time. The target of the activity is to talk to a peer about the six photos on the page and describe a key object in each photo.

The activity itself is not motivating enough to encourage task completion. If we pretend the child asks us 'But why?', the only answer we can really give here is, 'Because that's what the task is'. So let's consider how we can make this more playful and therefore more motivating:

In order to make worksheets more playful, for example, try some of these:

- **Adding a sensory tray:** Lay the worksheet at the bottom of a tray and cover it in a small amount of a dry sensory base like rice, sand or red lentils. Give the child a paintbrush and see if they can sweep away sections to reveal the page underneath. You could add a figure of a dinosaur/fairy to add extra magic and motivation to search for the missing worksheet.
- **Cutting and sticking:** Cut the worksheet into sections to create a 'puzzle' and allow the child to stick it into their book, or cut it into more pieces to explore. As they cut and build, they will naturally need to look at the details of the sheet and playfully, almost accidentally, complete the activity!
- **Hiding:** Cover parts of the worksheet up so the child needs to explore to discover it. You could use Post-It notes to hide sections. You could use blobs of play dough squashed onto the sheet that

need peeling off. You could fill a zip-bag with kinetic sand or paint (make sure it is securely closed and use sticky tape for extra security!), lay this flat over the worksheet and use fingers to carefully slide the sand/paint away to reveal the sheet underneath.

- **Making it a mission:** Offer the work completion as a role play mission depending on the child's play preferences – suggest they be a detective and find the items on the sheet. Or suggest the fairy king needs all the items identified before the castle's grand opening can happen. Use voices and actions to allow the child to become part of the mission.
- **Adding a prop:** Having something to hold during activities can make it feel more meaningful. If the activities involve searching on the worksheet, you could offer a magnifying glass to look through, or a cardboard tube as a telescope, or tokens/hoops/buttons to place on the items when you find them on the page.

You may be tempted to use a 'now-and-next' board for this type of activity, where the child completes the worksheet and then gets a preferred activity afterwards. This can often lead to quick task completion, however because the learning is not the drive itself (the motivator comes in the next part), this learning part is often rushed or done in an unsettled state either because of fear or excitement to get to the next part. This shifts the child's brain out of a learning state and into that fight or flight state, and so, although the task is completed, the learning goal itself may not be retained. In these ideas we have merged the 'now part' and the 'next part' together to *create an appealing academic playful task.*

Ideally, we want children to *choose and be motivated* by the learning activity itself. Rather than trying to race through it to tick it off and get to the activity they really want.

Within short therapy sessions, it is possible to make this a priority for almost every activity. However, at home and school, this may not always be possible with every single activity and instruction. It is about balance and mindfulness, understanding that these two types of attention exist and working these strategies into learning as much as possible.

Movement and regulation

Movement matters for learning

For most children, and certainly for neurodiverse children, being able to move their body to regulate themselves while learning is absolutely crucial. This isn't a preference; for them, it's an absolute need. It's what helps keep their sensory load balanced, it's what helps them stay in a calm and connected brain state, and it's what means they are at their most ready for taking on new information, tasks or requests. When we restrict a child's natural urge and need to move their body, we will often accidentally encourage a minimalising or more internalised movement, which can be damaging for them. When we ask them to stop wiggling on the carpet, they may remain more still in their body, but have their hands in their lap and pick their skin on their fingers – it's smaller and less noticeable to others, but the stimulation that is needed by the child is still received. This shift in movement is at the cost to the child's wellbeing and is not affirming. Once we know and accept that movement is an essential need, we have choices about how we then approach and apply this to our therapy or learning tasks.

The first option is to include movement as part of our play and activities, create tasks that include movement naturally as part of their flow.

For example, if we are playing a colour-sorting activity, we could place the box of coloured teddy bear figures at one end of the room and we can place the yellow, red and blue bowls at the other end of the room. We can encourage the child to take one or a handful of bears at a time and travel over to the bowls to sort them into colours. Our language aim here is to name colours, talk about size, work as a team to collect them. We are also working on logic and problem-solving skills as we sort and differentiate the colours. The child also needs to develop a transporting system using their hands or a pot to get the teddies from one end of the room to another. But more importantly, they will be moving around for the entire activity. Naturally, as part of the way we have laid out the resources, they will need to get up and move from one side of the room to another, so the regulating action of walking/skipping, bending lifting and dropping is already there. This act of movement will in turn mean their attention and focus can be sustained for longer. They will be being active *and* attending to a task/activity.

The second option is to know that the activity you are asking has an element of stillness to it and plan that your child will be in need of movement afterwards. Plan for movement after stillness and focus. Don't wait for dysregulation and then offer a movement break; instead, plan in the movement as part of your schedule.

For example, if you have a child who loves sitting with water, they pour and scoop and watch the water flow. They drop figures into the water and watch the splash. They engage and focus on the droplets and delight in the movement they see. They repeat the dropping and splashing over and over and it brings them real stillness and joy and focus. As their attention fades with the water, they will likely feel a drive to move. We can support this by anticipating that after stillness comes movement. We can offer a balance board, or some bean bags to throw, or we can have ready a busier activity idea. It is often helpful to notice this with them in a description like this: 'You were so still and so focused at the water tray, that was such a lot of calm for your body. I can see your body needs to move now! Let's find something busy for it to do!'

Both these options plan for movement to support attention but in different ways. We either have the movement as part of the play itself, or we have the movement planned for after period of stillness. Where children often struggle is if we have several still or structured activities in a row, because there isn't the release of movement that they need in order to create a feeling of calm for themselves. This leads to a build up of this need to move and then an explosion of movement or busyness, which we as adults can often view as 'disruptive or difficult behaviour'. In fact, what has happened is that our expectation for stillness has gone on too long, there's been a build up and build up and then, like a volcano, there's a fierce eruption. By adding movement into our play/learning or scheduling movement immediately after periods of stillness, we slowly and gradually release that need for movement in a much more regulated way and we see our children remaining steady and engaged for longer. (This links to discussions in Chapter 2 about grounding.)

Not *what* we use but *how* we use it

Using resources and programmes respectfully: keeping things neurodiversity affirming

It's not always *what* resources you use, but *how* you use resources respectfully that will mean you are being affirming for children. Some will argue that schedules and timetables are no longer affirming because they are a way to dictate to children what must be done. However, I consider this to be an example of two extreme viewpoints and that there is a middle ground that needs to place more value on *how* we are communicating things with children rather than *what* resources we are using.

There is a very clear difference between the two scenes:

1. Showing a child a now-and-next board and telling them their preferred activity is finished and that they must stop now. Then an adult strongly guiding them away from it while they are distressed, forcing a new task completion that an adult has chosen, allowing distress to remain the key feeling, but getting the task done anyway.
2. Showing the child a now-and-next board, explaining that their preferred activity will need to stop, giving them some notice, acknowledging that they wish they could do it more. Showing them the next activity to try and make it seem exciting. Adapting the next activity to their needs and interests to make it desirable even if it's not preferred. Carving out time for emotions to be felt about change and offering reassurance. Helping them regulate across the transition with sensory input, toys and connection. Reassuring them that the preferred activity can be returned to again soon. Working alongside the child to support them in completing a less-preferred activity in a regulated way.

Technically, both those scenarios are, on the surface, 'adults using a now-and-next board' – but the way it is done – the *implementation* of the visual – has been done in two completely different ways. With two different focuses. The focus in the first scenario above is task completion at any cost, the visual merely lets the child know it happening whether they are ready or not. Scenario two has a key focus on connection and support. The visual is there to guide and support an understanding of the transition, but the adult's implementation keeps regulation and connection as the key focus. The task completion is a secondary focus.

This is not true for all visuals, systems and structures, but does apply to many. It is not necessarily the system/schedule that creates distress and/or trauma for a child, but the way that it is implemented and what the adult has as their primary focus. It is easy to get carried away with the target focus, the schedule focus and the time-keeping focus. However, to be truly affirming, we must always have the child's wellbeing and regulation as the main focus of our decision making and the way we implement our strategies.

It is helpful to ask ourselves as supporting adults, 'What is my focus here? What benefit to the child does this bring? What will be their takeaway message from this interaction?'

That last question will really make you stand back and revaluate actions – 'What is the take away message here?' For a child who makes rules about life after every experience they have, to a child whose brain is perfectly programmed to remember patterns and recall past experiences, to a child who will remember this as positive or negative and associate it with you – what are they taking away?

In scenario one, the takeaway message will likely be:

- That adult doesn't understand me.
- I am unsure if that adult is safe because I had an unsafe feeling with them that they ignored.
- When I see 'now-and-next' I need to panic.
- My feelings weren't the focus, getting the task done was.

In scenario two, the takeaway message will likely be:

- I didn't like the change, but that adult helped me.
- That adult is safe and understands me.
- 'Now-and-next' means change.
- Change feels hard but I get help.

When children live scenario two, they are learning key life skills. They are experiencing small change in a safe and supported way. They are learning that supporting adults understand their needs and struggles. They are learning to trust and to ask for help when big feelings happen. These skills are transferable to other times in life and are ultimately what we hope and aim for as supporting adults at home or at school.

Chapter 13:

Outdated advice for play and communication therapy

Things *not* to do – we now know better, so we can do better!

You may still hear some of the outdated advice highlighted in this chapter given out, by therapists who are not up to date with current research, or by therapists and companies who are not willing to change or listen to the voices of Autistic adults. I wanted to highlight these key strategies as warning signs for practice that is *not* affirming for neurodivergent children.

Historically, in therapy, there have been a few key pieces of advice that have never felt right for me. Even as a newly qualified therapist, I could see families question the logic and reason behind the advice they were being given and I found it hard to justify it. I found it even harder to demonstrate it or to model the advice I had heard. Very quickly, I looked for alternative ways to support children's interaction with play and connection at their heart.

In more recent years, now that we have taken time to stop and listen to adults who are Autistic, we can listen to their voice and their experiences of therapy and how it feels – we have this as a very real reason to change our practice and adapt how we support children in therapy.

Outdated advice 1: Any communicative reaction is wanted

This was the idea that as adults we could look for any ways to get a reaction from children, because all reactions are a form of communication – what this translated to often was that adults could look for ways to mess up play patterns, intervene with ideas and systems that children were creating because it got them noticed. The child looked up from the line they had made, when you destroyed it and screamed at you – that was seen as a positive thing, that it was communication, so it was OK.

What we know now about the brain and the nervous system tells us that these extreme reactions are harmful and hurtful for children. It's distressing and it destroys a child's trust and relationship with that adult. They no longer see the adults as safe and predictable, but as unsafe and a possible threat. Although in the short term you may get a few moments of interaction, what you end with is a child in 'shutdown' mode, where they refuse to let you in because you become a danger to their wellbeing. Toys are often huddled away into corners, children hunch over them and look warily for you, explosive emotions occur at any movement you make. Or worse, the child stops trying to play altogether and zones out. The child at this point is in survival mode and their brain and body are not in a position to learn. So you can model all the language you can and they will not learn or transfer any of these skills because their main aim is to survive this interaction NOT learn from it.

Outdated advice 2: Repeated exposure to unpreferred things will help them learn to cope

This was the idea that, if a child struggled with a situation, texture or skill, the best way to conquer this was to expose them to it lots. This stems from research and psychology around building new pathways for tolerance to unpleasant things and is really rooted in the idea that the responsibility for inclusion lies with the child – *they* need to learn and adapt rather than considering how the environment and community can be more inclusive of them.

The difficulty with dispelling this outdated advice is that, technically, you can see a change in the child's behaviour and reaction to the thing you would like them to cope with or achieve. Exposure and repetition does create new pathways and you can technically train a child to alter their outward reaction and response to something. Often the target that is set is met and can be ticked off. However, this change is usually *only outward*. They do not like the activity more, they do not find the loud bell less scary. Their body and nervous system *internally* respond in the same way. Often what we managed to do is condition them to mask their real reaction because they have learnt that the adults around them do not respond to their distress. They learn the behaviour pattern that, 'Even when I express distress, the expectation is that I do the thing anyway'.

As a neurotypical individual, this approach may work because the experiences encountered that are distressing are few and far between – and so the notion of 'powering through' is manageable. However, as a neurodivergent individual, as a child who is Autistic, the frequency and intensity of experiences are so high that distress levels are unmanageable on a daily basis. The result is an outward appearance of progress and change, but at a huge mental wellbeing cost. This is a frequently recalled experience by Autistic adults who now have a voice to help the next generation. It is so important that we listen, know better and do better.

How might this look in therapy

Exposure behaviour based therapy might show a child a noisy pop-up toy, and notice that they are consistently distressed by the build up of music and then the toy popping up. It gives them a fright, they don't enjoy the rush, their body takes a long time to recover. Behaviour therapy approaches that use repeated exposure would suggest that this sequence must be repeated a set number of times every session. It may suggest that an adult uses hand-over-hand to get the child to press the button themselves. The rationale would argue that this is helping the child acclimatise to sudden noises, that they will get used to the sequence, and that they can practice recovering from the shock.

A play-based neurodiversity-affirming approach would notice the destress and stop the play, but leave the toy available for the child to explore in their own time and on their own terms. Model and demonstrate advocating phrases/visuals/AAC 'It's too loud', 'Stop', 'Finished', 'I don't like it'. It may be that you leave the toy available but offer ear defenders alongside it. It may be that you leave the toy available but already popped and allow the child to hide it away but then request 'stop', allowing them to experience the toy but remain level and curious without shock.

Both these sessions teach life skills. Both these sessions get a child ready for their wider environment. However the exposure approach comes at the cost of the child's nervous system being lit up and at the cost of the child's trust in adults. Coping and masking is learnt.

The neurodiversity-affirming approach gives the child tools and skills to safely express their needs and advocate for themselves. It's putting the child's wellbeing at the centre of therapy aims and shifts the focus from short-term outcomes to long-term skill sets.

Yes, the child may never use the noisy pop-up toy via this approach, but they will learn to say 'stop', they will learn to notice that noise is a sensitivity for them, they will learn that ear defenders can help, they will learn that adults can help find solutions collaboratively, they will learn they don't need to hide how they feel, and they will learn that they have the right to choose their experiences.

Outdated advice 3: We need to get them ready for the real world

A lot of the theory and explanation above also applies here. This is really a mindset shift in terms of expectation and inclusion.

Our children are already living in the real world. They are already trying to access it within their skill set and capacity. What is needed is a shift in responsibility. Rather than the expectation and load being on our neurodiverse children to get ready for a world that doesn't understand them. We need the world to take responsibility, to learn and be better educated about how to accept, support, include and nurture all individuals.

Outdated advice 4: Withholding items will make them talk

This was the idea that, in order to encourage a child to talk, adults needed to keep items of interest out of reach as a way of motivating them to request them verbally. This was often advised to be done very strictly where children were not given the item they wanted if they didn't ask for it. Sometimes this is referred to as withholding or 'friendly sabotage'.

As with other outdated advice discussed, it can be hard to dispel this strategy's validity because it can seem, superficially, very effective. Children get frustrated and make noises, they reach and cry and may even say the word in an act of desperation to be given the thing they want being held out of reach by an adult. Communication happens, but its drive is frustration and distress. What this tends to teach children is that communication isn't enjoyable and that it isn't a choice. It becomes more of a means to an end. For them, communication and distress become linked.

What we want to do as an alternative is to *create a chance* to talk. Communication is how we join together and connect. We want it to bring us joy. We want it to be a choice. We don't want it to feel like a power struggle, like a consequence of upset or frustration.

In play-based therapy and strategies, I therefore consider whether communication happening because we've created connection, or is it happening because the upset and frustration is so intense they have to.

Communication can be the result of connection.

Communication can be the result of frustration.

Both methods result in an act of communication – words or sounds or actions – but the motivation and reason are so different. The communication occurs, but at what cost to the child? The takeaway message we are teaching children about why we communicate and why we share messages are opposite. The strategies and system we explore in this book keep connection, regulation and joy at the centre of a child's communication journey.

Outdated advice 5: Signs and symbols will stop their talking because they don't need to try ✗

Studies have shown time and time again that using signs and visuals does not slow down or hinder a child's ability or motivation to use spoken language. In my experience, these tools accelerate and increase motivation and enjoyment of communication which has a positive impact on spoken language. What these tools *do* offer is a way to express themselves while on the journey to talking. They reduce frustration. They encourage children to experiment with different ways of connecting with other people. They allow children to explore the enjoyment of communication and play before they have spoken words. They support relationship and friendship building, and they give a voice to children who are working hard to find theirs.

This outdated advice shows again a shift in perspective. The idea that children don't talk because they don't have to, or are being lazy, really doesn't appreciate the effort and work that young children and/or children who are Autistic have to do to acquire skills that, as adults, we may take for granted. It is important to shift away from this mindset and always believe that children are working as hard as they can with the skill set and capacity they currently have available to them. So often, if they *could* use words, they absolutely would, because it would be quicker and easier for them to be heard and understood. So if they are using a sign system, an AAC app or a combination of system and strategies to get their message to us, they are actually working even harder than a spoken word system and we should honour and nurture that resilience.

Outdated advice 6: Stimming needs stopping ✗

This was the idea that stimming was a behaviour that children could be taught not to do. What we know now from listening to neurodivergent adults and being more observant and holistic of neurodivergent children is that stimming is a much-needed and purposeful act. It helps an individual the regulate their body and their nervous system. It helps an individual to express their emotions in a physical and freeing way. In my experience, the body movements themselves are not something that can be stopped or supressed; what happens instead is that the individual experiences bigger waves of emotions expressed through melt down or shut down. Or the movements become smaller but more intensive, which may result in a more harmful self-stim, like skin picking, biting or pinching.

We should be celebrating our children's stimming as a beautiful and pure way of them expressing themselves and responding to their bodies' requests for regulation. If you notice that a child is stimming in a way that puts themselves or someone else in danger, we can support them collaboratively. Notice the behaviour and the need with them and help them to find a safe/healthy alternative.

This might sound like, 'What a lot of wonderful spinning you've done, your body is starting to bump into people and furniture now. Let me help, do you need more wooshing? We can go on the swing, or to help you settle we can roll in the heavy blanket.'

This might sound like, 'I see you are picking your toenail lots during bedtime story today... Let's put a sock on to keep it cosy and safe and find a fidget toy for hands to play with instead. It's so important we care for our bodies.'

This may sound like, 'You love these bubbles so much! I can see your happy jumps every time they pop! Hooray for bubbles!'

This might sound like asking other children to make a space – 'I can see that X is absolutely loving how the radiator line looks while he runs up and down... Can you give him a little bit of space while he enjoys that play feeling, please?'

This might look like explaining stimming to other children – 'I can see X is so happy about his line of cars, his hands are moving and flapping in a happy dance to tell us all about it.'

Outdated advice 7: Obsessions need stopping ✗

Our children who are Autistic will often show a strong preference for a certain type of play or character, and these will become a great source of comfort and repetition for them. They may enjoy only to explore numbers. They may prefer only to talk about Pokémon, or Kilimanjaro or WW2. Out-of-date advice suggests that we should reduce contact and exposure to this to try and widen a child's play opportunities or create more 'neurotypical play'. We now understand more about how distressing and isolating this can be for individuals. We understand that an Autistic brain is wired differently, and these favourite topics and themes are not an obsession for us to squash but a specialist skill for us to nurture and support to thrive. These areas of passion are a crucial part of a child's skill set that can unlock communication, connection and interaction skills if we lean into them, rather than pull them away. In Chapter 11, I talk more about layering favourite and preferred themes into therapy.

They say 'we are all a little bit on the spectrum'

This isn't outdated advice as such, but it is something that is said often and isn't accurate, so I've included it here.

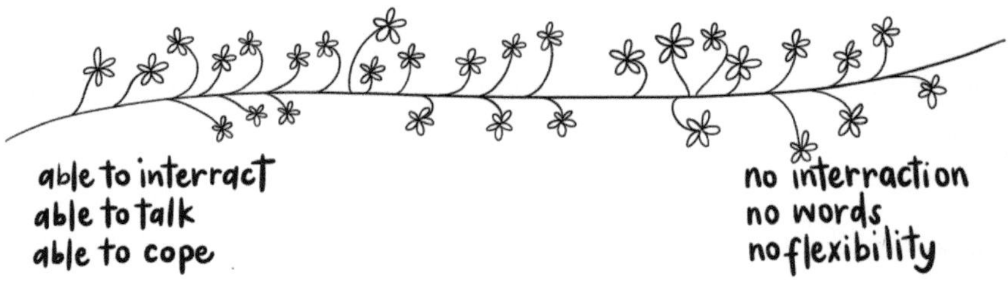

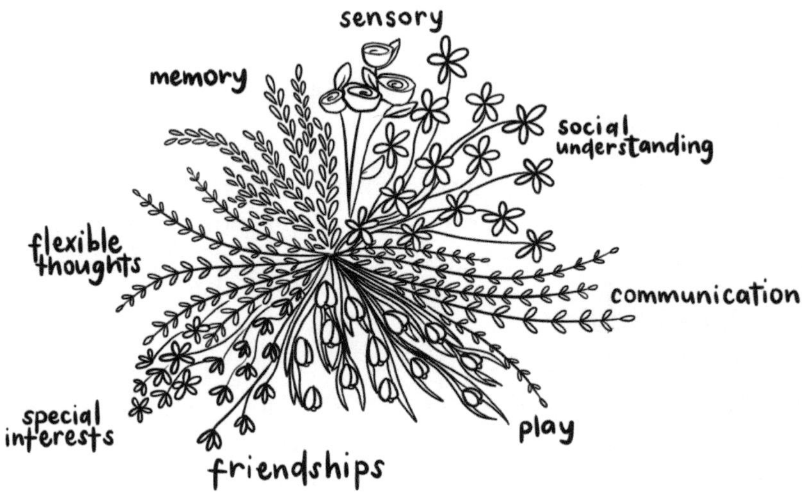

There is an outdated view of Autism and the idea of a spectrum being a straight line, like a vine of flowers. This idea implies that, at diagnosis, you are placed on this line. Maybe you are a flower at the far end of the vine and have no words and many struggles. Or maybe you are a flower at the other end and have many words and few struggles. But this just isn't a true reflection of what Autism is. When you are Autistic, you are not one type of skill set. You do not exist as a single flower stuck on a vine in that position forever.

Being Autistic means you are a glorious bunch of flowers that bloom, wilt and constantly change. Your set of skills and struggles are different to everyone else, even within the diagnostic umbrella of being Autistic. Your bunch of flowers blooms in an entirely different way to the neurotypical.

But just the same as everyone else, there are a collection of skills that are constantly growing. There is no stillness, you are not stuck as a single flower on a vine. Your potential blooms constantly.

The problem with viewing people who are Autistic as a single flower is that others may feel like they hold that single flower in their neurotypical bunch themselves. Then this dangerous illusion of 'we are all on the spectrum a bit' feels plausible. I think what people mean when they claim 'we are all on the spectrum' is that they can relate to a single struggle. Maybe one or two struggles. The outdated line visual of Autism lends itself well to this misconception and that's what makes it so damaging. The key difference, though, is that that one struggle doesn't impact their entire life. It doesn't impact the growth of all their other flowers, so it is not the same at all.

This is such a huge topic for discussion, and many will feel very passionately about it. I hope that this visual can help. When supporting children who are Autistic, it is important to remember and understand that it is not a vine of flowers that we pluck one from and hold forever. It is a glorious bunch of flowers that grow and change and bloom and wilt. New buds grow and old petals fall. Every configuration will be different, and the growth will differ too. This way of visualising Autism will help supporting adults to be more affirming of skills and development. It will help us to appreciate areas of struggle and celebrate change and growth.

Chapter 14:

Ready to play – therapy ideas

Language through making

An easy way to create connection is to create something together. Simple baking, mixing and making - naturally has so many language opportunities, just by the nature of the activity itself.

There are instructions to follow, language concepts, sensory exploration, mistakes and giggles, mess and textures... Then whatever you've made gives you a second play opportunity and a chance to extend your connection further.

Make crispy cakes.

Make play dough from scratch.

Junk box modelling.

Arts and crafts.

Stacking cups and lights

Use a torch and some stacking cups to create lanterns of different colours and light towers. It's so simple but the play and language opportunities it creates are wonderful! As you play, talk about colours, the tower, the light. Make patterns, line them up, crash them down. Sing, make silly noises.

Play foam or play dough to make clothes

All you need for this play is some figures and something that moulds. Start squishing the clay/play dough/foam around the figures and create outfits or characters! You can even add hairstyles or themed costumes – such as making them into a clown with hair, a nose and large shoes.

This activity is great for language learning. Making things lends itself to chat about 'doing'. This chat has a lot of verbs and adjectives in. For example, you can talk about what we are doing – squashing, moving, building, hiding, fixing, bending. Talk about what it's like – soft, sticky, big, tiny, funny, quiet, rainbow coloured.

Because of the nature of this play, the chat is very vocabulary rich!

Other ideas include:

- Make outfits.
- Create characters – clowns, dancers, police officers.
- Make events – a party, a school, Halloween.
- Make hairstyles and a hair salon.
- Make shoes.
- Hide the figures and find them.

Painting toys!

Get some plastic figures, some paint and explore!

This is a great activity because it is so curious! It is not something we are usually allowed to do and that evokes connection and an opportunity to communicate about the unusual.

You can link this to stories like painting a grey elephant patchwork like Elmer.

You could design your own mythical creature. Create patterns. Create camouflage.

You could use this as a sensory tray where the pint and toys mix and the textures/colours are explored.

Offer instructions using body parts and colours, like, 'Let's paint the head pink' or 'Paint the tail blue and the tummy yellow'.

Wrap up a puzzle

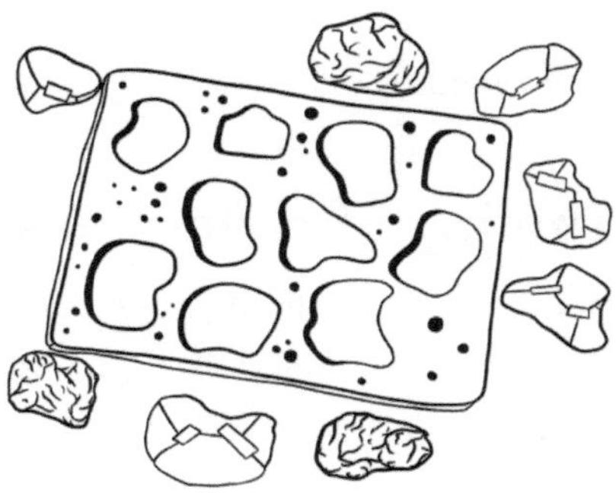

This is quick to set up and is just too curious for children not to investigate!

Insert puzzles can become too easy for children quite early on, and I find that, for many children, often seeing the picture on each piece is enough at a glance which means the play ends very quickly.

This idea helps extend attention and focus, it encourages joint attention – we are both a bit curious and intrigued about it, and allows for lots of lovely phrase repetition!

A few ideas for wrapping:

- Use masking tape or washi tape for children to pick off.
- Wrap in tin foil for a lovely crunch!

- Wrap in tissue paper.
- Wrap in packaging/paper shreds.
- Wrap in play dough!

Post-It note flaps

This is a simple and effective way of creating an extra opportunity to pause and engage on each page of a book. Put a Post-It note over key parts of the picture and explore together what is underneath – it's like a lift-the-flap book but it doesn't matter if they rip them out!

This play lends itself really nicely to using a few set phrases – perfect for little ones who learn and copy language as a whole sentence:

Try saying things like:

- 'Look! It's hiding!'
- 'Who's there?'
- 'Hello X.'
- 'There's the xxx.'
- 'Let's open it.'
- 'Hiding again.'

The joy of collections

One of my favourite therapy play ideas is taking a big collection of similar items for open-ended play. Plan to have a language or communication target in mind, such as using the terms 'big' and 'small', for example. Or asking for help. Or using colours. Or answering a question on size or location. But the actual play itself can be left up to the child.

If you had a collection of ducks in different sizes and colours with plastic eggs, here is an example of the language opportunities:

- Make colour collections.
- Look at size.
- Set up a pond and have play sequences develop.
- Copy each other putting ducks in a line or pushing them off the edge of the table.
- Act out the five little ducks song.
- Place ducks inside the eggs and need help to click them shut.
- Take on different roles in play – like one to put the ducks in eggs and one to break them out.
- Hide the ducks under half a shell.
- Add water or shaving foam and splat them into puddles.

The ideas could go on, but each play idea lends itself to infinite targets.

Simple sensory exploration

Here are different ways to play using dry pasta, spoons, pots, tubs or trays.

Stage 1:

- Encourage scooping from one container to another.
- Encourage mixing.
- Watch the pasta fall.
- Use simple words like 'mix' 'more' 'gone'.
- Give one instruction at a time in play – 'Some for the BLUE POT' 'Stop... Go!'

Stage 2:

- Encourage pretending.
- Mix like you're making a cake.
- Pretend to eat it.
- Spill some and have to tidy up.
- Give cakes to each other to eat.

- Use describing words like 'big cake' 'it's hot!' 'the red bowl'.
- Give instructions with two parts – 'Can I have a BOWL and a SPOON, please?'

Stage 3:

- Encourage role play sequences.
- Take on character roles like a baker and a customer.
- Make cakes for your shop and act out buying one for a party.
- Use longer and more detailed language – 'Hello, do you have any big cakes? It's my birthday and I'm having a party!'
- Give more abstract instructions – 'This chair is my delivery van. Can you put the cake in the boot for me, please?'

As discussed in Chapter 5, you can add things to this type of set up that will capture your child's imagination. If they like dinosaurs, have a Dino tea party! If they love superheroes, pretend there's a problem at the cake shop to be solved!

Hiding and searching

Hiding and searching for toys and parts of toys is about creating curiosity. Curiosity is your best friend when it comes to communication. If there's a chance to explore something then there's an opportunity to talk about the adventure.

An easy way to create curiosity is by having parts of a toy missing and going on a search for them. For example, have a Mr Potato Head toy, but have all the pieces in different bags and boxes set out next to it. This is really simple. Just popping each part of the game into a different box/bag but it adds so much to the game.

Instead of just quickly popping each part into the potato's head and it being finished, we get to go on a journey!

Exploring each box/bag, its texture, its noise, wonder what could be inside, ask for help, anticipate, share success, name what it is... then add it to the potato head.

The journey is where the language is. Not the completion of the task. This play strategy works with almost any activity. If they love cars, put a few in lunch boxes. If they love puzzles, hide a few pieces in tissue paper. If they love Barbie, put some of her accessories in tubs/handbags. Lay it out so it's an invitation to explore. As always, make sure this is playful not upsetting, there is no pressure to use spoken language to access the toys and if a child appears upset by the incompletion of a set then support and resolve this swiftly.

Here are some ideas for containers:

- Take away boxes.
- Old handbags.
- Party bags.
- Lunch boxes.
- Plastic tubs.
- Tins.
- Tea bag box.
- Upside-down cup.
- Coffee tin.
- Zip-bag.

Toy rescue

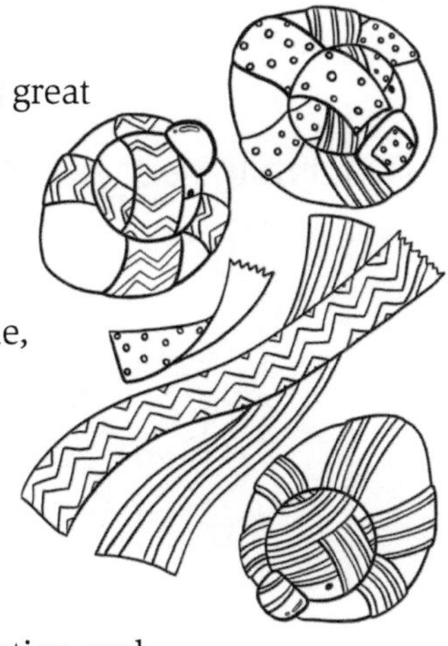

Wrap toys up in masking tape or stickers. This is great for communication as it naturally covers skills across the communication pyramid (see Chapter 3 for more on this).

Attention: Little ones focus intently on the rescue, it's unusual and they are curious about the task.

Social: It's tricky for fine motor skills so they may need help. They may need to ask and request you to be part of the activity.

Understanding: They may need to access instruction and watch to learn how to problem solve.

Talking/communication: We can model and offer verbal information and key words as we play, learning vocab and verbal reasoning language. We can model using signs, action and AAC as we play.

Following instructions in a sensory tray

Choose items that range in size, such as a big giraffe toy and a small giraffe toy, a big elephant toy and a small elephant toy. Add a sensory element such as shaving foam or kinetic sand (see p.108 for a list of ideas for sensory bases).

To play, explore the animals and the sensory base. You can set them out in their pairs and offer a verbal instruction such as 'splat the big giraffe' and encourage your child to find the right animal and splat them into the shaving foam.

Once they have finished exploring, you can play in reverse by adding a tray of water and cleaning them! 'Let's clean the little zebra.'

Swap between you offering requests and allowing your child to instruct you who to find.

This activity helps children listen for key words within instructions – the size *and* the type of animal.

A straw tea party

To play this game cut up straws, paper or plastic, or use pompoms if you prefer. Add these to a plastic tea set or plastic beakers or sippy cups you already have. Practice filling the cups with the straws and pretending to drink from them. You can pretend that the tea is too hot and doing a big blow into it. As you do this, all the straws will fly out and float all over the floor creating a lovely sensory experience.

By playing this game we work on:

- Waiting and watching.
- Anticipation.
- Following a sequence (crucial for storytelling and literacy later on).
- Using key words and signs.
- Using facial expressions.
- Responding to another person's reactions.
- Pretend play which can be extended to role play.

Depending on your child, you can make this play sequence much longer by pouring the tea and making straw tea for teddies. You could try adding a song like 'I'm a little tea pot' or 'Polly put the kettle on'.

Play dough building

Use play dough as the cement for building blocks to create houses, castles, towers, igloos and more. While children play and create, you can ask them simple questions, encourage them to tell the story of their build and develop creative ideas together. It's a fabulous activity for problem-solving discussions too. You can add figures, characters or animals to extend the theme and explore even more language as you play.

Use curious language like:

- 'I wonder what will happen if we put this on the top.'
- 'Imagine if we built a bridge too.'
- 'I think this could be even taller.'
- 'If only there wasn't such a big gap here.'

This phrasing starts a collaborative conversation with children. It doesn't hold the same pressure that adults asking a lot of questions can hold. This makes the play and talk feel equal and joined up, rather than like we are testing them.

Just add water

Create a playful experience by adding water to any of your other play ideas. The reason this works is because it immediately creates a curious but familiar experience and naturally extends language and play ideas. For example, if you have a little one who loves farm animals and you add water, they now have a pond or a swimming pool to play in. If you have a little one who loves cars, you now have a car wash. If you have a little one who loves lining items up, they can now jump or fall into the water afterwards. If you have a little one who loves to throw, there is now a spectacular splash to explore after the throw. Adding water to a play is naturally soothing as a sensory regulatory tool too, so it often offers a moment of calm for a child in play alongside the learning.

Epilogue:
Play is the language that connects us all...

In this book, we've explored theory and knowledge that tunes us in to becoming part of our children's world through play. My hope is that with all this information, you feel inspired to watch and learn more about how your little ones experience the world, and look for how we can work with them to enhance their lives, nurture their skills and enjoy it with them.

This is a book jam-packed with theory and knowledge and ideas and strategies that we hope to use to help our young people thrive. It's important to notice that it is hard to do all these things all the time. That's actually an impossible standard to set yourselves, so please make sure it isn't one you are striving for. Read and learn and know how to do better now you know better. But also understand that we are all human, and just as we need to support our small humans with compassion and care, we also need to support ourselves with the self-compassion to get it wrong and still want to try again. Knowing the theory and the strategies and the skills doesn't mean you will be the perfect parent or practitioner. Knowing the ideas doesn't mean that you won't feel the deep emotions and find the strategies hard to implement from time to time.

When things don't go to plan, and emotions run high or when burn out is imminent, remember to play. Remember that play connects us all, no matter what our age or skill set. If your relationship with a child needs repairing, find a way to play. If a session has not gone to plan, find a way to play that connects you again. If they are tired, find gentle and restful play. If they are full of energy, find busy play. If you are both full of emotions, find connective and collaborative play to restore you both.

In play, therapy and life, let's aim for connection, not perfection.